SUPERMIND

A  BOOK

SUPERMIND

The Ultimate Energy

by BARBARA B. BROWN

HARPER & ROW, PUBLISHERS

NEW YORK

Cambridge
Hagerstown
Philadelphia
San Francisco

1817

London
Mexico City
São Paulo
Sydney

FIRST EDITION

Designer: Sidney Feinberg

Library of Congress Cataloging in Publication Data

Brown, Barbara B
  Supermind, the ultimate energy.
  (A Cass Canfield book)
  Includes index.
  1. Mind and body.   2. Subconsciousness.   3. Con-
sciousness.   4. Stress (Psychology)   I. Title
BF161.B764   153   79-2614
ISBN 0-06-010518-6

80 81 82 83 84 10 9 8 7 6 5 4 3 2 1

Contents

Preface: Organization of the Book   ix

PART I
MIND, BODY, BRAIN: THE STATE OF THE ART

1. The Mystery of Mind   1
   Enigmas and Paradoxes • New Awareness of Mind

2. The Realm of Mind: Knowns and Unknowns,   8
   Beliefs and Attitudes • Untapped Skills of Mind and Consciousness • Compartments of Mind and Consciousness • Exploring the Resources of Mind • Discovering the Healing Mind

PART II
THE BODY CONNECTION

3. Keen Mind, Simple Body   29
   Mind Over Matter • Controlling the Body • The Primitive Nature of the Physical Self • The Nature of Mind-Body Operations • Central Control is Mind Control

4. Body Sense: Cradle of Awareness   42
   Awareness Begins with Perceptions • Biological Awareness • Other "New" (Evolved?) Senses • Body—the Mirror of the Mind • Conscious vs. Unconscious Judgments • The Body Responds

5. The Unconscious and Body Behavior   58

   Awareness of Internal States • "Teaching" the Unconscious to Control the Body • Unconscious Control of Intelligent Behavior • Intelligent Unconscious Control of Body • Benign Interference • Reacting to Placebos Is Intelligent • Victimizing the Unconscious • Permission to Become Aware of Internal States • Body Awareness and Well-Being of the Body

6. Stress: The Uninformed Mind   81

   The Stress Illnesses • The Current Consensus About "Stress" • Insights from Common Sense • Stress Is Manufactured by the Mind • Mental Steps to Distress: (1) Expectations • (2) Perceptions • (3) Worry • (4) Uncertainty • (5) The Images of Worry • Between Reason and Unreason • (6) Rumination • (7) Self-Deception • Back to Square One • People with Stress Are 100 Percent Logical! • The Second Illness

   PART III

   THE BRAIN CONNECTION

7. Mind and Brain   117

   The Mind-Body Problem • How the Experts See Mind and Consciousness • Brain-to-Consciousness Theories • To Know Mind Is to Know Man

8. The Creation of Mind   132

   Mind, Brain, and the Evolutionary Perspective • Foundations of Biological Evolution • Survival of the Fittest • Genes and an Evolutionary Inheritance • Biological Communications Systems: Their Effect on Genes • The Communication Systems • Expanding Communications • From Neural Substance to Brain • Learning and the Evolution of Behavior • Evolution of the Social Mentality • Best-Fitting Hypothesis?

   PART IV

   THE UNCONSCIOUS CONNECTION

9. Tracking the Unconscious Mind   171

   The Invisible Fabric of Mind • The Unconscious Reality • Historical Insights • The Approach of Psychology • The Roots of Consciousness • Does "Primitive" Behavior Mean "Primitive" Mind? • Communicating by Time-Space Patterns • The Evolution of Awareness

10. The Nature of Exceptional Mind States   196
    Dissociations of Consciousness: Unexplored Resources of Mind • Nonordinary Mind States • The Nature of Altered States • Mobilizing the Unconscious Resource • Visions of Hidden Intellect • Glimpses of the Caring Unconscious • Sleep Walking • Thoughts on Out-of-the-Body Experiences • Life After Death • Flying Saucers • The Idiot Savant • Hypnosis • Sorting Out Altered States

11. Quintessential Consciousness   232
    Mystical States • Imagery, Imagination, and Mental Images

12. The Intellect of the Unconscious   248
    New Insights • Learning to Control a Single Cell • A Summary of General Observations • The Unconscious Intellect: The Information It Uses • Clues to Unconscious Abilities from Observing the Performance • A Sense of Order as a Fundamental Property of the Mind Brain • The Will and the Will Executor • The Brownenberg Principle • The Unconscious Mind—Master of Mind Functions

    Appendix A   265
    Appendix B   267
    Appendix C   269
    Appendix D   271
    Bibliography   277
    Index   281

Organization of the Book

There is today a good bit of excitement about the powers of the human mind. New ways to use mind have literally been showered upon us as we have begun to gain insight into our neglected talents for controlling both state of mind and state of body.

We are, in fact, uncovering two quite different phenomena of mind. The most immediately useful is the power of mind to regulate the functions of the physical body. We have come to know something of these powers from the new body-awareness techniques, from bio-feedback, meditation, imagery, and other techniques that help the mind control the body.

The second phenomenon is the remarkable intelligence that can emerge in altered states of consciousness. The two phenomena may be related. The ability of mind to shift its consciousness and allow the mysterious inventions of the unconscious to surface may be simply a different manifestation of the action of mind that changes the physiology of the body. That is, if we agree that mind is generated by—but is not the same as—brain, then when mind controls mind, as in meditation or hypnosis, what we observe is, in effect, the mind controlling the physiologic activities of the brain.

Even though the underlying mechanisms of these two operations may ultimately be found to be the same, their effects are manifest so differently—one producing physical changes and the other changes in consciousness—that they can be considered most comprehensively as separate subjects. Thus, I have chosen to discuss the two phenomena in two sections, parts I and II of the book dealing with the relationship of mind and body and parts III and IV dealing with psychobiological arguments for the emergence of a new potential from the hidden recesses of the "unconscious" mind.

Part I of this book—an introduction—notes the qualities of mind that mind and body experts for so long have spurned as imaginary, impossible, illusory, or accidental, but which are at last being recognized as valid, useful qualities important to the course of human development. Part I also describes the surprising gap between what is known and what is not known about the capacities of mind, and sets out the objectives of this book: to present a brief for the preeminence of mind, not only as the supreme force in man's physical nature, but as the ultimate resource for sustaining both physical and mental well-being.

Part II provides the evidence and argument for the potential of mind to control the vital functions of the body. This review prompted consideration of an allied inquiry: the possibility that the germ substance of mind (neural tissue) has guided the entire evolutionary course of all life; thus part III examines evolutionary and genetic theory, supporting the notion that evolution is primarily an evolution of psyche, consciousness, and intellect and the need to recognize the primacy of man's cerebral nature. Part IV contains an analysis of operations of the unconscious mind and explores new conceptions of its role in the repertoire of intelligent human behavior.

Words describing mind and consciousness can have many meanings. The following short list describes what I have intended as the meaning of such words in the following pages.

Mind: The operational system of interacting processes within human beings that produces thought, perception, feeling, memory, imagination, and intention.

Mind-brain: Used to indicate the idea that "mind" represents the product of activities occurring between mind and brain, i.e., the idea that brain affects mind and mind affects brain.

Consciousness: A state of recognition of one's own existence, sensations, and thoughts; a product of mind-brain activity.

Awareness: Recognition of things and events in a way that can be communicated either to one's self or others.

Consensual consciousness: That part of both conscious awareness and the unconscious shaped by one's society and culture.

Supermind: The complex of innate capacities of mind-brain to appreciate, organize, understand, and control both body and brain.

—BARBARA B. BROWN

PART I

MIND, BODY, BRAIN:

THE STATE OF THE ART

CHAPTER 1

The Mystery of Mind

Enigmas and Paradoxes

What flows from the mind of man can be as awe-inspiring, prodigious and miraculous or as fearsome, odious and intimidating as what flows from nature itself. The progenitor of man's schizophrenic nature is the intangible effluence of an animal substance called brain, a part of the physical being so exceeding the bounds of physical evolution that the magnitude of its capacity to determine the course of all nature, including its own, is scarcely acknowledged.

The evolutionary leap from great ape to the genus *Homo* was a trivial feat of nature compared to the genesis of an unexpected new form of life: the psyche, the inner self, the self apart from physical substance that made the species *sapiens*. The creation that became mind brought into existence faculties of being only faintly foreshadowed by man's phylogenetic forerunners: his uniquely human abilities to abstract the essence of complex events and patterns, to create images and abstract symbols and then transmit them from generation to generation, and the supreme achievement of mind, equaled only in the creation of the cosmos—the capacity to impose order in the universe where order never existed before.

The mystery of the mind is so gigantic that it renders even the best of minds helpless to absorb its magnitude, let alone set a proper course for exploring the endless reaches of its power. This, more than

1

anything perhaps, explains why for centuries human beings have failed to be much more than passingly curious about the power and potential of their own mental apparatus. For perhaps five millennia man has skirted the mystery of mind, sometimes treating it like an imponderable, inaccessible echo of the Absolute, sometimes like a mechanical puzzle whose operation is complex but nonetheless ordinary. Neither view has been concerned with exploring the origins of the seemingly inexhaustible energy of mind, nor with probing sources of the mind's power to order and master the entire material universe.

For most of man's existence these powers of mind have been shrouded behind ignorance and myths, or held sacred and unknowable by philosophy or assumed to be predictable and trivial by science.

In the religious philosophies that accept mind-spirit as the handiwork of a superior spiritual power, the rights of ordinary mortals to manipulate and nourish the potential of mind to understand its own nature are ceded to the spiritual goals of life. Yet insight into the cosmic consciousness or knowing God by divine communication is mainly, if not exclusively, an act of mind. Revelation is a case in point. We stand in awe of saints, trusting divine communication, for who dares to ask of saint or swami, "What is the proof for your revelation, for your enlightenment?" There is no proof, no witness; revelation is an event within the mind. It is the mind that recognizes an Ultimate Reality, or feels an understanding of the Absolute, or becomes aware of the nature of Beingness. It is the mind that interprets and reports, the mind that believes and prompts changes in consciousness and behavior. Whether by supernatural infusion or manufactured by mind (a miraculous feat in itself), before any insight, natural or supernatural, can be appreciated and communicated, the powers of mind must cooperate. We still do not know whether the mind perceives the "supernatural" or is itself the "higher spirit" because we still do not know with any certainty at all the role the mind plays in knowing what seems so far beyond the ability of the mind to know. The hesitancy of philosophic authority to probe the natural mind has been an unfortunate barrier to understanding how to nurture mind to strengthen and fulfill its abilities. The philosophies teach us the shadows to look for, but they fall short in teaching us the methods to see.

Science, too, treats the mind as untouchable, even unstudiable; for the most part science denies the very existence of mind. Science Says (like a computerized Simon Says) that mind is simply the product of the mechanical activity of the brain. The scientific study of the brain is to look deeply into the chemistry and electricity of brain cells. It is difficult, if not impossible, to relate the atomic universe of the brain to the immaterial realms of thought and feeling and self-awareness. Although science talks a lot about the brain, it can say little, if anything, about the mind. Science cannot explain how the mind functions, how it can be nourished, how it can be expanded, how its faculties can be used more efficiently, nor what its ultimate destiny may be.

In the end, with millennia of philosophy and science behind us, we can say very little about the mind. The sages of science and philosophy alike leave modern man trapped squarely in the netherland of a precarious perplexity about his identity, foundering between science's idea of his primordial, unchained nature and the philosopher's unattainable ideal of union with the universal spirit.

Even with ever-expanding insights into man's nature and abilities, no trend has yet emerged that uses his sophisticated, humane qualities of mind. The shame of war and poverty, the laxity of democracy, the suspect probity of leadership, the oppression and slaughter in the Third World, the neglect of the wise or sometimes foolish elderly, the callous economics of modern medicine, the persuasion by the media to base behavior are only a few of the victories of the animal roots of mind that have ravaged the beauty and energy and power of the uniquely human mind to fulfill its own potential.

The dilemma of modern society is to be torn between the philosophers' ideal of humanity and the biological scientists' insistence that man is only a more complex animal. The dilemma underscores the extremes of our mental capabilities. On the one side is the mind that can project a just, fulfilling existence for all life. On the other side is the basest of caged emotion, stripped of all intelligence. How is this dichotomy of human nature possible? What is it that has let man understand a Golden Age yet destroy every possibility of reaching it? It is, of course, the activity of the mind that lies behind both the growth and destruction of man. No other species contains within itself the ability to control its own survival or death.

"Mind," "consciousness," "thought," "spirit," and "awareness" are words that illuminate the dialogues of man like sunbeams in a looking glass. They are the signs for things without substance, but they speak more of the qualities of man than do any of the labels for his body or his tools or his habitats. Of our Western history, for example, we remember the most about those human beings who symbolized the complex uses of mind and consciousness: the Leonardos, the Galileos, the Darwins, the Pavlovs. We honor those who have embodied the summits of awareness or of spirit or of thought: the Saint Johns, the Platos, the Einsteins. Yet today we know little more of the mind and spirit of man than we did in the beginning. The one aspect of his vital substance that man has failed to explore is his own mind, his sole unique feature in the universe of living things.

New Awareness of Mind

From time to time modern science and philosophy express opinions about the nature of mind, yet as imposing as their speculations may seem, none has substantial proof. None of the theories about the origin or essence of mind is defensible, and none can account for the outreachings of mind we call awareness and images and insights. Behind the cryptic façades of scientific and philosophic pronouncements on the essence of the human mind lies a chaotic jumble of fragmented and unexplored half-guesses about what may be the greatest power in this or any other universe.

The 1970s, we might say sometime in the future, was the beginning of the Age of Mind. Certainly the widening scope and electrifying speed of today's communications give man more food for thought than ever before. But not even the daily flood of information about human activities in every niche and level of society can account for the swelling interest in mind and consciousness. Quite suddenly, it seems, people everywhere are looking inward with a new freedom and confidence. They are discovering long-hidden powers of mind.

These are not the elusive, ephemeral, supernatural emanations of spirit we collectively call ESP; these newly discovered mind capabilities are substantive. And useful. Even in their embryo state they have guided many of a new generation to inner peace, and the new recognition of the potency of mind is vastly improving understanding relationships among peoples.

Nearly everyone today has felt the stirring of a new awareness of mind. Words like awareness, altered consciousness, meditation, holistic health, the healing mind are word-signs of a new interest in the inner resources of the human mind. The widening interest in mind techniques of self-suggestion, imagery, healing powers, changing consciousness, body consciousness, inner games of sports, mind-body integration, the meaning of Zen writings, yogic meditation, and other variations on the theme of mind all signal a new perception of mind as the energy and savior of life.

Beyond the excitement of self-discovery, behind the enthusiasm for exploring the inner being lies a profound change in the nature and behavior of man. The stream of consciousness of a substantial part of society has turned to a unique game of introspection, awareness and assertion of the self. It has found unrealized talents of mind, new mind tools that are surprising in their effectiveness for achieving personal fulfillment, for growth of mind, for harmony of mind and body, and for realizing the dreams of the human potential.

The new attention to mind and consciousness is, in a very real sense, a rebellion against the strictures of mind and consciousness laid down by the powerful authoritative opinions of science, philosophy, and religion, whose intellectual communities have for so long appropriated the domain of mind as their absolute province. Today's generations have, despite the admonitions of these authorities, found that the mind within can be supreme.

Their interest in things of the mind is not without support. The voices of a sprinkling of scientists also suggest the preeminence of mind. Who the scientists are is important, for they are not the overburdened laborers in the fields of science, buffeted by the whims of recognition politics. The scientists now speaking out about revelations of a powerful inner mind that exists apart from the organic matter of the brain are scientists who spent their lifetimes studying a brain they believed was the basis for mind, if mind existed at all. They are among the foremost who have ever studied the intricacies of the brain: Sir John Eccles, Roger Sperry, Wilder Penfield, Hans Selye, Karl Pribram. Their words are cautious, as befits scientists of integrity; nonetheless, the words ring with the promise of new vistas for conscious experience.

Now that science is discovering the ability of mind to heal the body, control the substance of dreams, and improve awareness, what more unknown talents of mind may be revealed? Is man, indeed, evolving a higher level of mind?

In speaking to nonscientific audiences, I am still surprised to realize the average person is not aware that the sciences and scientists believed to study mind in fact deny its existence, assigning mental functions to the tidy mechanics of the brain's myriad nerve connections. And until perhaps ten years ago I, too, failed to question very seriously this universal scientific premise. Spending my life in these unyielding physical-only sciences, however, never prevented me from appreciating the wonders of the human mind. Over the years I often sorrowed because the genius of man, his great visions, the power of his beliefs and faith were rejected by science as illusion or imagination, misperceptions of what science could reduce to ordinary chemical, mechanical changes in brain cells.

But finally I, too, have come to the conclusion, and quite analytically and logically I believe, that the scientific consensus that mind is only mechanical brain is dead wrong. I have become reasonably convinced (the word reasonably betrays the traditional scientific skepticism ingrained in me) that the research data of the sciences themselves point much more strongly toward the existence of a mind-more-than-brain than they do toward mere mechanical brain action.

I believe I can make a solid case for the existence and potential of a superior intelligence within every man, a mind born of brain but existing apart from brain, a mind with extraordinary, unacknowledged potency and range of powers. I will rest my case on data and logic. This is not a book that will spin theories from the unusual, or from the paranormal, or from the miraculous, although I may cite such from time to time. Rather, I will rely on observations, analyses, scientific fact and experiment, and the deductions that can logically be derived. Even if science ultimately concluded it can account for every feat, fancy and phenomenon of mind and consciousness, it will, in the meantime, be unqualifiedly invaluable to work at knowing mind *as if it operated differently from the workings of the brain.*

The focus of the chapters that follow is first on a discussion of the nature of the mind's absolute, innate ability to regulate every aspect of the body, from the flow of nerve impulses and directions of the brain's activity itself to the mind and body's responses to the stresses of life. I turn then to the other side of the mind—the extraordinary innate intelligence that lies hidden in the unconscious, examining first the facets of concealed intelligence that have not, but can be, deduced from the existing annals of science and natural biology. I note the remarkable hoodwinking we suffer when science speaks of its theories of evolution and genetic influence, suggesting instead a more coherent view for the evolution of mind. Lastly I inspect, from a new persepective, the multiminded nature of various *nonpathological* states of consciousness that may underlie the evolution of supermind.

I have attempted to organize both what authoritative science knows and what it does not know about mind and consciousness, and, in particular, I have analyzed the existing scientific information for the legitimate conclusions it contains that imply mind is an entity more than can be accounted for by the functions of the physical brain. Along the way, it became clear that the evidence for the supremacy of mind over the matter of the body, including that of the brain, is a hundred-fold more valid and more precise than the evidence science uses to insist that mind is no more than the mechanical action of the brain.

The sum of evidence about mind signals, I believe, the emergence of a human superpotential, a "new" mind. If a new mind is emerging, or if the old mind has not reached its potential, then the signs exist. And if the signs exist, they can be put in order, and we can begin to understand the role of mind in the evolution and fulfillment of the human species.

CHAPTER 2

The Realm of Mind: Knowns and Unknowns

Beliefs and Attitudes

In the introductory chapter, I fretted about the sorry state of knowledge about the mind. I chided science for declining to acknowledge the idea of a self-directing mind apart from brain—if only tentatively for the sake of a research perspective more relevant to the needs of modern man. It is time now to begin the argument—not just for mind—but that sleeping within everyone is a mind of superior intellect and ability, a mind that modern man, preoccupied with the wonders of physical nature, has neglected, and virtually silenced.

There is some groundwork to do first. The average person who speaks confidently about the mind (and that includes many a scientist) is remarkably unaware that the bulk of scientific authority considers mind a foolish and unwarranted concept. Most people believe that science recognizes and studies the mind. But when science speaks of mind, it means brain; when the average person talks about the mind, he really means the mind. This confusing difference in views about mind and consciousness between science and the public is reinforced by social and political influences exerted by the scientific community itself.

Within science there is an unvoiced and rather rigorously suppressed conflict between the ruling hierarchy that denies mind-as-more-than-brain and scattered groups of scientists who live and think outside the consensual stream of scientific thought. These "other" scientists are torn between logical, substantive ideas and data about the potency of mind and their practical need to conform to the convictions of their scientific peers, who disavow the idea of mind-apart-from-brain on the argument that there is no physical, demonstrable proof for mind, only for brain-is-mind. Because the establishment dictates, by its scientific-social-political consensus, what is acceptable scientific thought, any effective argument against the prevailing ideas of the scientific establishment is almost impossible. Deviates from consensual scientific thinking tend to be culled from the scientific community and relegated to relative oblivion (although occasionally some may receive a good bit of popular press). Put yourself in the intellectual-social-economic place of the "other" scientist and ask the question, "As an aspirant to scientific achievement and recognition, should I challenge the vested theoretical ideas of the leaders in my scientific profession and argue for mind-as-more-than-brain?" Obviously not, unless I am prepared to risk my career, lose my scientific credibility, be laughed at or ignored by the people who control my scientific fate.

It is, perhaps, not so surprising that the human needs to survive economically and psychologically can dominate the course of science. These needs have prevented many a first-class scientist from stirring up scientific dialogue about the most impressive attributes of man's nature: mind and consciousness. The practical needs of scientists to survive permeate the scientific community so completely in modern times as to concentrate most of its intellect on achieving economic and social security before it can consider the real work of science. It is the social demands of individual survival that skew science and account for the meagre knowledge about the mind. (We should remember that the scientists now disagreeing with the established consensus that mind-is-brain were first recognized for their expertise in the ideas of the consensus.)

If there is to be any hope for understanding the mind and for exploring its true potential, there must first be a clear understanding about how much is actually known about the mind, what is myth and what is useful theory, what is ignored or neglected, and above all, where science has overreached fact with theory. Once the broad unknowns of the mind are outlined, once it is understood how very little is known about the extraordinary dimensions of the mind, it will be clear that mind cannot be rejected as merely a self-fulfilling invention of unknowledgeable men on the basis of what science does *not* know about it. On the contrary, freed from the indefensible prejudices of science, mind and consciousness emerge as not only realities, but the substance of man's future life and evolution.

Untapped Skills of Mind and Consciousness

Neither science nor philosophy has provided us with much insight into the unique resources of the human mind, nor into the complex operations of mind and consciousness. We know little, for example, about how to improve mental imagery or how to promote creative thought, how to encourage the ability to form and recognize concepts, to develop a sense of self- and other-image, how the unconscious mind functions, or how we recognize art or innately understand harmony and order. Nor has science studied to any degree such well-known manipulations of consciousness as turning off pain, our often ingenious reactions in emergencies, dreaming or daydreaming, summoning the body to perfect performances in sport or the arts, the curious mind state of hypnosis, the power of positive thinking, or subliminal perception.

Science knows virtually nothing about what makes a child genius, why genius can be lost, nor about prodigious memories, how mystical states can be sustained, how dream logic can solve nondream problems, nor the mental processes of persuasion and self-deception, nor why social stress can cause physical illness.

We know nothing of the mechanisms of intuition or insight, why we can recall dreams that take place in deep unconsciousness, how consciousness is both there and not-there in sleep walking, nor do we know what makes precognitive dreams. We do not know why faith healing and placebos can heal the sick, how hallucinations develop, what happens in the mind in déjà vu or hypnotic imagery or to cause hysterical blindness or the synthesthesias, where stimulation of one sense makes images in a different sense. We cannot explain neurasthenic fatigue or general malaise, nor the mind-body split of transvestites. We have little if any understanding of how the mind-brain slips into the many neuroses and psychoses, from free-floating anxiety to paranoid schizophrenia where consciousness is multiple. We do not yet understand love or grief or conversion or illumination, nor what makes special kinds of minds, like the artist's or musician's or mathematician's mind.

We do not know why our behavior can change to surprising extremes when we work or play as groups of human beings. At times we can be persuaded by a group will or crowd mass to base behavior and offend our own human nature. Yet at other times, when there is a group spirit or team momentum, or the home advantage in professional sports, in groups we can perform with abilities we scarcely knew we had.

We do not even know much about the things of mind we have studied most: the rise of intellect from the depths of depravity or oppression or apparent lack of mental capacity. There is more than one example of intellect springing from the most impoverished generations of primitive minds, like the outcast baby girl of the degenerate Jivaro tribe who, adopted by archeologists, became an outstanding archeologist herself. Or my friend, the son of impoverished, late-of-Africa sharecroppers, who received no education at all until in his teens, yet became an outstanding professor with many professional degrees. Or cases like that of Larry, the boy judged to be mentally retarded and so never educated, but who was discovered at age thirty to have educated himself to high school level with neither the tools of education nor even human attention.

These are only a few of the possible feats of mind and consciousness. The spectrum of the mind's capabilities is enormous, its potential power prodigious. Yet all that society or science or religion has done about this ultimate resource of man and its universe is to poke at it gently with touchproof gloves, like an astronaut timidly probing at moondust.

Only the tiniest portion of the mind's skills and secret arts has been tapped. At today's frontiers an occasional courageous psychologist or therapist works with engineering the content of dreams, another with guided imagery to change the body's physiology, another with mind control of pain, and others with meditation or self-hypnosis to alter consciousness. But this is about the extent of any serious effort to tap the faculties and talents of the mind for anything other than the ordinary ways of coping with the ordinary circumstances and demands of life. We have developed no systematic approaches for improving the faculties of mind and none for using the insights and understandings that come from altered states of mind and consciousness.

Compartments of Mind and Consciousness

The lack of official biomedical and psychological research interest in the mind and consciousness means that we have relatively little definitive knowledge about the subjective and subconscious universe of man that would enable him to improve his innate mental capabilities and use them productively. The extensive information we have about the electrochemical reactions of human organisms to stimuli contrasts strangely with the meagre knowledge we have about mental processes and states of consciousness. Scientific knowledge about vision, audition, obvious emotions, types of learning, and other facts of human behavior is extensive, but the countless mental activities and variations of consciousness has scarcely been touched by science.

Once, out of curiosity, I listed some of the operations of the mind-brain and consciousness most studied by science but about which we have, in fact, little or no truly vital information useful for developing the full capacity of the human mind. The list is very long.

We know, for example, little about perception, that mental process of attaching meanings to sensations. Science knows a great deal about the physical and chemical nature of sensations, the way the energy of the environment affects the sense organs, and is translated into other energy in nerve impulses, about what influences sensory information and where and how it may be modified in the brain.

But little if anything is known about the most important mechanisms by which people give meaning to what their senses detect. One of the most intriguing actions of perception is its ability for subjective appreciation, the process of putting "I" into what we detect through the senses, the way in which events and objects in the environment come to have special, private meanings at different times and under different circumstances. The private and very personal interpretations of experience are often, possibly always, processes occurring at the margins between the conscious and unconscious minds. The entire, elaborate process by which we evaluate our sensory information is, except for occational bits of information captured by conscious attention, guided by a subconscious (unconscious) activity. And with the infinite levels and labyrinths of sensory, perceptual, and mental association processes all working, circulating, and shifting below the level of conscious awareness, the conscious mind is hard put to translate the feelings and internal associations of mind activity into objective terms. It follows that subjective appreciations of the self and experience and being are difficult to communicate and to study, but they are, nonetheless, the most vital activities of human beings.

One particularly important and still unknown aspect of perception is selective perception, that often life-serving but occasionally pernicious way people seem automatically to select scenes, sounds, or happenings to perceive and are blind and deaf to other obvious events. Sophisticated mental processes are used quite unconsciously to block out any awareness of what the eyes see or the ears hear. Selective perception is a mind device we use to eliminate distractions and focus our attention on the things we feel are most important to well-being, as when we need to solve problems, concentrate, or rest the mind by daydreaming.

Physiologists tend to believe that the brain circuits used to appreciate the environment can handle only a finite amount of information, and that concentrated attention can tie up the circuits and prevent appreciation of events that exceed the limits. Yet we all know that we can recall things and events we paid no attention to at all, a phenomenon that suggests, contrary to the scientific view, that the mind may contain a mechanism that can not only narrow one's focus of attention but at the same time store other perceived information without bringing it to awareness.

Another quite extraordinary kind of perception neglected by experimental psychologists is subliminal perception, that remarkable ability of human beings to sense complex visual and auditory information and even ideas, understand them, and react specifically and appropriately without any conscious awareness of either the perception or the response.

Science has ferreted out almost every chemical and physical process concerned in the way organisms detect information from the environment; it is *how* individuals interpret the personal and social meanings of sensory information that eludes research. Most researchers seem to be content to show how nerves and brain conduct and react to sensed information, but such bare-bones mechanics cannot account for the way in which information sensed is used to produce personality, intelligence, or any other complex social behavior.

Scientific contentions that people learn and are shaped by their experiences are also distressingly superficial; it is still unknown *how* experience and training are incorporated into the personal repositories of the mind for human mental development. Experience is multi-tiered and multi-faceted, and it does not occur instantaneously for nerve sensors to deal with, as neurology researchers seem to believe, but develops through time and human spaces. There must be very complex brain and mind mechanisms to form and test a thousand kinds of associations, systems that compare the associations, ways to analyze patterns of things and events and to recognize them, varieties of logic, and mind-brain systems that provide for access to the memory pools for both adventitious and nonpatterned information as well. From time to time research tenders us a morsel or two about mental logic or pattern recognition, but as yet science has given us no unifying themes around which we might systematically explore these myriad sophisticated mental operations.

Despite decades spent in memory research, the critical operations of memory—storing information in logical sequences of meaningful associations, and then recalling exactly what we intend to recall—also remain unknown.

The operations of human memory are extraordinary. Some scientists estimate that virtually everything one experiences in life is put into memory. Both hypnosis and stimulation of certain brain areas during operations can evoke memories that individuals can either barely identify with or sometimes feel are actually foreign to them. These "buried" memories are astounding in their logic and meaningful strings of associations. If it is true, as seems likely, that the memory stores of the brain are filled with information from every experience in life, the operations of the mind-brain that keep the data in orderly sequences and arranged for usefulness and relevancy must be staggering in their complexity. Research has discovered a great deal about what brain structures are involved in memory and the conditions for long-term and short-term memory, but science knows virtually nothing about why or how some memories become buried in the deep unconscious mind while others linger, unwanted, at the edge of consciousness. Research has shown the importance of attention and need for remembering, and has shown physiologic and genetically programmed influences on memory, such as imprinting in the very young or the pathology of memory defects. But none of the scientific knowledge can account for how different bits of memory become associated in a coherent manner, nor how the chaining of memories occurs, nor how forgetting can be learned.

The other side of memory contains the remarkable ability of the mind to recognize—to have an awareness of events or people or things that mind has experienced before—and the ability to recall, to retrieve meaningful information from its endless banks of memories. The elegance of the memory retrieval systems is so mysterious that we have only the faintest appreciation of their operations. When we recall voluntarily, as when we try to remember a friend's phone number or what he was wearing yesterday, the conscious mind gives some instruction to the unconscious mind to look in the memory files for very specific bits of information. In psychobiologic theory this feat is usually passed over as a mechanical operation of mere association, but what the theorists neglect to observe is that before any mental process, however mechanical, can locate the right memory file, there must be some prior knowledge by the searching activity about where to find that file.

Scientific research can describe many factors that influence memory and recall, but it has little idea about how an intention to recall something can locate the appropriate memory; certainly we have nothing concrete to explain spontaneous or adventitious or unwanted memories, or the mental mechanisms that can interfere with retrieving memories that can usually be easily recalled.

The remembering and the recall or recognition of abstract concepts is even more miraculous. If one wants to use a certain complex, abstract concept in a specific situation (such as the formula for calculating compound interest), what is it that triggers memory to produce the concept? Many brain scientists liken the brain to a computer, neglecting the obvious: that something outside the computer decides what to ask the computer to do.

The conscious mind identifies some quality related to the concept, then commands and directs a search of memory buried in the unconscious for clues until the correct word or phrase struggles up from memory and presto, the concept appears—whole and coherent. Something in the mind must know how and where to search memory before it commands the search that ends in recall. Even then the process is not complete, for some other memory must "recognize" the recovered concept as the one that matches the intention. If there were no supervisory brain director, the mind might be flooded with irrelevant concepts and would need to make an extraordinary number of comparisons in order to select the right concept. If this were the case, it would essentially defeat the entire learning process and belie the principle of parsimony in mind-brain operations.

It is in the realm of human thought—productive, voluntary thought—where our scientific knowledge is most meagre.

Science has studied the *input* of information to thought mechanisms, such as sensations and learning materials; it has studied the energy transformations in neural tissue and dissected mechanisms of the intelligence systems that can be modeled after computers or other physical phenomena; it has studied changes in neurons and behavior when speech is recognized, how attention affects productive thought and the influences of organization of information, of images, of laws of learning, rules of problem solving and decision making. But science has only guessed at mechanisms of thought.

Science uses models to gain insights into the mechanics of brain function, but the models have yet to explain intuition or rumination, and the models cannot explain logical, away-from-reality fantasies, the creation of images, the projection of images into past and future time, and how and why individuals develop different thinking styles. And the ultimate activity of thought—the faculty for introspection, for self-awareness, for self-analysis, and for analyzing one's own thought processes—is still the mysterious "black box" of mind miracles that no man seems to dare to try to open.

The phenomenon of consciousness is perhaps the ultimate magical property of mind that defies understanding. It is a battered concept. "Consciousness" is used to label both the definable and the inexpressible inner feelings and appreciations of the world and our relationship to it. Consciousness really includes many varieties of awareness, from the awareness of what one is doing and thinking that can be communicated (by which many scientists define the word) to a sense, a sensation far beyond anything one is able to verbalize. The sense of identity, the awareness of the physical being, the sense of "otherness," the senses of harmony and order and continuity are all integrated, sophisticated sensations about the totality of mind and body beingness that transcend the mere connectedness of physical parts and functions.

The "unconscious" part of the consciousness spectrum is relegated by science to primitive animal nature and is, science would infer, relatively unimportant. It is, however, but one aspect of the continuum of consciousness that elides from the unconscious awareness-of-nothing state of deep sleep to the conscious awareness of wakefulness. Whatever we fail to understand about thought or behavior we shunt away into the obscurity of "unconsciousness." Yet the unconscious mind has its own reality and substance, however ethereal that reality may be, and I will show that it is the source and the machinery of nearly all we call mind. One of the curiosities of modern science is its apathy toward the miracles of the unconscious mind, the stuff of creativity and artistry, of insight and intuition. In the realm of consciousness and the "unconscious" mind, it is mainly their pathology that science studies.

But it is from the unexplored expanses of the unconscious mind that also arise the unusual states of mind: dreams, fantasies, detachment, peak experiences, illusion, ecstasy, the inner sensations of joy and peace. These marvels of an active mind have yet to be claimed by science.

Science does, of course, know something about the necessary conditions for thought that can analyze and synthesize, and something about the necessary conditions for making decisions and evaluating our information, for establishing goals, formulating intentions, and developing defenses for personal survival, for formulating our ethics and social conscience. Science has tabulated the conditions. But lists and descriptions do not throw much light on *how* the intelligence can abstract the essence of an experience or form symbols or become hypnotized or self-actualizing or exploratory. Nor does science know the nature of curiosity or what motivations are made of. We have no clues about how the mind recruits the body to perform its wishes, how intention is turned into action, how mind can modify instinct. We understand nothing of the operations of mind that lead to the human qualities of loyalty, of love, of identity, of power or pleasure or understanding.

When I began to list the unrealized resources of mind and consciousness, and then list the operations of mind for which, despite much study, we have so little understanding, I was aware of many gaps in our knowledge about human mental activities, but even I was surprised to find the lists so long. As I scan the texts and treatises on human behavior and brain and on the nature of man, the store of accumulated knowledge seems impressive. There are a million volumes in a thousand universities, books written about the brain and emotion and human behavior, but what the books do not say is what they cannot say about the functions of mind and consciousness and intelligence.

In a way, realizing the vastness of the unexplored territory of mind is a realization shocking enough to be frightening. If the mind can, for example, reveal its infinite capacities in the exquisite formation of complex symbols in dreams, or in an occasional genius, or create within itself a supraconsciousness or end the agony of pain, if mind can accomplish such things, then the reluctance of science to explore man's supernature for the benefit of man may be a form of intellectual suicide.

Perhaps the species man is too young. As the sole species with the power to control its own destiny, perhaps man has needed time to prove he *can* control his own destiny, as he has learned to control the elements in the physical universe. Science is a new tool of man. It has discovered the laws of nature and learned to use them to ease the strain of physical life—and to destroy life. It may now be at the edge of new discoveries about the true nature of the human psyche and the untapped sources of mind.

Exploring the Resources of Mind

The mind, as we can see, is capable of far more than we have been led to believe. Like the glitter of gold from the distant hills, the precious potential of mind beckons with a flickering light that from time to time reveals the deepness of its veins. The ways we now search for the mother lode of mind, like self-hypnosis or imagery or T.M., may well be as crude and chancy as those of the old gold-rush muleteers with their heavy picks and leaky sieves.

Serious mind explorers face stiff social prohibitions against adventuring with the mind. Science, all nuts and bolts, studies mainly the mechanics of brain, blinding itself to the countless miracles of mind that fill the literature of the world. And then, because science sees no evidence that miracles can occur, it disavows every suggestion that the mind has abilities beyond what can be accounted for by theoretical physics and statistics. And at the other pole of the community mind, ecclesiastical authorities issue injunctions about the moral sin of interfering with God-given natural endowments.

The other troublesome problem for people wanting to explore the breadth of mind is their disadvantaged status. The experts allow them no useful information or knowledge about the mind. Every scrap of relevant information has been hoarded and tucked away in the invisible vaults of what we call science. From the safety of exalted position, and with critical information safe from public scrutiny, science keeps itself safe from challenge about what the mind is and what it can do.

So it is no wonder that the average person, the nonscientist, is fearful of exploring his mind; he has been taught that doing so violates commandments of both science and religion. With no information and no experience about the far reaches and wonders of his own mind, and the minds of others, neither individuals nor society in general dare argue to authorities that new minds are real and powerful and what, perhaps, being human is all about.

I have a dream that soon man can begin to experience the wonders of his mind and learn to use consciousness to fulfill a greater potential of his being and of his species. My passions for this dream are undisguised, but they are passions for liberation of mind and consciousness as deeply rooted in science and philosophy as they are in personal experience.

Personal experiences have given me to wonder; the sciences and philosophy have given me the reality of the present and the past. Together they give me visions of the future, one vision the evolution of supermind and supraconsciousness, another vision the alternative course of mind stagnation and social suicide. The two alternatives temper my passions, but at the same time they catalyze my desire to communicate what my experiences, both personal and scientific, have led me to accept as evidence for a superior mind and limitless spirit lying within the reach of every mind.

Through the many years of my research into the physiology and behavior of man and animals, I have come to understand some of the obstacles to understanding the human mind. Science learns and grows in frustratingly tiny bits of knowledge, and when it comes to the vagaries and whimsies of the mind, the myths and confident authority of the medicine men are difficult to dispel. I have been fortunate to be in the vanguard of much new research about bodies, minds, and behavior, with the almost inevitable result of a growing awareness about how narrow and limited serious thought has been about the nature of consciousness.

The paradoxical shortcoming in the approach to mind and consciousness by specialists concerned with human nature is their almost exclusive attention to pathological states. For as long as I can remember, psychiatry, psychology, and biochemistry have concentrated their relevant major reserach efforts on schizophrenia, while psychologists have dissected emotions into every animal root they could think of. Medicine, psychiatry, and psychology, all developing from the ancient tradition of treating illness, naturally use their growing technology and expertise to study the causes of illness and to search for improved therapies. There has not been much room left over to explore other qualities of the human mind and consciousness.

What I think the scientists have missed—and for good reason, because pathology is a serious problem—is that the universe of man is also filled with illustrations of quite remarkable variations of mind and consciousness that are either useful to man or instructive and enlightening. Genius, special talents, and mind sets for art or music, states of ecstasy, extraordinary physical or mental performances under stress, hypnosis, subliminal perception, imagery, dreams, unusual memory, déjà vu, and creativity each manifest states and operations of mind that contribute to the growth and welfare of society. These are good reasons to take seriously the systematic study of the unusual attributes of mind and consciousness that are *not* pathological.

Discovering the Healing Mind

We—you and I—may be changing science. When exciting new information about the nature of human beings *does* become generally available through nonscience routes, science becomes challenged— there arises a kind of public pressure on science to perform more relevantly to human needs. The last ten or so years have seen a remarkable reversal of science's domination over ideas of what human beings are and what they are not.

Washed with the waves of new discoveries that yoga really "works," that meditation can improve body functions, that relaxation training can relieve the physical symptoms of stress, and that biofeedback training can repair a host of disabilities, there is no turning back for science. And while a share of the medical community may still resist the idea that ordinary human beings can, by their own decisions and with a bit of direction, change the physical functions of their own bodies with extraordinary ease and simplicity, almost everyone else is convinced of the reality of mind over body.

Whether they admit it or not, biomedical scientists have been shocked right down to their metatarsals by the rich consequences of changing life-styles on human health. Surprised reports come out of government agencies or from scientific societies to tell us that coronary heart disease has suddenly become much less frequent, that effects of aging have been pushed back by years, or that some willful people have staved off fatal illnesses. Not all the physical problems of man may be yielding to the mysterious forces of self-control, but when hard-core medicine admits that "better living" is saving lives, you can bet there is something to it.

Perhaps only medicine has been surprised. For decades, perhaps from the time that medicine became a science, it never seriously examined its rather arbitrary doctrine that the functions of the body's vital systems did not and could not ever come under control of the mind.

Science has tended to justify its prolonged apathy about the potential of the unconscious mind by claiming that such activities cannot be documented with the kind of precision science demands. As a matter of fact, all that science demands is a *systematic* examination of phenomena. Physical data are the most convenient and accurate means to document phenomena, but not the only means. After all, psychology uses emotional pathology to deduce unconscious conflicts; it could as easily use mental productivity to deduce unconscious harmony and creativity.

I have long felt that medicine and psychology have had a kind of hysterical blindness to the compelling evidence for mind control of body functions. It is as if the collective unconscious of science has feared an intangible power to which it might lose its authoritative influence over society's minds and bodies, and so it contrived a hundred excuses to avoid exploring the less obvious abilities of the mind.

There has been, perhaps, a dual difficulty: mind control of body functions is carried out mainly by remote processes of mind rarely accessible to conscious awareness, and unconscious mental processes are more difficult to measure and study than, say, spirituality. Hysterical blindness illustrates both of these difficulties. It is an ideal example of how revealing even the simplest analysis of mind-body phenomena can be. Anyone, in fact, can tease out startling data from this example about the critical faculties of the unconscious mind and demonstrate, at the same time, the remarkable power of the unconscious to cause profound changes in the body.

Hysterical blindness is an ailment fabricated solely in the mind. As one of the hysterias that occur when mind functions become displaced from their normal relationships with body or consciousness or reality, it is a striking example of the inexplicable schemes mind can contrive to assume absolute control over the most vital functions of the body.

The most widely accepted explanation of the hysterias is that something in the unconscious mind perceives a threat to the security of self, and to preserve its image of self the unconscious contrives the best way it can to protect self against the effects of imminent harm to well-being. The problem in the hysterias is that the perception, the creation of the defense, and the means to implement the defense all take place within the dark recesses of the unconscious mind, with scarcely ever a clue to conscious awareness.

Take an incident I personally witnessed. One day, when I was a student, the news swept our campus that an exceptionally intelligent and popular girl had suddenly become blind. We, her friends, were torn with emotion about the disaster, and because we were all struggling with school work, we were particularly awed by the unfortunate coincidence that the blindness struck a week before final exams. Day after day we pressed the hospital for news, and soon came the second shock. The girl was not physically blind, she was suffering hysterical blindness.

It is a stiff jolt to young belief systems cultivated by the certainty of physical causes for physical ills to experience the total power of unknown dangers latent in the human mind. We were told then, as we are told today, that the unconscious mind can become so disturbed by the problems it perceives that it manufactures ways to protect itself against threats, real or imagined, to its personal safety and security. It was obvious then, as it is today, that the unconscious mind is the secret place of the power of the human mind. And while we are convinced today about the master magician within the unconscious mind that can distort understanding and make emotional logic seem real, experts (disabled by their hysterical blindness?) still know virtually nothing about the internal operations of the unconscious mind nor about the extraordinary potency of a mind that can order unfailing obedience of the physical being.

Based on her demonstrated abilities, my college friend had every reason to expect continued success and happiness. It can be guessed, though, that a part of mind, that dark unknown unconscious, did perceive and certainly did create a problem. But the problem was not shared with conscious awareness, and left to its own devices, unconsciousness manufactured an absolutely foolproof answer to the problem its logic had led it to believe existed. Blindness is an automatic antidote to the pressures for performing when sight is essential. The ability of the unconscious mind to enforce an otherwise impossible control of a physiologic, physical function (*not* seeing) is, without question, one of the most prodigious but ignored faculties of the human mind.

When a part of the mind can (1) so deftly use something it perceives in its world to contrive a problem between itself and something outside of itself, and then (2) design a logical, appropriate solution for the problem it has created, a defense that can resist further impact of the problem on mind and emotions, and (3) order the body's cooperation to express the behavior needed for the defense, this is what we expect of man's intelligence. But (4) when recognizing and solving problems occur when conscious awareness does not recognize either the problem or the solution, we can only conclude that unconscious intellectual processes perform the elaborate operations of thought for the entire sequence of mental actions.

The blindness of so many experts to the genius of the hidden mind may be an unconscious process much like that in hysterical blindness. Psychodynamic theory does recognize unconsciously contrived conflicts and unconsciously developed protective devices against their effects, but just how the unconscious accomplishes these complex feats of mind is still unknown and unstudied. Science still recognizes the unconscious only when it is disturbed enough to cause obvious disorders of mind and body, and even when, through psychotherapy or chemicals, the unconscious mind returns to an acceptably normal state, all the credit is given to the conscious mind.

Unconscious mental activity, contrary to popular thought, does *not* usually produce unfavorable results. Most of the time unconscious mental processes are productive, positive, and benign. If we review the mental activities of the unconscious listed for the "neurotic" example above, we can see that each stage of the process is carried out in an eminently logical and efficient way except for (1): the perception of the problem (my college friend perceived what she interpreted to be a problem).[1] Suppose, however, that one's perceptions are correct and a problem does exist between one's self and something in the environment. In this case, the rest of the sequence is exactly the same. We design solutions to the problems or devise ways to defend against emotional assaults, and we direct the body to assist by giving our solutions or defenses behavioral expression. The only difference between the neurotic and the normal process is that in the first case certain perceptions are inaccurately evaluated. The chief reason perceptions are inaccurately evaluated is lack of enough relevant information to determine whether or not what one perceives does project a difficulty for one's well-being. When perceptions are inaccurate, the mind cannot produce effective solutions. But in both cases it is the logic and intellect of the unconscious mind that plays the principal role in problem solving.

There is, in fact, in the vast archives of the sciences of human behavior, a wealth of scientific reports that gives exciting testimony to the extraordinary range of the powers of mind over body. Some of the evidence is obscured by the ritual terminology of the behavioral sciences; some is unrecognized by the scientists themselves. Because of the constraints and traditions imposed on scientific reporting, a great deal of the evidence is not specifically noted, but it is, nonetheless, obvious, showing incontrovertibly that the physical, physiological activities of the body do change with mental activity, and how unconscious intellectual activities dominate the physiologic mechanisms that attend to regulating body functions when the mind doesn't wish to be concerned with directing the physical operations.

In the following pages I will describe some of the evidence and the logic leading to the conclusion that the unique nature of the human mind extends at least to the awesome power to guide and

---

1. The term perception is confusing scientifically because it is used in two ways, one to mean the recognition of qualities of objects and events the senses detect, and the other to mean knowing the *meaning* of objects and events. I use the latter.

control and extend the physical functions of its own living resource, the brain. I will argue: (1) that a part of mind, the unconscious, can be aware of every event in the body, from the actions of a single cell to the state of the integrated body itself; (2) that the unconscious mind is an elegant, sophisticated aspect of human intelligence; (3) that the physical (physiological) functions of the human body continuously express the mental activity of thinking, that they, in fact, reflect intellectual activity; (4) that when required by circumstances, the unconscious mind can exert control over biological functions (through unconsciously directed intentions and attention, through increased unconscious awareness from experience and learning, and by the directed attention and intention of conscious awareness); (5) that the unconscious mind in turn can be influenced by conscious awareness, particularly by the consensual consciousness; and (6) that the process of thinking itself is the exerting of voluntary control over the physical activity of the brain.

PART II

THE BODY CONNECTION

CHAPTER 3

Keen Mind, Simple Body

Mind Over Matter

Quite possibly, the most exciting change bubbling in the American consciousness is the move to life-styles that focus on becoming aware of what is good for mind and body. Many people optimistically assume that if you "take care of the body," the body can resist the ills and distresses so common in modern society. Yet taking care of the body is only the tangible, obvious act. The real instrument that works to protect and care for mind and body is the still latent and little-used ability of the human mind to know and control the operations of the internal being.

Nonetheless, the potency of mind to affect the body, however convincing to the people involved, has never been very convincing to science because personal anecdotes always end with the result. Few, perhaps no, scientists have attempted to organize the special features of mind-over-body experiences that could point the way to understanding them. I believe it *is* possible to examine reports of mind-over-body experiences in a way that can succinctly describe their special features. Because I have thought long and hard about the possible causes for my own experiences, I will use these to show how such experiences can be probed for clues that could guide more systematic explorations of mind-body phenomena.

Controlling the Body

My personal experiences in control of the body are not too different from those of many people, although, being a researcher, I've been more inclined to experiment and so my experiences may seem more dramatic. My outstanding accomplishment occurred during a tonsillectomy done when I was an adult.

When I was in medical school, a professor in an ear-nose-and-throat course consistently used me to illustrate diagnostic procedures, thrusting large laryngeal mirrors down my throat until I developed an extreme sensitivity to, and anxiety about, any probing in the mouth. So, told that a tonsillectomy was absolutely necessary, I panicked. I asked the surgeon to give me three months to prepare my emotions. From time to time I would silently tell myself that the operation would be easy, cause no pain, and there would be no problems.

At surgery, the tonsil areas were so friable that it was almost impossible to inject the local anesthetic. "Oh," I sputtered in frustration, "Yust cgut um ought," which, speaking through a mouth filled with hardware, was all I could manage, but meant, "just cut them out." Amazed, the surgeon began removing the hemostats, asking me if I really meant it. I assured him that I did, and to hell with the anesthetic. Irritated, and calling my bluff, he reloaded the mouth with hemostats, his fingers, a scalpel, and a few gauze swabs on strings. As he worked, I reached up and dragged the swabs out of my mouth.

"Hey," he rebuked me sharply, "you're contaminating the field."

"Yeah, but I'm not bleeding either," I gulped out, trying to smirk.

He worked, and I grunted, looking at my watch.

"Better hurry," I said, "You're supposed to be the fastest surgeon in the West. It's almost fifteen minutes."

He grinned, yanking off the drapes to show me he had finished.

"Damnedest operation I've ever been through," he laughed.

I had felt no pain, didn't bleed, and had absolutely no recovery problems. Mind over matter.

This hidden capacity of mind to control the vital functions of the body has been useful to me at other times, although I confess I do not know what happens in the mind to accomplish such remarkable effects. I do know that I will it, and that in some curious way the conscious mind keeps out of the way of the magnificent operations of the unconscious mind.

This particular power of mind can be called upon in emergencies, such as the time I nearly amputated a thumb when the sharp edge of a car door cut it neatly. Keeping the parts together until I reached surgery, I gasped to the surgeon that I was hypersensitive to local anesthetics (having become so sometime after the tonsillectomy). So he sewed up the damage while I concentrated on avoiding pain.

The surgeon was so impressed with my Spartan attitude he neglected to prescribe pain medication for the swollen, throbbing, bandaged mass that had been my old reliable thumb. At home I realized I would have to cope with the pounding pain all by myself.

With none of the conveniences of pain pills or sedatives, I decided to use mind power. Over and over I repeated to myself that I would feel no pain. And because the surgeon had advised me the thumb would be disfigured and have no feeling, for good measure I threw in some commands to myself for the thumb to heal whole again, without scars. The pain would break through my concentration, but I continued to intensify my mental effort, and literally sweated through the entire day trying to convince the thumb not to hurt and to heal perfectly. By evening I was exhausted by the mental effort, and decided to have a cup of soup, give up, go to bed and just cry if that was what it took to get through the night. As I went to the kitchen, I passed the liquor cart. A light bulb floated brilliantly over my head.

"You and your persistent mind," I scolded myself. "A few drinks of that ancient soporific and there would be no pain." So I drank, believing in moderation in all things, including mental effort. Sometimes mind power should yield to a more efficient force, especially if that mind power is immature. But liquor or not, the thumb healed quickly, with only a faint line left as reminder.

It seems strange for me to be telling mind-over-body stories. I recall, as a youngster, my great-aunt occasionally having the confidence in a selected group to reveal her secret thoughts about the power of mind. She had adopted the simple philosophy of Émile Coué, and would repeat the "I'm feeling better and better" formula a hundred times a day. She and some of her intimate friends were convinced they could evoke unknown powers in some way hazily connected in their minds to spirits or God (I was never sure which) that could perform miracles for the mind and body and spirit.

Yet today rather much the same idea is becoming recognized as legitimate therapy and preventive medicine. We are simply becoming a good bit more systematic about using the abilities of the mind, and because of the successes of the new mind and body awareness techniques, we are much less hesitant to discuss our personal techniques and successes and thoughts about the potency of mind.

Mine are *not* unique experiences. There are thousands of stories like mine hidden away in family circles and personal archives. It is sad indeed that no one has taken a critical look at the apparently innate potential of every human mind to insist upon a healthy body.

While we may not be able here to solve the puzzle of how mind can direct the physical operations of the body, we can, nonetheless, take a first step in the systematic study of this human potential, isolating the more conspicuous features of mind-over-body experiences. For it is the logical analysis of data that leads to insights about the mechanisms of natural phenomena. The understanding may be a long way off, but we can at least begin the search for understanding by making simple lists of observations. We can, for example, define the distinctive qualities in the experiences I recounted above.

They were, first, therapeutic processes carried out without external intervention of any kind. They were, too, analgesic effects exerted mentally that were at least the equivalent of moderately potent analgesics, such as codeine. Second, although the intent and commands to the body were known to conscious awareness, nothing else of the cognitive or physiologic activity was appreciated in conscious awareness. We have no choice but to conclude that the critical operation, the execution of the intentions, occurred in the realm of the unconscious. Third, fourth, and fifth, the unconscious mental acts involved were purposeful, intelligent, and productive; and, finally, they had survival value, i.e., they improved the well-being of the individual.

Here we have isolated the important qualities of the experience. No doubt everyone else's mind-over-body feats have exactly the same fundamental qualities. The analysis does not yet reveal ways we can use this potential unfailingly, for that will come only with a deeper probing into what we know and what we do not know about relationships between mind and body.

The Primitive Nature of the Physical Self

Nowadays most people are no longer content just to know mind can influence body. They are eager to understand the ability—to know it well enough to "feel" it and learn to use it to realize the best of their being.

Most people, however, find it difficult to untangle the jargon psychology and medicine use to describe the extraordinary complexities of mind and body functions. The sciences are much too occupied with the details of such complicated mechanisms to take the time to reduce them to easily understood statements. Yet it is exactly these concepts that are needed if we are to use the energy of mind to accomplish its full potential. Distilling the essence of mind-body operations has been one of my particular interests, and in the following two sections I offer a brief summary of mind-brain operations that, even in skeleton form, demonstrate the imperative to explore the skills and resources of the unconscious mind.

Let me first review briefly how the vital body systems operate. Once we have an understanding of the basic operations of body, it will not be difficult to explain how the unconscious (and conscious) mind works to change the functions of the body.

One of the most fascinating and imaginative "popular" scientific books ever written about the mechanics of the human body is H. Chandler Elliott's *The Shape of Intelligence.* [1] The neurologist-author captures the essence of the great interacting networks of the body and reduces them to streamlined, elemental, orderly systems that perfectly explain the role of every cell, every tissue, and every organ in the normal functioning of the human body. The body is, in this extraordinary analysis, a completely automatically adjusting mechanism. When it is broached (stimulated), it reacts with infinite appropriateness to ensure its own survival. It is a complicated piece of machinery, and its operator is the brain, the specialized control centers which process the information about the body's environment and initiate the adjustments necessary to maintain life effectively.

There is no mention of mind. The sciences that deal with brain

---

1. New York: Scribner's, 1969.

rarely admit to the concept of mind. And indeed, if we dispense with the idea of mind, we come to a startling conclusion: that the organization and operation of the human body are primitive and simple—indeed, machinelike. It is only the processes of mind that give the body and brain versatility and sophistication.

Reduced to their basic operational principles, the functions of the body are astonishingly unsophisticated—not much more elegant than a cat's or rat's or elephant's body. This is illustrated by the general agreement in medical science that the major systems (divisions) of the body are only three in number: the skeletal muscle system, the autonomic nervous system and the organs (viscera) it innervates, and the central nervous system.

The skeletal muscles, so called because they are attached to the bony skeleton, make up the main mass of the body. They are the effectors of commands emanating from the brain, and they can do absolutely nothing without the nerves that come from the central nervous system (brain and spinal cord). And, in fact, even with nerves, all they can do is contract. In body function relaxation is simply not contracting. Muscles appear to be specialized, but this is actually not an attribute of muscle tissue; rather, whatever specialization muscles have is directly dependent upon what happens in the nerves that supply and stimulate them. For example, in order to execute a smooth muscle movement, such as tapping the finger, exactly the right sequence of muscle fibers must become active and contract, and this is dependent upon the right number of nerve impulses reaching the right muscle fibers at exactly the right time from higher coordinating nerve centers in the spinal cord and brain. It all goes back to the central nervous system, leaving the entire skeletal muscle system as a helpless puppet, useless without the apparatus of the brain pulling the strings.[2]

The second system is the autonomic nervous system (ANS), a special nervous system regulating those internal organs which support life through a normally autonomous feedback system involving a primitive central control that adjusts visceral activities by reacting to sensory information, such as activating reflex motility when pressure in the intestine is increased. The viscera can actually function

---

2. There is a small neural system in the spinal cord that can *actively* inhibit muscle contraction, but it is used principally within the spinal cord–muscle feedback systems.

fairly well without the ANS at all. Normally the ANS controls all internal functions along with such functions as body heat, water balance, blood pressure, waste disposal, sexual responses, digestion, etc.

There are two divisions of the ANS, the sympathetic and the parasympathetic, sympathetic meaning that the function is sympathetic to (protective of) life function, and parasympathetic meaning that there is another set of nerves of similar origin which tends to compensate for the actions of the first set. When body functions are challenged, as during eating or exercise or during danger, it is mainly the sympathetic division of the ANS that mobilizes the internal body activities toward action, and when the need for action is over, the parasympathetic division is automatically activated to return the internal system toward a normal state.

The ANS has been likened to the nervous system of insects, and it is, in fact, quite a primitive kind of nervous system. Anatomically the ANS can be seen to begin and end in the lower brain, in the region of the hypothalamus and with connections to the central endocrine organs (pituitary). From here in the lower brain, the neural connections are diffuse and almost impossible to trace, but there is physiological evidence that the ANS interconnects with many, if not all, of the higher brain centers. This is fairly obvious, since even imaginary thoughts about danger can excite the ANS and activate the viscera to action. Nonetheless, the ANS, like the muscles, is primitive and undistinguished in its actions without the coordinating activity and direction from the brain.

The third and most important system is the central nervous system (CNS), consisting of aggregates of nerve cells with similar functions housed in the brain along with all of the functional nerve junctions that connect with the brain. It is truly the nerve center of the body's organization and function. The CNS includes everything concerning nerves, from the special nerve "receptors" in all sense organs which send information to the brain to all terminal nerve cells which excite and activate the organs (muscles, heart, etc.). As the collector of all the information about changes in the environment of the human organism—through sight, sound, smell, touch, vibration, and from muscle, and visceral and other internal sensors—the central brain core sorts out the information critical to making effective changes in the organism so it can survive and function in the changing environment.

The Nature of Mind-Body Operations

One of the most miraculous systems of the human body is the orderly and endless communication between the higher mind and all of the elements of the body's vital being.

Between brain and body are endless networks of nerves that carry information between the brain and every organ and muscle of the body and between the scores of specialized areas in spinal cord and brain. When most of us studied physiology and neurology, we learned that sensory nerves carried information from organs and peripheral parts of the body to the brain and that motor nerves and other efferent (carrying away from the central neural core) nerves carried information from the brain to guide the activity of the body.

It is hard now to believe how naïve biomedical experts were such a few short years ago. Gradually we have come to learn that the operation of the body involves more than nerves carrying information to and from the central nervous system. We have come to realize that the operations of the body depend upon feedback systems (also called control systems), in which the effects of a regulating system are governed by information returned to the system about its effectiveness.

For every "automatic" regulating feedback system of the body, whether it is the neural-biochemical mechanisms that regulate gastric acid secretion or brain neurons of the cortex alerting other brain neurons to be attentive to new incoming information, there is always (postulated) a yes-or-no control mechanism that decides whether a body's ongoing functions are proper and appropriate or whether they need to be changed according to information the central control receives.

A feedback control system is a system that performs a function, almost always by using information fed back to it about the effects of its performance. It is as fundamental a principle of the behavior of natural phenomena as are the principles of thermodynamics.

The feedback control systems that regulate all animal and human body functions and all behavior correspond in principle to mechanical control systems, such as the household thermostat for heat control

or the computerized guidance systems for automatic pilots in air-
planes. The "control" is simply a mechanical device that compares
the information about the relevant environmental condition with
what the system is doing. If the control system is a heater thermostat,
for example, the control compares the heat level in the selected
environment (the information "fed back" to the central control) with
what the thermostat is set for. If there is a difference, the "on" part
of the system is activated; if the outside temperature is about the
same as the thermostat is set for, nothing happens. A similar system
exists in the body for body temperature and, in fact, for all the
functions of the body, from stomach acid to pupil diameter to blood
sugar levels to blinking. If differences between actual and desired
activities are found by the central controls (brain), then appropriate
mechanisms of the body are activated to ensure that body function
is maintained in a way appropriate to the environmental conditions
that exist.

All operating systems have goals, and for automatically operating
systems the limits of the values for the goals are preset. If one's hand,
e.g., touches something hot, the information about the hotness is
sensed and fed back to central control of the body's system (the
brain), which detects that operating limits are being exceeded. Central control then adjusts its operations to return to within normal
limits by activating the neural switches that remove the hand from
the heat. The goal of the system, of course, is to maintain its state of
well-being, and so the limits of heat it can stand are already preset.

For people excited about mind and consciousness, this kind of
analysis is welcome relief from the reductionist approach which studies complex phenomena by analyzing their parts or basic elements
and explicit responses to stimuli. Almost everything about human
beings has been studied by reductionist techniques. Not until long
after World War II did the science of system analysis (cybernetics)
and feedback control systems begin to influence the behavioral
sciences, and even today few scientists who study human behavior
are versed in the quite simple principles involved in analyzing systems as wholes. Feedback system concepts allow study of living organisms as wholes with self-regulating systems.

Cybernetics, from the Greek word meaning "steersman," is the
science of communication and the manipulation of information in
controlling the behavior of biological, physical, and chemical sys-

tems. Probably the most fundamental outcome of cybernetics has been the demonstration of the critical role of feedback information in systems with automatic control.[3]

Central Control Is Mind Control

If it is true, as it seems, that the systems of the body do operate by simple, automatic mechanisms, the critical question then becomes, How do the hundreds of "automatic" systems work together for coordinated activity and intelligent human behavior? To account for the way different physiologic systems interact with each other to produce a smoothly operating whole organism, it is assumed that there are organized, graded classes of feedback systems, each with a "higher" control.[4]

If you have ever struggled to understand the structure and interacting functions of the human body and become mired in its complexity and detail, whether in high school or medical school, the schematic description in figure 1 may give you a surprising new perspective. Simplifying the intricate meandering maze of biological structures and physiologic functions to schematic representations of their most fundamental and important elements (as in figure 1) creates a finite, comprehensive framework from which it is easy to grasp how completely the mind-brain complex controls operations of the human organism, discussed in the immediately following section.

The diagram in figure 1 schematically represents the major feedback systems of the body and shows how higher-order mental functions dominate and can control all other functions of the body. Be-

---

3. Feedback information is information that relates events influencing the behavior of a system from the outside to operations inside the system. All systems, whether amoeba or electric stoves or human beings, possess sensing devices that detect changes outside the system relevant to their operations, and the relevant information detected and sent "back" to the system about its operation is the feedback information.

4. An example of how "higher" (more cerebral or intelligent) systems operate to control more basic physiologic feedback systems is staring fixedly at something. Normally the eyes blink and shift their gaze, actions which are automatic and prevent the eyes from drying and becoming excessively fatigued. But when one's attention becomes fixed on some object or scene because of its unusual meaning, one sometimes stares so long the eyeballs tend to dry and eye muscles fatigue to the point of discomfort. In this instance, a "higher," more cognitively related system has inhibited the normal regulating action of the eyes' physiologic feedback systems.

cause it is certain that virtually all brain and body mechanisms operate by means of feedback, it becomes obvious that the operations of
brain we call mind are in a position to affect *all* physiologic activities
of the human organism—including the electrochemical activities of
brain itself. That mental events affect actual brain activity is clear
when the character of the interaction between higher-order mental
processes and the environment is examined. While the integrative,
interpretive functions of mind use information perceived from the
environment to adjust the behavior and the physiologic activities of
the individual, at the same time the same integrative, interpretive
functions act upon and can (and do) easily modify the information
they sense and perceive from the environment (e.g., being so involved in planning the day's activities you fail to notice the toast is
burning).

In the more highly evolved species, functions of the body and its
behavior are controlled by two different mechanisms: the functions
that "automatically" adjust to environmental change (all the vital
functions) by means of feedback control systems; and the *intervention* in these automatic functions by the higher-order integrative
mechanisms of the mind-brain complex for purposeful, intentional
change. (Intervention of the intellectual mechanisms in physiologic
activity may be beneficial or detrimental, conscious or unconscious.)

The feedback theory of brain-body operations culminates with
the eternal question: What is the ultimate control?

Most theorists propose that the ultimate control of behavior and
vital functions lies simply in the decision-making capacities of neural
networks concerned with judging, associating, and comparing more
and more complex or abstracted information. But, like the age-old
question of how life began, the question for feedback theory is, What
sets the master control of mind-brain activity? My diagram in figure
1 shows that the integrative, interpretive, higher-order functions of
the brain interact with the environment (both internal and external),
and by using the information from the environment adjust the behavior and activities of the individual. But the higher-order mental
processes also influence what they themselves perceive from the
environment. Thus mind-brain activity continuously modifies perceptions and perceptions continuously modify mind-brain activity.

The implication of figure 1 is that the critical function of mind in
relating the individual to the environment is its ability to integrate

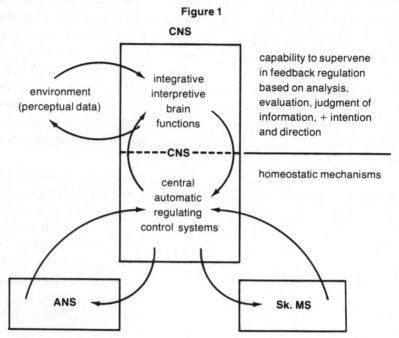

Figure 1

ANS = viscera innervated by autonomic nervous system
Sk. MS = skeletal muscles innervated by sensory-motor nerves
CNS = central nervous system

and interpret information from the environment. Because individuals function as integrated wholes, no *single* decision-making process of brain activity can support integrated behavior that depends upon so many interacting pieces of information needed to appraise and respond to the endless variations of our physical and social environments. Only a product of brain activity such as a *pattern* of activity that contains the capacity for simultaneous control of many functional systems (mind) is capable of relating the extraordinary elements and variations of environment to the endless number of elements and variations of the human organism. The essence of mind is this capacity that can extract the thousands of bits of information we need to regulate body activities by mind and order them to a highly specific effect on the physical elements of the body that carry out our physiologic functions.

The automatic operation of the body via its nerves became automatic only through the good offices of a central nervous system that also evolved mind. As animal life became more complex, primitive reflexes were "left behind," but neural connections multiplied to coordinate the actions of all physiologic systems with each other and became brain. As brain evolved mind, it left instructions for the physical being about how to regulate its own activities through appropriate feedback circuits and be automatic (within limits). But like the Executive Board of any organization, the mind retained its ability to assume command over body whenever it was appropriate or needed.

CHAPTER 4

Body Sense:
Cradle of Awareness

Awareness Begins with Perceptions

The idea that mind can regulate internal states is an idea of bewildering proportions. Informed scientists are no different from anyone else in their awe when finally faced with the seemingly inexorable force of an apparently intangible energy that can move the molecules of one's own being. Trying to understand how an "invisible" nonsubstantial mind can command physical nature is a task fraught with ambivalence. The evidence is clear enough; the problem lies in untangling the inaccuracies in a vigorous and dogmatic scientific mythology and explaining why understanding the phenomenon has been so difficult. There is so little truly known about the depths of human mind capacity that explanations of the mind-over-body phenomenon become mired in rebuttals of old beliefs and the need to redefine complex mental activities.

The situation is unnecessarily complicated. The average human being has invariably experienced the power of mind over body. Nearly everyone, for example, has had the experience (or knows someone who has) of wishing away warts. It is a common magic of mind, a magic that plagues the best of scientific reason.

Recent experience in controlled research suggests that mind-over-body phenomena all begin with focusing the attention, actually with merely drawing attention to the source of information: the interior physical self. Once the attention is directed toward the source, the remarkable number of man's senses begin to detect the myriad physical exertions of the internal being to which the attention is directed. With perhaps twenty-two different kinds of biological senses,[1] and many of these cooperating to detect and interpret the intricate networks of moving biochemicals, it is not surprising that the information the sensory apparatus detects can flood the brain with data about the body functions. The brain gathers the information, puts it together in a way that localizes the sensations, estimates the degree of ongoing activity, fits it with previous experience, evaluates it for relevance, and fashions a final product of brain activity we call perception. Perception is the beginning of mental activity.

Even this early in the explanation of mind-over-body, however, we must detour because of gaps in our knowledge about that most basic, critical operation of mind: perception. The snag is, as we have seen, that science has been preoccupied with studying the mechanics of *sensations* of discrete, *external* physical events (feeling heat, cold, pressure, etc.) with little if any attention to how *meaning* is attached to sensations to translate them into perceptions. Nor is there a whisper in science about the perceptions of internal events.

In a typical advanced text, for example, I read that perception is sensation plus the way experience, learning, and motivations alter the information detected by the senses. I search the book for explanations about how such mental actions do indeed affect sensations and find no further mention of these powerful influences of mind.[2] Science seems to be happy that we have learned a great deal about *how* we sense our environments, and leaves the important issue of what sensations *mean* to us up to someone else.

We have to pick up the threads that can tie mind and body together and make perceptions out of sensations from other sources, and when we look, the threads are skimpy at best. Our most useful

---

1. Described in Roger W. Wescott, *The Divine Animal* (New York: Funk & Wagnalls, 1969).

2. Two of the few scientists who ever dared to speculate on the way we really perceive our worlds are Charles Solley and Gardner Murphy, and although their data have been available for some time, scarcely a note about how sensations are interpreted for the mind's appreciation is made in most science texts (C. Y. Solley and G. Murphy, *Development of the Perceptual World* [New York: Basic Books, 1960]).

data come from documented anecdotes, a form of evidence not generally or willingly accepted by science. The most powerful illustration of how mind can *innately, unconsciously,* abstract the meaning from many interacting senses (sensations) to form perceptions and then complex concepts and understanding (one of the most difficult mental tasks) is the mental feat, at age seven, of Helen Keller, the famous blind deaf-mute who achieved a level of intellectual genius still marveled at today. Once a suitable tutor was found, with no instruction other than forming letters on the child's hand to spell out the names of objects, in an incredibly short time the child grasped several of the rules of syntax, the basic structure of language.[3]

One really needs no other example to illustrate the innate human capacity to form complex concepts from elemental sensory information. If the mind can create a synthesis that expresses the very essence of human intelligence from the raw elements of sensations, as the child Helen Keller did, it should have no trouble understanding information about its own body. With the intelligent, unifying, purposeful integration of even the most elementary and physical mechanisms of the body by the unconscious mind, the understanding the unconscious achieves is the instrument that can achieve successful management of the forces that affect the physical being.

Some of the most fascinating properties of man's being are rarely considered for understanding either the nature or potential of man. Almost completely unrecognized are two highly complex, vitally important operations occurring within the unconscious domain, operations that generate our awareness of self and body and relationships to all outside the self and being. These are: (1) that awarenesses depend upon the integration of information about events in widely separated parts and systems of the body; and (2) that we possess evolved senses that depend upon an integration of information of events and qualities in widely separated parts and systems of nature.

I suspect that these "senses," or kinds of awarenesses, which reason and evidence point to as fundamental capacities of mind yet which are never conceptualized, are important guides to unconscious mental activity. Exploring them is another detour, but I think

---

3. Children learning to talk also innately grasp rules of language, but the relationship of this kind of conceptualizing to unalloyed sensory stimulation is obscured by other, simultaneous influences.

a necessary one, to the goal of understanding how the unconscious mind can perform its intelligent control of the body.

Biological Awareness

The sciences of human behavior have surprisingly poor definitions for the most fundamental properties of mind. Awareness and consciousness are used interchangeably, usually to mean a state of the individual characterized by knowing or understanding a good part of what goes on around one's self. It is an imprecise definition, and does not distinguish the many levels of awareness with which we are all familiar. Some kinds of awareness can be communicated, some can be only hinted at, and many feelings defy communication or even description to one's self.

I have proposed there exists a kind of awareness about the physical being that does not communicate directly with conscious awareness,[4] an awareness so remote from normal consciousness that it communicates only with the unconscious mind. I have called this kind of consciousness biological awareness, meaning that somewhere in the mind there is the means for knowledge of every physical operation of every physical part of the body at every moment in time.

Take, for example, the common experience of being gnawingly, cravingly hungry for a special food or taste that you can't describe even to yourself. As a child I used to drive my mother to distraction by insisting I was starved, but didn't know exactly what I wanted to eat. I would turn down her every suggestion of food until the hundredth or so finally placed it. In later years I would analyze this experience, and find it wasn't so much a hunger for food as simply a craving for one very special kind of taste. I would search the refrigerator and cupboards endlessly, look at the market ads for ideas, and sample everything in the house without any satisfaction at all. Sometimes the answer was a poached egg, sometimes a breakfast cereal, sometimes stewed tomatoes (which I dislike). The puzzling part of the craving is that absolutely nothing satisfied the "hunger" except the specific item that consciousness is helpless to identify. If this kind

---

4. "Biological awareness as a state of consciousness," B. B. Brown, *Journal of Altered States of Consciousness* 2, no. 1 (1975).

of experience were simply wishing for a certain kind of food, it could be labeled as nothing more than a whim of mind. But when the whim is satisfied only by a highly specific taste, yet the sensations are associated with hunger but are not hunger sensations, the most rational explanation would seem to be that there is some biological need recognized in the unconscious, an awareness that consciousness responds to but cannot express. And once the need biological awareness detects is satisfied, the sensation vanishes.

Animals can be observed to respond to biological awareness. One of my dogs, a lhasa, has very long hair that parts precisely down the middle of his back. When I rumple his hair, he immediately shakes vigorously, and in a second his hair is neatly parted down the middle again. I suspect he has an innate awareness of the "part" in his hair. Most human beings do, too, and they experience considerable uncomfortableness trying to wear their hair with a part on the opposite side of the head. It is an expression of an awareness of how biological elements behave when they are part of a biological "whole."

This kind of evidence for a special biological awareness operating below the level of consciousness is fragile evidence. The awareness is assumed to exist only because no other explanation seems plausible enough to account for sensations strong enough to make a dog shake its disturbed coat or people recomb their hair because of an uncomfortable part.

But now from biofeedback comes startling evidence that the biological awareness of ordinary people is so powerful that awareness of the actions of a single cell can be achieved. One of the most dramatic examples of the ability to recognize even the most obscure, cryptic, and highly complex physical functions of man was related to me by a neurologist friend.

He was asked to do an EEG diagnostic analysis of a seven-year-old mentally retarded girl, to try to trace the origin of her seizures. The child was wired around the head for the EEG recording and, for some obscure reason, was able to watch a TV monitor of the brain wave recordings. These are complicated squiggles written by a pen on anywhere from eight to sixteen different channels, and are difficult to interpret under any circumstance. The first ten minutes or so of the little girl's recordings were normal; then, as the child watched the wiggly lines passing by, one single abnormal brain wave occurred in the maze of lines flying by. It was over and done in a quarter of a second. The child stared, put her hand over her mouth, and exclaimed, "Oh, excuse me!"

She had perceived the impossible, the misfiring of a few brain cells that had only mildly distorted the brain wave recording, and she knew immediately that something in her body was misbehaving.

Many of us in biofeedback have observed something similar as we have worked with hundreds of people to help them learn how to control their brain wave activity, particularly alpha and theta brain waves. Probably the most amazing outcome of their learning experience is the inexplicable identity they develop with these very special brain waves. Once they have learned to control them, there is no possible way to deceive them by substituting other brain waves or anything else we might pretend are alpha or theta brain waves. People are trained to control specific kinds of brain waves mainly by showing them a light signal when that wave is present in their EEG pattern. Normally alpha waves appear somewhat sporadically and are present in the EEG for only a second or two at a time. Yet, if we try to manipulate the light off and on artificially on a time scale much like that for alpha waves, our trained subjects almost invariably become upset and scream that something is wrong with the apparatus and shout, "That's not my alpha!"

This is very unsettling behavior for a psychophysiology theorist to explain. *No one* has ever had a prior sensory experience with his brain waves. After all, not only is the recording of them rather arbitrary electronically, but the subjects doing the learning see only a light signal to tell them when alpha is present. During their training, of course, they have the opportunity to associate the light signal with the way they feel when the light is on, and one can only deduce that trained subjects have come to identify this feeling with extraordinary precision. They cannot, however, express the feeling in language. It is simply a body feeling that we have not yet learned how to describe.

Many people learn about their "delayed" allergies in much the same way. Some people with allergy to chocolate, for example, do not develop the symptoms of their allergy for some 12 to 18 hours after ingestion of the chocolate, so that usually sleep intervenes between eating the chocolate and the onset of the symptoms, most often a vascular headache of the migraine type. This is a very long interval of time over which to make associations between one of many foods eaten and waking up the next morning with a migraine headache.

Eventually most of these people become aware of special internal sensations preceding the headache and gradually come to associate the feelings with chocolate. The sensations defy verbal expression, and the best description so far has been that it feels as if some chemical is irritating the nerves all over the body. Although the sensations cannot be expressed, they can be conjured up as feelings in imagination so vividly that the mere sight of chocolate can eventually become revolting.

Other "New" (Evolved?) Senses

Feelings of body image and personal space may be intimately related to the innate awareness of one's own biological being. Most psychologists interpret body image as how one feels one's being appears to someone else, while physiologists, occupied with the physical body only, tend to explain the sensation of body image on the basis of the senses of position and motion. Physiology may be able to explain how one or another sense, such as the sense of location or relative motion, gives the brain information about where the body is and what it is doing, but what physiology doesn't tell us is how we are able to appreciate, i.e., have the *sensation of the total body as an harmonious whole.* No one has bothered yet to define how we experience the sensations of many senses acting together, such as an awareness of the physicalness of our being, sensations that are quite different from the sensations from any one sense, such as touch or heat.

The self also has a sense of its physical boundaries, but more, human sensations also include a sense of the totality of the functioning of its being. There may, in fact, be two evolved senses, one a *feeling* the principle of life and the other a *knowing* the unity of being. Descartes' "I think, therefore I am" might just as well be said as "I am aware of the livingness of my total being, therefore I am." The sense of self is not the kind of sense science explains, except to infer that it is learned by experience and through the effects of one's culture. I would argue somewhat differently.

One argument is that if we follow the development of animal life, we see the evolution and creation of new and specialized senses in different animal forms, such as the radar sensing system of bats or the special thermal sensors of snakes. It stands to reason that if survival of a species depends on the evolution of special sensory apparatus, then the senses of his animal heritage would be developed and modified in the species man to fit him for survival in new environments. And man's survival may well depend in part upon the continued expansion of the capabilities of his senses and the evolution of new senses.

A sense of physical body image and the sense of the totality of one's being may be senses that have been sharpened, or possibly created, by the complex social environment that man has created. It is an environment far different from that of any of his animal relatives, and different still from the social life of primitive man. Social demands today are much less concerned with the survival of the species man, or even with the survival of smaller groups of man. A large part of surviving today means individual rather than group or species survival. We can trace the growing importance of the individual, and with it we can trace important although subtle differences in the behavior of human beings. A sense of body image, that sense of personal identity, may be a sense developed to help individuals assert their identity and make them aware of the needs of the individual self in the struggle for social survival.

One of the new fascinations with body image and the sense of personal identity is with the characteristic dominance of one side of the body over the other in performing. The seemingly innate preference to use and improve the skills of one eye or hand over the other has recently been found to extend to other skills. New experiments have shown that people can learn to change the temperature of the dominant hand much more easily than they can for the nondominant hand. The implication is strong that the more skilled a body part is, the more the identification sense is abstracted and the more it is appreciated by the central nervous system and brain. It is a lot easier to wink with the preferred eye than to wink with the other eye. I suspect that when the less skilled parts of the body are called upon to perform (winking the other eye), because they lack eye-brain coordination memory, they excite the sensory organs helter-skelter, bombarding the normal nerve circuits with distracting impulses, and interfere with learning and performance. Whatever it is that puts certain skills on one side of the body over the other, it also gives us a sense of awareness of the dominance of that body side. It suggests, too, that we could develop other biological awarenesses and use them to maintain the body's well-being.

Another argument for the evolution of senses peculiar to man is based upon the capacity of the brain to associate and integrate and use information from *all* the senses in increasingly complex and specific ways. When we learn some new principle about mathematics, for example, we can apply the principle to all the problems that are based on that principle. This is called generalization of concepts. What surprises us is that complex concept formation can take place within the deep unconscious mind without any help from conscious awareness. The aesthetic sense of human beings is an example of a quite new sense, where love and appreciation of nature and of the creations of animals and man alike are abstracted and isolated as a very special sense of human beings, primitive or civilized. It also has the peculiar characteristic of being expressible only by creating things or by a very special feeling of satisfaction. Evolving new systems for sensing the new complexities of our world from old, more primitive senses is not an unexpected process, as we now know from cybernetics theory, which also explains how the evolved new systems may have quite different characteristics from the systems used in their evolution.

There are some senses integral to successful functioning as living beings that rarely appear to conscious awareness. Nonetheless, these senses might be deduced to be recognized by the unconscious mind and be involved in the "evolution" of more complex senses, such as the sense of self-image. An example is the sense of gravity, one of the more unfamiliar senses. The *awareness* of this sense may have been responsible for one of my most profound sensory experiences; I do not know. I once felt the earth's rotation. It was nearly evening, and while lying on the floor, gazing at the sky between two edges of roof, I became aware that the moon was beginning to peek just above the lower roof edge. The space between the two roof edges was not large, perhaps two feet, giving me a modest piece of sky to see. I began wondering how long it would take the moon to "travel" across the small expanse. I watched, and the moon rose, rather swiftly because of the small space, and after some fifteen minutes it had risen above the upper edge. My experiment over, I rose. Planting my two feet on the floor, I suddenly became aware of movement—a rotation downward, opposite to the "passage" of the moon. My God, I thought, I'm feeling the earth's rotation! My intellect was unbelieving, so I rushed to the phone and called a friend in Texas, a theoretical physicist and amateur astronomer. He was not surprised, noting that the sensation had been experienced by others, but was still rather a rare experience.

I still puzzle over how it is possible to absorb into a completely immobile body, whose entire experience has been in relationship to a "nonmoving" earth, the sensation, the feeling of the earth rotating on its axis. Probably what puzzles me most is that the sensation occurred *after* my attention shifted from the apparent movement of the moon. Until then I hadn't been aware of movement sensation in the body (opposite to the passage of the moon through the roof spaces). And even more surprising, I was fairly certain about what the sensation was. If my unconscious had made the association between feeling motion and the earth's rotation, it did so with amazing speed and accuracy, and despite the fact that the sensation of the motion was exactly the opposite from what I had observed visually. Calling my friend to validate the cause of the sensation was, no doubt, the result of my scientific training.

The point of reciting this experience is to illustrate that we have many kinds of senses we may never become aware of. Yet these same senses serve important functions in the business of living. It seems likely that how we perceive ourselves and our internal functions involves an integration of sensory information detected not only by the usual senses but by more sophisticated, socially evolved senses we scarcely know exist.

Body—the Mirror of the Mind

Information about the status of most of the body's internal activities rarely comes into conscious awareness, although, as I described earlier, under special circumstances an unconscious awareness of internal states can generate intentional but unconsciously appreciated behavior (like the biological "drive" for more coffee), and under other circumstances ordinary human beings can recognize highly specific internal change for which there has never been any prior sensory experience, as in biofeedback learning.

In the two examples of biological awareness of brain wave activity I described earlier, it was modern technology that made experiencing internal states possible. Curiously, the technology to detect even the faintest, most obscure activities of the body's interior has been available for most of this century, but it was only the accident of biofeedback that turned the instruments around to face the people being recorded and uncovered the ability to change internal functions intentionally. For a long time the science of psychophysiology has known that if sensitive instruments are used to detect internal activities, the physical changes of the body with emotions, beliefs, thoughts, and attitudes can easily be recorded. Unfortunately, these techniques were rarely directed toward studying the operation of mind.

Psychophysiologists have done hundreds if not thousands of experiments recording physiologic activity while people were challenged about their beliefs or thoughts, but the focus of scientific interest has been almost exclusively on measuring the "degree" or "direction" of shifting internal functions, assuming that all physiologic changes are caused by emotions and that emotions are, after all, nothing more than the body becoming "aroused." In all these thousands of experiments there is no mention of the role of mind, an oversight so gross and so persistent that it defies understanding by rational minds.

For example, using the lie detector, one finds that the electrical activity of the skin reveals not just intense emotion, but thoughts about emotions. Do you remember one of the first card games you played as a child, the simple game of trying to guess which card has been picked out of a deck? The one who picks the card tries not to give the game away by giggling or squirming. But the closer the guessers come to the right card, the more the youngster tends to wiggle and break into a smile.

With a lie detector, you can play the same game with adults who try to hide their thoughts and feelings. The person being recorded selects a card, and you ask questions about what card it is. As you come closer in suit and numbers to the card selected, the more there is a tendency for the body to react. If the card is the queen of hearts, and someone asks if it is the jack of hearts, the lie detector will show a change that could be interpreted as "yes" unless the questioning is continued and the queen of hearts is named. The very second the right card is named, the recording of skin electrical activity will bounce vigorously, and you know you've nailed the right card, although there are no obvious body signals to give away the answer.

Nothing, perhaps, is a more poignant testimonial to the disregard of science for creative insights into the nature of man than the blindness of psychophysiology to the original observations by C. G. Jung about the body's ability to reveal the unconscious mind. It was in 1904 that Jung reported his experiments with recordings of the skin's electrical activity while conducting psychologic interviews. Using an old-fashioned galvanometer, he found the electrical activity in the skin changed specifically and dramatically when he asked questions that penetrated the hidden emotions of his patients. He is reported to have exclaimed, "Aha, a looking glass into the unconscious!"

From then until now, research has shown that nearly every body activity reacts to emotions and activity of the mind. Heart rate, blood pressure, blood flow, respiration, muscle tension, and brain waves are all sensitive indicators of emotional and mental activity, most of which are used in the lie detector. It seems incredible that such a magnificent tool for exploring the unconscious mind has, for three-quarters of a century, been used only by police departments or the personnel departments of large corporations. Instead, the mind sciences have busied themselves with skin electrical activity to demonstrate the machinelike nature of the brain.

The following experiments are typical. They are also fascinating because they illustrate a continuing intellectual schizophrenia—the remarkable preoccupation of science with the physical characteristics of body and brain, and a surprising reticence about any contribution of unconscious activity to the reactions and activities of the body.

Conscious vs. Unconscious Judgments

How would you interpret the following pair of experiments? Groups of volunteer subjects participated in two similar tests. In the first test, they were asked to rate, verbally, the intensity of an electric shock applied to the skin of the arm. At the same time the electrical activity of the skin was being recorded. The subjects were told that the intensity of the electric shock would be changing constantly; actually, the intensity of the shock never changed, but the subjects reported that the shock intensity became less and less, even though the skin's electrical response always stayed the same. The usual interpretation is that electric shock excites physiologic processes causing the skin to react, and being mainly a mechanical event, the skin responds the same to each shock. The subjective reports of sensations of lower and lower intensity of shock, although the intensity was always the same, are explained on the basis that one expects each successive shock may be more severe, and when it isn't, the subjective appreciation interprets the intensity to be less (than expected).

That sounds straightforward enough (except for considering why awareness of shock intensity wasn't more accurate), but then comes the second experiment. The second experiment was identical to the first except that noise was used instead of electric shock. The subjects were asked to rate the intensity or loudness of the noise, and they were told that the noise level would be constantly changing, although in fact it always remained exactly the same. In this instance, in sharp contrast to the electric shock experiment, the subjects reported that the noise became louder and louder, but, surprisingly, the electrical response of the skin became smaller and smaller.

We have no choice now but to try to understand why the subjective sensations (perceptions) "manufactured" louder noises when the loudness never changed and why the biological response of the skin changed as if the noise had become softer and softer. Psychologists tend to believe that expectation is the major influence that skews our perceptions of reality, but they do not answer the question of why people would "expect" a noise to *increase* in loudness and an electric shock to *decrease* in intensity when they had been told only to expect change but both the noise and the shock were, in fact, always given with the same intensity. My guess is that the unconscious mental operations concerned with expectations are quite complicated. We have a learned fear of electric shock, and no doubt the fear raises expectations, so there is apprehension that each shock will be severe, and when it isn't the immediate sensation is compared to the expected sensation, and judged to be less than expected. The implication is clear that intellectually processed information (adding expectations and judgments) supersedes and dominates actual sensations and even over learned perceptions.

Just why the electrical reaction of the skin should decrease in response to a noise stimulation that never varied in intensity is even more interesting and contains implications that are enormously important to the understanding of the relationship between mind and body. Only one school of psychology offers a theory. Magda Arnold suggests that subconscious (unconscious) mental processes actually assess the significance of the stimulus (in this case, the noise) for the well-being of the organism and the resulting judgment then modifies the physiologic response. In the case of the noise stimulus, we assume that the unconscious mind judges noise as not very threatening, and when this judgment is confirmed with repeated bursts of noise, the body's physiology is instructed to ignore the noise.

This pair of simple experiments offers us new insights: the unconscious mind not only carries out complicated thought processes, but its reasoning can also directly and completely control the behavior of the physical body.

There is also the puzzle of why unconscious reasoning can make such an accurate appraisal of the meaning of events in the environment (noise) and direct the physical being to react appropriately (noise likely will not be harmful, so no skin electrical response), while the subjective sensations that creep into consciousness seem to misjudge the physical reality completely. If conscious interpretation fails to perceive the physical reality, yet the unconscious mind judges correctly, doesn't this suggest that under certain circumstances the intellectual activity of the unconscious is superior to that of the conscious mind? Or that the conscious mind contains some defect that prevents it from appreciating accurate information coming from the unconscious or from the body itself? Certainly there is a conflict between conscious and unconscious appreciations, and a conflict that can have serious consequences for the well-being of the body. The basic problem is that we social, communicating creatures rely upon our learning from the social consensus to interpret the meaning of private internal events rather than trusting unconscious judgments. The defect of the conscious mind is the inability to be aware of internal states, a defect that may come from our belief that the conscious mind is the superior instrument of man. Obviously this is not necessarily so.

The Body Responds

More and more people are beginning to learn how to tune into awarenesses of the unconscious mind. Most of the results of these exercises are spectacular. The most visible effect of tuning into unconscious awareness can be seen in competitive athletics, especially

when competition is one on one. We hear more about "concentration" and even "meditation" today as athletes prepare to perform.
Some athletes concentrate on concentrating, narrowing the focus of
attention and eliminating all outside distractions; some meditate,
giving themselves positive self-suggestions; some visualize, concentrating on images they project about their performances; others concentrate on body state. Whatever mind technique they use, the result is a striking effect of mobilizing both mental and physical energy
into a harmonious whole that coordinates intention and desire and
movement into a totally unified action.

I recall watching a track meet at UCLA. The runners for the 440
were in their blocks waiting for the starter gun. The gun barked, and
all the runners except one catapulted out of their blocks. The man
nearest the gun got up, puzzled. He hadn't heard the gun go off.
Concentrating on his form, on his strategy, he had failed to hear the
gun go off. His preoccupation with the interior self was so complete
he neglected to heed the one aspect of conscious awareness critical
to his goal. He had directed the physical being so completely he had
turned off hearing.

How can the mind so completely control the body? And why are
we only now beginning to learn that there are mechanisms within
the mind-brain that are the source of this marvelous "new" power
of man? If such mind power exists now, has it existed in our ancestors,
and if it has, why did we not discover it sooner?

I perceive our naïveté about mind power, as I noted earlier, as
the result of an hysterical blindness of the scientific community and
the fears that come from ignorance in the community of man not
blessed with the power of authority. More than we care to believe,
both science and philosophy have disadvantaged the common man
so thoroughly that he can mobilize no substance for his eternal yearnings for the supremacy of mind and spirit.

Take, for example, the basic understanding of the functions of the
human body. Science is wont to elaborate on the most minute details
of cellular composition or the exchange of ions between tissues, or
describe the mechanics of blood flow or the chemistry of digestion,
but it hesitates, indeed, it avoids, or perhaps is impotent, to speculate
on or explore how the elaborate machinery of the body invariably
bends to the will of consciousness. Even the aborigines of the
Kalahari Desert since ancient times have practiced mass self-hypno-

tism of whole tribes, in which healings take place, and this use of mind to heal the body is not unlike the way our own modern sophisticates, Hans Selye and Norman Cousins, used an intellectual determination to restore their ravaged bodies.

CHAPTER 5

The Unconscious
and Body Behavior

Awareness of Internal States

The ability of the unconscious mind to perceive and understand the external reality would seem to be the perfect tool to ensure the survival of the human species. Man, however, has evolved the quality of mind we call consciousness, or conscious awareness. There is no really clear, meaningful definition of consciousness. It is generally considered to be a state in which one is aware of events in present time. As I note elsewhere, the behavioral sciences are enormously vague about what constitutes consciousness. As a way of discussing consciousness, I have proposed,[1] for example, that there are at least two forms of conscious awareness, the principal form being what I call the "consensual consciousness," or objectively appreciated consciousness. This means an awareness of things, events, and experiences that is based upon agreement about one's perceptions with one's particular or general society. We have agreed that a chair is a chair or that a blue sky is a blue sky no matter how we *feel* about chairs or skies.

Conscious awareness of one's own internal states is much more difficult to describe. For most internal feelings we have agreed upon

---

1. "Biological Awareness as a State of Consciousness," *J. Altered States of Consciousness* 2 (1975): 1.

certain labels and descriptions, but the most provocative feature of these agreed-upon descriptions is that they are invariably in terms of analogies to external objects, i.e., to the objective world, and do not directly describe characteristics of the internal state from which the feelings arose. We express internal feeling states by approximating their sensation to sensations we have about or from reactions to external events, such as, "I feel peaceful" (echoing the sensations of peace after war), or, "my heart is pounding." These are limited ways at best to describe states of vital internal affairs, but we have not yet developed a more specific language. (Drug takers have probably the widest repertoire of expressions about internal states, the best known being "high" or "on a trip.")

There is yet another type of subjective feeling that cannot be expressed at all, the kind I call the subjectively appreciated consciousness, meaning the sensations we are aware of that cannot (yet) be put into objective terms. The best we can do to communicate these feelings is to express an awareness of a deeper awareness, such as, "I don't feel quite right, but I can't tell you exactly how I feel," or, "I feel strange, but I don't know why or what it is." It is an internal communication about the state of body or being. Biological awareness and awarenesses of other complex senses I described in the preceding chapter are examples of awarenesses that are subjectively, privately appreciated only and, for the most part, poorly communicated, if at all.

But we *do*, at times, have an awareness that meaningful events are transpiring within ourselves that conscious awareness cannot seem to capture, and we are becoming more and more interested in the potential of an inner intelligence to contribute to our human development and particularly to our well-being.

We are beginning, too, to become aware of a remarkable ability in the unconscious mind—with never a clue to conscious awareness —to direct virtually every facet of human behavior, including all functions of the body's vital physiology. There is, for example, the now classic prank played by some psychology students on their professor that shows the remarkable ability of the unconscious mind to respond appropriately and to direct complex behavior toward the reality it perceives. The students plotted to look attentive and wide awake during the professor's lecture only when he spoke from a particular place in the room, and when he wandered to other places in the room, they would squirm, look bored, or pretend to be drowsing off. Before the hour was up, the professor had firmly ensconced himself in the exact place where his students had driven him by their subtle changes in behavior.

In a somewhat similar situation, one researcher "directed" unconscious processes in a simple word test. He asked subjects to say aloud all the nouns they could think of for as long a time as possible. Every time a plural noun was spoken, he said, "Mmm-hmmm," and soon the subjects were saying mainly plural nouns.

Psychologists generally interpret such learning as the result of "social reinforcement," which is, of course, a basic factor shaping our behavior. But much more fundamental to understanding human behavior would be understanding the mechanisms by which the unconscious mind performs all the operations needed to react to obscure social demands with eminently intelligent behavior—without any conscious application at all.

For it is clear that in the two instances described above, the unconscious mental activities accomplished complex feats of perception, understanding the meaning of social events, making decisions, and taking action. These are the remarkable operations of mind, and an understanding of these kinds of unconscious processes can yield much more insight into the why and how of human behavior than the vagaries of social interchange and "behavioral reinforcement."

"Teaching" the Unconscious to Control the Body

From time to time psychophysiologists report studies that clearly demonstrate the ability of the unconscious mind to *learn* control over a body function, but invariably the reports fail to comment on, or even allude to, mental processes at all.

The failure of the behavioral science community to appreciate the significance of their own data owes in large part to what and how behavioral scientists have learned about the process of learning. The majority of researchers in human behavior for some time have been persuaded, as is indeed true, that learning commonly occurs through the association of ideas about things occurring in close association with one another. When most animals observe two events occurring at about the same time, in the same place, and under the same circumstances, the two events become associated, as for example the association between dark clouds and rain. Researchers, however, have believed that the process of associating *ideas* could not be measured, and because they felt physical evidence is necessary to guarantee any deductions made about the learning process, they "reduced" the complexity of learning to only those elements that could be measured and studied, i.e., by using physically measurable stimuli and physically measurable responses.

They then evolved the doctrine that the mind is made up of simple elements that can directly communicate information about sensory experiences, so that sensory information (including concepts) therefore quite mechanically becomes associated with appropriate behavior.

The experimental work of Pavlov was the first to document learning in terms of physical responses to controlled physical stimuli. By providing some nonrelevant stimulus, such as the sound of a buzzer, to a dog at about the same time a stimulus naturally producing a natural reaction (food and flow of saliva) was presented, it could be demonstrated that an association between the nonrelevant and the natural stimulus occurred: i.e., saliva flowed when the buzzer sounded without the presence of food. Pavlov always insisted (as do the modern, more mystically inclined Russian psychophysiologists) that this kind of learning resulted from "higher-order" brain activities (read "mind"); nonetheless, for nearly five decades behavioral scientists have been bogged down in the physical aspects of learning, and have not deigned to explore *how* ideas are associated in the mind-brain to produce learning.

Even in the face of this bias, the data accumulated over the decades since Pavlov, using his experimental learning technique, provide marvelous insights into the potential of mind for total dominion over body, despite the reluctance of academic psychologists to appreciate them. Take the following Pavlovian-type experiment, for example:

In subjects whose heart rates were being recorded, the spoken word "blue" was paired with a mild electric shock to the skin, i.e., the subjects heard the word "blue" spoken and a second later they received the shock. As a frightening, threatening stimulus, electric shock causes the heart rate to accelerate, while even a mental image of "blue" has little or no effect on heart rate. In the experiment, the two stimuli, "blue" and shock were repeated together for some time, until the heart rate began to accelerate when the word "blue" was spoken. Typically, at this time, if no further electric shock is given, the heart rate will continue to increase when "blue" is the only stimulus given, a demonstration that hearing the word "blue" and feeling the shock have become so intimately associated that "blue" literally means electric shock is coming, so the heart rate responds.

While most Pavlovian conditioning experiments end at this point, this particular experiment was carried an important step further. Now that the subjects were responding to the word "blue" with an increased heart rate, a blue light was paired with the spoken word "blue" and no more electric shocks were given. After repeating this combination for some time, the heart rate was found to increase when the blue light only was shown. As with the word-shock pair, these two signals, visual and auditory, had become so associated that the response of the heart rate was transferred from the word "blue" to the blue light.

It has always been most astonishing to me that experimental psychologists interpret experiments of this kind as the simple result of associating two sensory stimuli. Astonishing, because this interpretation assumes that the word "blue" and the blue light are simple sensory stimuli, like heat or cold or pain, and without any contribution from intelligent understanding, even though the understanding may be hidden in the unconscious mind. The word "blue," of course, is *not* a simple sensory stimulus.

There is much more to the above experiment than meets the average psychologist's scientific eye. Certainly anyone with any sense is going to take advantage of any clue that a shock inexorably follows, such as hearing the word "blue"; the apprehension about the expected noxious assault to the body should indeed arouse the body to be prepared. On the other hand, contrary to the psychologists' insistence that the word "blue" is a mental stimulus with no emotional overtones, the word "blue" is a symbol for a color, and almost always has pleasant sensations associated with it; so, during "learning" in the experiment that a shock will follow mention of the word, it is quite likely that there was also the mental process of developing a *new* meaning for blue: blue now means a shock is coming. That is, any previous association between blue and pleasant sensations had to be replaced. Although this displacement of a traditional association by a new association has somehow not been considered by psychology theorists, it is, nonetheless, a mind-brain process of considerable importance.

A much more complicated process in the experiment occurs when the physiologic response of increased heart rate first associated with shock later becomes associated with the blue light signal. Without carrying the analysis too far here[2] the data of the experiment suggest that, since at no time during the experiments were the subjects significantly aware of the heart rate change (although it's a safe bet there was marginal conscious appreciation), there was unconscious mental activity that could appreciate the new meaning of the word "blue" for the very special conditions occurring only during the experiment, and further, that could extract the new meaning of blueness from the light signal and associate the new (and temporary) meaning with the unconscious sensations just learned for the word "blue." The result of this unconscious mental activity was to direct quite specifically the appropriate change in body physiology, changing the heart rate. Moreover, after the special conditions of the experiment, it's a safe bet that the mind dismissed the provisional, temporary contingency meaning of the word "blue" and returned to the usual associations of blue with pleasant things.

Some insight into the complicated process of the unconscious that can so readily learn new meanings for familiar things (the word "blue" and the blue light) can be gained by considering the nature of subliminal perception.

Unconscious Control of Intelligent Behavior

Subliminal perception is probably the best-hidden secret of psychology. After the scare years ago about subliminal movie and TV commercials, experimental psychologists became so discreet about the idea human beings might be controlled by messages only their unconscious minds could perceive that we hear little about the subject these days. One always suspects government intervention when techniques to abuse man are suddenly banished from discussion. In any event, for some twenty years now there has been steadfast denial of this extraordinary phenomenon by the experts.

---

2. I have analyzed similar experiments in my biological awareness article and in *New Mind, New Body* (New York: Harper & Row, 1974).

The subliminal phenomenon is, nonetheless, quite real, and regardless of its potential for disaster, it contains a wealth of useful information about the operations of the unconscious mind and its remarkable capacity for intelligent activity. There are, as a matter of fact, many studies that confirm that human beings can and do perceive complex, even symbolic information in the absence of any conscious awareness and can and do respond to the information perceived in a highly appropriate, customary, sensible way.

The evidence for the actual perception of information subliminally comes from many studies using quite complex information presented to subjects either visually or auditorily at levels of light or sound below which it is possible to see or hear the material. Many researchers have recorded brain waves or heartbeats or skin electrical activity, then presented words with emotional meaning, such as "sex," "cancer," "Mother," "snake," etc., mixed in with words that rarely arouse the emotions, such as "building," "carpet," "necktie," and the like. When the emotion-producing words are presented subliminally, there are strong changes in the reactions in the physiologic systems, but no changes when the other, neutral words are given.

The ability of the unconscious mind to appreciate the meaning of situations perceived subliminally and react appropriately is illustrated by experiments such as reported by one group of researchers. A group of test subjects were trained ("conditioned") to react to slides of certain nonsense syllables with a skin electrical response when an electric shock was given to the skin at about the same time the syllable was seen. Other nonsense syllables were not accompanied by the electric shock. Once the subjects had "learned" to produce a skin electrical reaction to the particular syllables and not to the other syllables, the subjects were then given a tachistoscopic test with all of the syllables flashed on a screen too quickly to be recognized by the conscious mind. The results showed that most subjects reacted with a skin electrical response only to those nonsense syllables that had previously been associated with the electric shock. The only possible conclusion is that despite lack of conscious recognition of the syllables, there was an unconscious appreciation (and memory) that certain syllables had been associated with electric shock.

One interpreter of this experiment wrote that, because electric shock has painful associations (consciously), the unperceived anticipation "would enable the individual to avoid the painful situation, [and thus] this response would clearly be valuable."

This kind of limited vision about the significance of subliminal perception research is a striking example of the inability of so many researchers to understand the phenomena they work with. It takes little imagination to extract the critical elements involved in producing an appropriate response to a signal that consciousness cannot perceive. One can deduce that the unconscious perceptual apparatus of man is not only capable of accurately understanding the meaning of information, but some unconscious intelligence must also be able to make logical, meaningful associations with quite relevant memories, then activate exactly those brain nerve networks or mental processes that are appropriate to respond to what is perceived without any conscious awareness.

It is clear that most of the critical abilities of mind, with the obvious all-important function of judgment, can and do operate unconsciously with considerable efficiency. The threatening nature of subliminal research is no doubt the reason why there is tacit agreement to keep such research at a very low key.

Curiously, most research into subliminal perception is directed toward demonstrating that there *is* unconscious appreciation (understanding) of things in the environment (called subliminal stimuli) by recording the body's responses to the *learned* meaning of the stimuli. This narrow experimental approach evades the issue raised about subliminal advertising, i.e., whether perceptions of "new" stimuli containing meanings actually can *direct intelligent behavior*.

What is especially curious is that quite striking evidence for the influence of subliminal perception on both human behavior and on all physiologic functions of the body has recently been appearing in scientific journals but with never a mention of subliminal phenomena. This omission can be only partly justified. The new experiments are classified as "learning" research; nonetheless, the following illustrates that such research clearly deals with a more complex aspect of subliminal perception which involves the ability of the unconscious to detect a reality despite the lack of—and even opposition of—conscious awareness, and produce an appropriate behavior. The following is a case in point.

Intelligent Unconscious Control of Body

One of the strangest examples of unconscious learning to control body functions is an experiment in which subjects were prepared for the recording of heart rate (EKG) and were told that a loudspeaker in the room could be made to emit either high tones or low tones simply through some mental activity of the subjects. The subjects were told that when a red light signal appeared they should try to make the speaker produce high tones, and when a green light signal was given, they should try to make the speaker produce low tones. What the subjects did not know was that their heart rate recordings were connected to a tone generator, so that when the heart rate increased, high tones were produced, and when the heart rate slowed, low tones were produced. With only a relatively short practice time, all the subjects learned how to produce high or low tones "by mental means." It was claimed that they never suspected that the tones were produced by their own heart rate changes.

This is a delightful example of how human beings (and animals as well, even without instructions—see below) in some way use the unconscious mind to direct changes in body activities with exquisite specificity . . . and upon demand.

The implications of such experiments are, however, as disturbing as they are revealing of the processes of the unconscious mind. They suggest that the conscious mind has no appreciation of the unconscious mind's ability to understand and *respond appropriately* to factual circumstances. In the experiment described above, the precise relationship between high and low tones, when they occurred, and a biological awareness of very specific physiologic change (heart rate) was not only perceived and understood by the unconscious processes, but the exact physiological change the unconscious determined to be appropriate was evoked appropriately and at will in response to the different signals.

Despite such reality-relevant behavior by the unconscious, many therapists tend to blame unconscious learning for many of our psychologic and stress-related difficulties. I suspect this negative attitude about the unconscious mind stems from taking research data too literally and the lack of theoretical speculation about the nature of the unconscious. There is a further difficulty as well—lack of under-

standing of the very complex relationships between conscious awareness of the self and unconscious awareness.

The following discussions illustrate these difficulties, particularly
how certain operations of the unconscious mind can be manipulated
by that part of the unconscious that has been previously shaped by
experience and the consensual consciousness. For the evidence suggests that when conscious awareness pays attention to information
about its physical and mental being, it can change the natural operations of the unconscious—whether or not that information is valid.

What we find, in fact, is a three-part operation between mind and
body: (1) an innate unconscious intelligence that can absorb information from the environment, recruit both physical and mental abilities, and act on the information quite appropriately no matter how
complex (see p. 38); (2) a conscious awareness that can sometimes
appreciate events in the unconscious with an understanding awareness that does not interfere with unconscious decisions and actions
(such as in perfect performances, acting on intuitions); and (3) a
conscious awareness that relies on the social consensus about the
proper behavior of both mind and body.

Since conscious awareness rarely knows *how* it becomes aware of
a sensation, thought or decision, it rarely discriminates between internally derived information (body sensations, intuitions) and information from the consensus about its own sensations and behavior.
The latter—conscious awareness—is the tool that allows man to survive as individuals, and if we subscribe to the survival principle that
evolution entails accruing flexibility and a repertoire of alternatives,
it would seem likely that conscious awareness might possess the
option to overrule certain unconscious decisions just as it can control
external behavior.

Benign Interference

The extent to which consciousness, as a reflection of the consensual
consciousness, can interfere with the successful operation of the unconscious mind on the activities of the body can be illustrated by
simple experiments.

It is well known that when most people are apprehensive and
anxious about something, there are many unperceived changes in
the body functions. One of the quickest to occur is an increase in the

heart rate. The pattern is so invariable that behavioral science always assumes that acute apprehension and anxiety are accompanied by an increased heart rate. The formula would seem to be that even such mild fear as anxiety arouses the mechanisms of physical survival, i.e., to react by preparing the body to take some action (the old fight-or-flight reaction). But witness the following:

Groups of volunteer subjects were subjected to a procedure that made them acutely anxious. Their heart rates increased, as expected. As part of the experiment, however, the impulses of the heartbeats had been converted electronically to produce sounds such as one hears through a stethoscope. Once the hearts were beating faster because of the anxiety, unbeknownst to the subjects the device producing the sound of the heartbeats was changed to a mechanical device and only slow beats were heard. When the subjects heard the slow heart rate, their anxiety diminished, and with it, their own heart rates decreased.

Why should *hearing* slow heartbeats cause people to relax and lose their apprehensions and anxieties? The answer is not an easy one, but I suspect it harks back to the intelligence of the unconscious mind. In the first part of the experiment, the conscious perceptions correctly recognized a threatening situation and transferred this information to those unknown mechanisms of the mind that stimulate the body to respond in an appropriate way, i.e., by preparing to defend itself against the recognized threat. As the body reacted, the reacting organs of the body passed information back to the central nervous system about their changed conditions, as is normal, and the sensation of changed body state intensified the feelings of anxiety.

But in the second part of the experiment, the information that the central nervous system received about its body state through the auditory sense was essentially that the body was okay, not anxious. Since most of us are naïve about internal body signals and have not learned to discriminate their messages, we consciously and unconsciously accept the information *about* internal states as valid even when that information does not come from the organs involved and is false. When information about internal body states is received through eyes or ears, the information must be "processed," i.e., it must be routed to brain areas that can associate the information with previous experience to give it meaning, so that the significance can be perceived. Since the conscious mind has had no experience in recognizing its own internal body states, and is now being deceived, it initiates body reactions that are appropriate to the information it has, even though it is false. These body reactions occur in both mind and body, and in the anxiety experiment with false heart rates, the mind accepted the information it heard that the body was no longer disturbed, diminishing the sensations of anxiety; this in turn reduced the messages from mind to body for the need to prepare to defend, and so the heart rate slowed, i.e., returned to normal.

When the anxious people heard the false heart rates, the information relayed from the mind to the physiologic control mechanisms was that the heart rate was slow, and if the heart rate is slow, the information relayed back to the interpretive mind is that the body is not aroused, as the emotions relax. The result: no anxiety. This tends to confirm Jacobson's conclusion that body tensions and anxiety go hand-in-hand and that when there are no sensations of body tensions, there is no anxiety. This case also exquisitely demonstrates the potency of the intellectual mechanisms for control of body. The significant factor for physiology and psychopathology is that the perceived auditory information overrode the internal visceral information (from the viscera to central control) signalling the presence of tension.

It is remarkable that "sensations" about the body's state received by the conscious mind (the sound of a slow heart) can supersede the actual sensations stemming from actual, true body activity, and that the effect on the body can be the same *as if* the sensations were true sensations caused by direct communications from internal receptors via proprioceptive impulses to the brain.

If you remember the statement on page 47 that people who have learned voluntary control over alpha brain waves cannot be fooled by any signal they could legitimately believe to be alpha, the reason why false information about internal states can have such dramatic effects may become clearer. If people *can* identify and be (unconsciously) aware of internal functions, they cannot be deceived by false information in conscious awareness. But they can be easily fooled about their own internal states if they have never learned to identify the internal sensations of body functions in conscious awareness.

If it is still puzzling why false information about one's body can actually change body functions to become consonant with the false information, there is still another way to explain the phenomenon. The experience can be thought of in terms of mental images. Hearing a fast heartbeat evokes sensations of anxiety while hearing a slow heartbeat evokes sensations of relaxation or relief from anxiety because this is what we have learned through experience. Situations evoking such memories also evoke mental images associated with apprehension or with relaxation, and when mental images of body activity are present, it is the mental activity associated with the image that activates the body's physiologic mechanisms to respond.

Awareness of the exact state of an internal function—even one, such as alpha brain waves, that cannot be sensed by the body's internal sensory systems—is a special ability of mind that can learn and improve just as mind ability improves as it learns more about the meaning of muscle feelings when muscles are trained for special activities like violin playing, painting, soccer, or acrobatics.

The nascent ability for internal awareness is apparent at birth, in puppies and kittens as well as in human beings. Putting a ticking clock in the baskets of newborn puppies or babies to keep the newborn calm is a homey remedy based on a learned awareness of the relationship between the feeling of security and the body's physiology. In the womb the fetus has a stronger sensation of the mother's regular, slow heartbeat than of his own faint heartbeat, but once born and, especially when alone and in a strange environment, the infant may have the sensation of loss of security. Its own heart rate is rapid —not the reassuring slow beat it has grown used to. The ticking clock supplies a benevolent deception of the unconscious through conscious perception.

Reacting to Placebos Is Intelligent

The placebo is an elegant example of how consciousness can deceive the unconscious mind yet benefit the body activities. The placebo, of course, is a completely inert substance; nonetheless, when administered to patients its significance is quite falsely confirmed to be effective medicine. The unsuspecting patient, with a very real physical or emotional complaint, is given the medication; he trusts the medical environment and the medical expertise; medical deception is unheard of. The information "input" to both the conscious and unconscious thought processes is a complicated mix of clues, all indicating an unquestioned confidence that the medical experts know best and relief is justifiably expected. Every clue is positive, and with no reason to question the information, the unconscious accepts the data that it (through subliminal perception) and the senses of consciousness perceive as accurate appraisal of the relationship between its state of non-well-being and the secure promises of the therapeutic environment.

Given these assumptions that the medicine will do some good, the unconscious mind becomes preoccupied with digesting the information implicit in the therapeutic situation; and also being expectant, it no doubt becomes more attentive to internal body signals. It begins to appreciate that the tensions accompanying the illness no longer are as important as they were. Before the medicine (placebo), there was the need to worry about relief of the illness; after the medicine (placebo) the mind believes to be real, the situation no longer demands as much body tension it needed in preparing for the worst. The tensions of anxiety are relieved, for there is always the stress (tension) of being ill, and at the same time there are implicit suggestions from the unconscious that relief is here. With both subjective and physiologic relief, the patient begins to perceive the sensations of feeling better.

It is the unconscious mind, prodded by conscious appreciations of the situation, that uses the information it receives quite logically. Essentially it concludes that if relief is at hand, there is less reason to keep the body prepared for the worst. It releases the tensions, and as tensions are lifted, the physical operations of the body, freed from this handicap, can perform more efficiently and effectively, and can assist or even evoke normally occurring recovery mechanisms.

The labyrinthine puzzle of unconscious-conscious awareness intercourse that makes our social lives so complex is, in fact, the crucial substructure of all mind and body control. It is so delicate, so observing, so responsive, that this lacy, elusive organization of mind can be shown to respond subconsciously *even to the mistakes of science.* After all, the mind does depend upon information to make its conclusions and direct its activities, and when the information is sanctioned by authority, the mind uses it. This explains why so many volunteers for psychophysiological experiments so often produce the results researchers want; why Milgrim's obedience-to-authority subjects could unflinchingly inflict pain on others upon command; and why placebos can relieve real physical problems. The ingrained belief in authority by conscious awareness can indeed overrule the innate intelligence of the unconscious mind.

Deceiving the intellectual processes of the mind may not be so bad after all, under limited circumstance. There is always, however, a latent danger that the mind, with false information, can interpret its information in a way that could cause harm to both mind and body. This is what we see often in emotional and physical ills due to stress (see chapter 6).

Now that we are awakened to the crucial role of mind for the well-being and survival of human beings, we should take note of the reasons why the innate potential of mind to ensure its well-being has been so ineffective and unused. If we do possess such abilities, then some understanding of why they have not been exercised can be a logical introduction for understanding how these abilities can be revived or energized and developed for improved operations of both mind and body.

The unconscious mind does, in fact, frequently yield its power to preserve the well-being of the body. It submits whenever it is misinformed or when it is denied the information it needs to perform properly; it submits also whenever the conscious mind has beliefs adverse enough to override the delicate processes of the natural mind.

Victimizing the Unconscious

Deception of the unconscious mind by appreciations in conscious awareness can be subtle yet can produce devastating effects on body functions. In one experiment, for example, subjects were deceived about their body's internal state as they viewed pictures on a screen. It is well known that pictures especially interesting to us cause an increase in heart rate. In this experiment, while the subjects were led to believe that they were listening to their own heartbeats as they viewed the pictures, the loudspeaker system had been rigged so that the subjects heard false slow heartbeats accompanying some pictures and fast heartbeats for other pictures. The subjects were asked to rate each picture for degree of interest.

The results of this experiment were surprising indeed. Regardless of the nature of the picture, if its showing had been accompanied by false *fast* heartbeats, it was rated as more interesting than pictures accompanied by false slow heartbeats no matter what the subjects' real heart rates were. Moreover, this subjective contradiction lingered for some time. Some weeks later the subjects were given their choice of the pictures shown during the experiment, and in nearly every case they chose the picture that had been accompanied by false fast heartbeat sounds.

This begins to have frightening implications. It seems quite possible that certain types of propaganda or techniques of persuasion take advantage of this vulnerability of internal awareness. Two extremely important phenomena are involved: the unconscious awareness recognizes a body signal (fast heart rate) that is normally associated with something special in the environment, and this is a signal to pay attention and see what it is. Since the environment in the experiment was restricted to viewing pictures, there was a high probability that the pictures accompanied by the fast false heartbeats would become the object of the increased attention, and thus could easily be interpreted as "more interesting."

At the same time, however, *the externally directed (conscious) awareness overrode any inner (unconscious) awareness of the true state of heart rate.* It is not difficult to understand how the sensation of increased attention produced by hearing information about one's heartbeat and assumed to be valid could affect subjective reactions and impressions, and be dominant over the internally appreciated sensations of no-change in one's own heart rate. But it is much more difficult to understand why the subjects *didn't* rate highly pictures they found interesting and their heart rates actually did increase.

For it seems quite probable that the subjects in this experiment found some pictures interesting that *weren't* accompanied by the false fast heartbeats, and this raises the question: Since this would increase their own heart rates, why didn't they rate *those* pictures as interesting as the pictures accompanied by the false heartbeats? The fact that the subjects ignored their own increased heart rates and responded to the false heart rates clearly demonstrates that unconscious recognition and awareness can be prevented or overridden by conscious appreciations under certain circumstances. Conscious awareness is heavily influenced by authority and represents what individual consciousness has learned from the consensual consciousness. It is, nonetheless, a surprise, and a disturbing surprise at that, to learn that the errors and myths of the consensual consciousness can distort the natural appreciations of the unconscious mind.

Conscious awareness can also become so occupied with the stimulation of the present and the images it creates that it screens out the messages from unconscious appreciation. When a student, for example, develops an anxiety neurosis about examinations, the unconscious associations and understandings about his professor's peculiar behavior around exam time can easily be interpreted by the unconscious as a signal of a difficult exam coming up, and the unconscious signals the body to tense and prepare for another battle for survival. The conscious mind, however, listens to other signals ("the exam will be easy"; "this grade probably doesn't mean anything"), and in its delusion ignores the anxiety signals the realistically oriented unconscious mind is generating.

This failure of consciousness to know what unconsciousness knows may well be the basis for many conflicts between consciousness and unconscious activities. Freud once said that we would have no problems if there were no consciousness. But we do have conscious awareness, and the solution to conscious-unconscious conflicts would seem to be to learn how to become aware of the depth and breadth of unconscious appreciations and understandings. This is exactly what is happening now in a society that has become interested in body awareness and in exploring the interior self.

Permission to Become Aware of Internal States

A fascinating example of how the human mind can be fooled about itself is shown in a series of experiments in which people were asked to describe the activity of different visceral organs during different emotional states. Situations contrived to make people anxious, for example, also increase the heart rate, yet most people described their heart rates as slowing. To the surprise of the researchers, most people "guessed" wrong about what was happening in most of their internal body systems. There was no conscious awareness about internal states. A subsequent study revealed that some of the inaccuracies occurred because the researchers had used too loose a terminology, but even with better clues, people simply do not recognize signs of internal (and vital) body functions.

Why? This lack of awareness about one's own internal status may be a chicken-and-the-egg problem. We know that during biofeed-back training people can develop a keen sense of how internal body systems are behaving, and they can learn to describe most accurately what the activity states are. Moreover, with the information they get about internal activities via the biofeedback techniques (feedback of biological information), and their developing awareness about internal states, people can fairly easily learn to control those internal activities or functions. Why not before training? Laboratory evidence suggests that the awareness deficiency is of a cultural or environmental origin. That is, the beliefs of our society, accepted from scientific authority, have suppressed *both* conscious and unconscious awareness of internal events.

It is quite different in India. One observation I have made about social life in India is the unaffectedness of discussions about the human body. I have not really observed any restraints about discussing parts or functions of the body. I have begun to realize that Indians not only pay attention to internal, interior activities, but, with no inhibitions to talking about what the West considers to be the private self, they have also, at the same time, educated themselves about the meanings of different internal sensations and feelings. There is reason to believe that this training in internal awarenesses is especially useful in their system for treating many distresses of mind and body. As we know from yoga, a large part of Indian therapy uses techniques that expand awareness and the energies of consciousness.

Indian attitudes about mind and body are in sharp contrast to those of the West. For most of us it has been taboo to speak of internal states, except where community experience has given us license, such as talking about back operations or ulcers or sinus headaches. But when it comes to internal physical activities, we speak disparagingly of things like runny noses or gas or sexual fantasies, and we are too chilled by fear to talk of heart attacks or cancer or epileptic seizures. We have been trained to expunge any awareness of internal states from all consciousness.

As medicine and psychology became absorbed in pursuing the serious ills of man, they concluded that mental activities were of little use in treating illness, and in fact could be a hindrance. This dogma reinforced the general hesitancy to recognize and to accept feelings about internal states as valid.

The upshot of the cultural and scientific attitudes was that most

Westerners never tried to use the mind to influence the body, and not until the recent developments in yoga therapy and biofeedback was the possibility entertained that an informed mind might indeed benefit the body and could be systematically studied.

One of the most crucial questions we face in trying to understand how the mind affects the body, especially when the changes interfere with our normal functioning and cause personal distress, is why we weren't aware that our internal functions were malfunctioning until we felt real pain or discomfort or until the doctor told us. It stands to reason that if we have no adequate research about the quality and extent of people's appreciations of internal activities, there isn't much science can validly say about awareness of internal states. From the objective measurements we make, such as asking questions in questionnaires, or trying to correlate subjective reports while measuring different levels of internal activities, the general impression is that we have a very poor perception of internal activities. Our lack of awareness is seen in every variation of reaction to stress we may have. The tension headache is the breaking through to conscious attention of the muscle tensions that have been accumulating all day, tensions that did not penetrate conscious awareness until they began to cause pain.

The plain fact that we can develop pain and distress because we have poor perceptions about internal states should be incentive enough to examine this deficiency of ours more thoroughly. If we, perhaps, can discover some of the reasons why we have poor perceptions of our internal physiologic activities, we can be halfway on the road to preventing untoward reactions to stress. The average person is educationally disadvantaged when it comes to the inside of his body; he is as handicapped as the navigator without a sextant.

There are times when our ignorance of internal states and our perception of them can have positive consequences, like using the sugar-pill for insomnia; but suppose that, as used to happen years ago, a pain in the abdomen is perceived as a sign of constipation, and the laxative taken bursts the inflamed appendix. It seems to me that a better route to health would be to allow the mind to use its innate body-regulating capacities by removing the traditional inhibitions against knowing the inner physical being.

The yogis, of course, get around all this because their philosophy of yoga stresses the need for mental discipline. You begin with the mind disciplining the body, and the best way to ensure the body's obeying commands of the mind is to develop an intimate awareness of the parts. Those of us in the West live under quite different philosophic injunctions. We have specialists, and as I so often comment, the body belongs to the AMA, the mind to psychology, the spirit to the Church, and we have nothing left to call our own and come to appreciate and understand. We have not, like the yogis, *tried* to use the mind to become aware of the interior physical being, nor tried to use the mind to change the functions of the body.

There is, I have discovered, a frightening consequence of our ignorance about the internal workings of the body and our inability to appreciate them and perceive their needs and changes. Part of our disadvantaged status is the false information we often apply to ourselves because we pay more attention to the opinions of consensual consciousness than to our own internal realities. Sex functions, for example, are surrounded by myths, and many a sexual dysfunction is the direct result of false information of consensus shaped by prejudice or misplaced morals about what one should feel rather than what one can and does feel.

One of the reasons, I suspect, that we so mistakenly interpret the state of internal functions, like believing the heart rate to be slow when in fact it is fast, is that our culture prizes good performance, and so we assume we are performing well. In the case of heart rate (and all the misinterpretations in those experiments were on the side of good physical performance), we've all been taught that a slow heart rate goes with long life or with good athletic ability, and we assume, or wish, that our own hearts behave for our well-being.

Body Awareness and Well-Being of the Body

It seems to me that there is no longer any lack of data on which to build a legitimate concept of how the mind affects the body. Perhaps I am more venturesome than most scientists to take leave of traditional explanations, but I am, also, too much a devotee of intellectual truths to try to bend new insights into old formulas. This mix of motives has prompted me to organize some rather precise scientific data that we now have about the relationship of mind to body and propose what I believe to be logical descriptions of the process by which mental activity affects biological activity.

The biofeedback phenomenon is the starting point because, unlike other body awareness techniques, its effects can be measured precisely. By way of a brief review, biofeedback is the label for the procedure in which signals about an individual's physiologic activity are "fed back" to the individual. Usually a special instrument is used to detect internal body signals, such as unfelt muscle tension or brain waves, heart rate, blood flow, or temperature and so on. These are signals that can be converted electronically to operate lights or tones or counters. The biofeedback instrument does two things: first, it magnifies body signals we normally cannot or do not consciously perceive, and second, it converts these signals into forms we *can* easily perceive. These signals represent certain physiologic changes and are used by the individual to become acquainted with internal events, especially since the instruments are designed to follow the dynamic activity of the physiology as it varies and changes over time.

The biofeedback *phenomenon* is what happens when people have the opportunity to spend time observing the ongoing changes in their own internal states, and especially when the individual has been instructed, or asked, to change the physiologic function by some voluntary action. The kind of muscle tension detected by biofeedback instruments, for example, is unfelt muscle tension. With the signals of the instrument as guides to changing muscle tensions, even though unfelt, individuals can readily cause changes of the muscle tension. The means they use to produce the changes are chiefly mental, such as imagining relaxation, or using self-suggestion to change the tension, or shifting consciousness to a passive state.

With practice, people can develop full voluntary control over the selected physiologic activity, whether muscle tension or heart rate or gastric acid secretion or particular brain waves. The process is probably identical to learning how to control muscle activity as in ice skating or tennis or typing. Unlike learning muscle skills, learning to control internal states requires special devices to detect the normally unfelt activity, but once learned, no device is needed and the control persists, much as do muscle skills.

When we analyze the biofeedback learning situation we can recognize a number of features in the situation quite new to the average person. The most novel feature is the availability of very accurate information about the ongoing activity of a particular and unfelt internal physiologic function. This is a new experience for most people, for the only information they have ever had about their internal functions is from the samples medicine takes (blood samples, yearly health examinations), and these are infrequent and mere samples at that. Other new features of the situation are the instrument being attached to the body, the instructions to use some mental means (!) to change body function, and the new responsibility for working with one's body rather than leaving it to the expert. These new features require some explanation, and explanations about the instrument, the procedure, and what is expected all constitute a framework of background knowledge into which the biofeedback experience is set. There are, in addition, implicit clues from the environment: the friendly treatment, the tacit understanding that anyone can learn to change body activities, and change them before the learning hour is up.

The novelty, the atmosphere, and the clues are more than enough to ensure attention to the biofeedback signals displayed by the instrument, and with the new knowledge that the mind is *expected* to do something to the body function, the mind has most of the tools it needs to do its work.

The mind does do its work, and people do learn how to control certain body functions at will, but the performance that is learned gives us few clues about *how* this extraordinary feat occurs, *how* an energy of mind changes the physical processes of the body. Most people have little idea about how they accomplish the feat. The secret lies hidden below the reach of consciousness.

We can, however, make some reasonable deductions about the process because the entire operation of mind influencing body takes place inside the individual and yet is not appreciated by conscious awareness. At last we are forced to confront the issue of the unconscious mind and its prodigious capacities to manipulate the physical elements of the body. We have little recourse but to infer that the unconscious mind perceives, i.e., is capable of an awareness of, the state of internal activities. At the same time the conscious mind is focused on the biofeedback signals displayed by the instrument, taking in information about the behavior of an internal physical activity as it changes through time.

Since the circumstances of the procedure are limited to exploring the mind for ways to affect the body and to watching or listening to the signals of the biofeedback instrument, these two tasks of mind begin to coincide, and this is the occasion for additional information about both mental tasks to be appreciated within the unconscious. That is, an awareness is initiated about the relationship between the two kinds of processes, between those processes that attach significance to the perceptual information (signals) and the processes of the search to find ways to alter the activity causing the signals. We might call information from the latter processes the experiential information because it involves experiencing whether or not what the mind is doing has any effect. With practice, the relationship between the internal experiences (feeling states) and the perceptual information about the signals tends to become established, and a firm association between feeling state and signal is made.

Once the relationship between the subjective feeling state and the biofeedback signal is established, continuing the practice continues to confirm the association. The isolation of the tie between perceptions and feelings, magnified by the confining situation of watching biofeedback signals and trying to become aware of what they tell about the body, helps to distinguish one particular feeling state from all others that bear no relationship to the signal of the physiological activity being focused on. It seems likely that this sequence of mental appreciations operates to define and identify the exact internal feeling state and once identified, the states can be recalled at will.

The biofeedback procedure is a radically different experience for all human beings. It is the first time that they have been given reliable, accurate information about their internal physical dynamics, and they are given this information, moreover, in a form that is extremely easy to perceive. When the signals change over a well-defined range, and the individual has the opportunity to perceive a reflection of his own unfelt interior activities, he is given the experience of interacting with his own internal states. The indisputable fact that anyone can learn to exert willful control over unfelt internal functions yet have no awareness of this purposeful activity can only suggest that it is the intelligence of the unconscious mind that carries out the feat.

CHAPTER 6

Stress: The Uninformed Mind

The Stress Illnesses

Without question, the recent dark decades when scientific research neglected the powers of the mind have their most serious consequences in the failure of the health professions to understand the causes and cures for the distresses of modern man. It is overwhelmingly agreed that the majority of today's emotional and physical problems have their origins in the stress of life. Yet nowhere in the therapeutic worlds of medicine and psychology is there more confusion of understanding, nor such misinformation about the causes of stress disturbances and lack of coherent principles, than in the treatment of stress problems.

Stress illnesses comprise perhaps as much as 75 percent of all of today's illness.[1] This sizable estimate comes largely from the new understanding that more psychological and medical problems than ever before realized can be traced to the effects of what we call "stress."

---

1. Some estimates of the incidence of stress-related illnesses in our society run as high as 90 percent. There is not, contrary to common belief, a preponderance of other kinds of illness, mental or physical. Other categories of illness are those from infection, from injury, from abnormal tissue activity, or from congenital or birth defects. Taken as a group, these physical problems constitute a relatively small proportion of today's illnesses.

Take a look at table 1. To the best of my knowledge, this is the first time that illnesses and emotional distresses caused by, or in some way related to, stress have been brought together and classified.[2] I have recently claimed that all of these stress-related problems have their beginnings in normal, reasonable worry, and I have gone so far, in fact, as to label worry as a problem of the intellect, meaning that it takes intellectual processes of the mind to create and sustain worry. Worry, as a matter of fact, is simply problem-solving activity fraught with uncertainty.

There is an interesting difference between the psychologists' definition of worry and the standard dictionary definition. Psychologists define worry as "an emotional attitude characterized by anxiety about the outcome of future events." While I agree that worry *can* lead to feelings of obvious emotion and anxiety, I would argue that worry, as we usually think of it, is more like the dictionary definition, that worry is "to feel distressed in the mind; to be anxious, troubled, or uneasy." Worry, I will show below, is first and mainly a process of the intellect, and only when problem solving is unproductive or frustrated does worry cause overt emotion and anxiety and the signs of stress.

Table 1   Some psychologic and physiologic disturbances believed to be caused by or related to or aggravated by psychosocial stress

---

Emotional: anxiety, insomnia, tension headache, aging, sexual impotency, neuroses, phobias, alcoholism, drug abuse, learning problems, general malaise

Psychosomatic: essential hypertension, auricular arrhythmias, ulcers, colitis, asthma, chronic pain, acne, peripheral vascular disease

Organic, triggered by stress: epilepsy, migraine, herpes, angina, coronary thrombosis, rheumatoid arthritis

Psychological adjustment problems: e.g., anxiety of classroom learning (moderate interference in satisfying/fulfilling human potential)

Sociologic problems: e.g., chronic unemployment; delinquency (socially undesirable; socioeconomic impoverishment and instability)

Aggravated or prolonged distress in illness of any origin

The intellectual exercise of problem solving that is worry is the source of all stress reactions. To a good many academic theorists this

---

2. B. B. Brown, "Perspectives on Social Stress," in *Guide to Stress,* ed. Hans Selye (New York: Van Nostrand Reinhold, 1980).

may seem to be a flippant disregard of traditional concepts of the origins of illnesses, but largely, I suspect, because it violates the old tradition of using unpronounceable, ununderstandable names for the causes of illnesses.

Even the most cursory glance at table 1 reveals two generally unrecognized but nonetheless quite distinctive features of stress. The first is that "stress" can cause or provoke an impressive number of disturbances of mind and body. The second and even more provocative feature is that "stress" causes a surprising variety of *very dissimilar disorders.*

How do the health and medical theorists account for so many different types of disorders from a single cause, stress? They don't; and as a result there is, surprisingly, no unified therapeutic approach to these many different stress problems *all from the same cause.*

One problem seems to be that health scientists never bother to define what they are talking about when they talk about "stress." They tell us that "stress" is tension and the "stress of life"[3]: work problems, job competition, family problems, ethical problems, love problems, worries about "making it." The experts can recite endless examples of what kinds of things cause stress, but they can't define what is "stressful," i.e., they have not identified the special qualities or properties of things or events that make them stressful. Worse still, when the experts do research on stress, they often work with the kind of stress that has no possible relationship to what we *and* they call "stress." A recent abstract in *Science News,* for example, reproduced the researchers' report that they induced stress by placing the subjects' feet in ice water! That is stressful all right, but scarcely the kind of stress we mean when we talk about "stress."

Usually, when we try to explain stress and what is stressful, we say that some situation or some person makes us nervous or tense. But that description is simply a description of our *reaction* to something that causes stress in us, and we have to write a short story to communicate what it is about the situation or person that makes us feel stressed. Trying to define stress is quite different from defining something like electricity or vegetables or other elements of the physical universe. For these we can describe the specific properties or features or qualities of a whole class of things or events that identify any

3. As in Hans Selye, *The Stress of Life* (New York: McGraw-Hill, 1976).

thing or event as belonging to that class. Trying to define "stress" is more like trying to define what is appealing about certain pieces of art or literature. For these kinds of human creations we almost always have to describe how we *react* to the art or literature. And that should give us a clue about the nature of stress.

The Current Consensus About Stress[4]

Both medicine and psychology deal with stress as emotional and psychosomatic disorders. Both rely largely on the data and theories from psychophysiology to account for physical changes under stress, and both assume that the emotional reactions involved stem mainly from unconscious conflicts and inadequate coping devices along with unconsciously generated, and inappropriate, ways to protect the psyche. Medicine, psychosomatic medicine, and psychology also consider emotions to be either a direct or a related or a concomitant response to physiological "arousal" caused by "stress."

A great deal of the theory dates back to the old fight-or-flight concept, developed from studies of animals and people subjected to provocations strong enough to be an immediate threat to physical well-being or survival. When animals are faced with threats to their physical survival, they react, according to species and circumstances, by fighting (aggression) or flight (escaping), or by submission. In order to do any of these things, the body must first have the right kind of preparation.

The body prepares for action by first tensing the muscles, as we tense up in races when the starter says, "Get ready, get set," before he says, "Go!" At the same time the body mobilizes its vital supporting activities to support the anticipated activity. The cardiovascular system reacts by shunting blood to the muscles for increased oxygen supply, the heart beats faster, the blood pressure rises; the stomach and intestinal activities slow to stopping, and many of the body's secretions stop. All of the body's resources are mobilized for its life-saving task.

Human beings show similar reactions during intense fear, and it is not surprising that lesser degrees of fear, such as apprehension and

---

4. See also Appendix A.

anxiety, might cause lesser degrees of the similar kinds of physiologic changes. Take a horror movie, for example. If the acting is good, you identify with the actors and the action, and when the action gets to some danger point, your heart beats faster, breathing becomes irregular, blood pressure is up, the mouth dry, butterflies in the gut (motility has stopped), and the muscles are very tense. After the movie, you breathe a sigh of relief, slump down in the seat, just to relax from the sustained tensions the body has been through.

Psychophysiologists prove this in the laboratory, using stimuli strong enough to evoke obvious emotional reactions (anxiety, fear), and so the theory was developed that such emotions are the result of the body's physiologic "arousal," the preparation phase of the fight-or-flight reaction. They believe that when people are stressed, the body responds by activating its defense mechanisms, i.e., tensing the muscles, increasing the heart rate and blood pressures, and other body changes that can help the body to defend itself.[5]

I believe the arousal theory does help to identify the endocrine and biochemical changes that can occur during some stress reactions, but it doesn't account for how "stress" can stimulate nerves and endocrines. Nor can it explain why the physiological arousal can be so specifically limited to one organ, as in gastric ulcers or asthma. Nor does arousal theory explain why different individuals have such different susceptibilities to stress, nor why the same stress can affect the same individual differently under different circumstances. It would seem that the current concepts about stress have quite a few holes in them.

As a matter of fact, there are a score of intellectual boners in what you and I and the psychologists and the experts in psychosomatic medicine call "stress." Stress is (a) *not* a physical stress such as Selye worked with in his research and used in his theories; (b) *not* any kind of immediate threat to our physical well-being or survival. Instead, (c) the physical defense mechanisms of the body, the biochemical and

---

5. Scientists support this notion about the way human beings react to "stress," with the stress research of Selye showing that no matter how organisms are stressed physically, there is always a similar kind of general, nonspecific reaction that accompanies the specific biological reaction to a specific physical assault. Selye discovered that the nonspecific reaction involved the neuroendocrine system. He called the initial outpouring of neurohormonal substances the "alarm phase," and most theorists assumed that this was the way the body became "aroused."

the physiological arousal mechanisms, are *totally useless* in defending against the kind of stress we mean when we talk about "stress."

It seems not to have occurred to the stress theorists that something is missing in their amalgam of popular concepts. How do non-physical "things" (the stress of an exam, the stress of a lover's quarrel) penetrate the skull and so selectively excite the physical nature of the pituitary, the hypothalamus, the autonomic nervous system, and the nerve-muscle systems to produce the physical signs of "stress"?

A minor but nonetheless troublesome complication in understanding stress lies in the confusion about how stress is defined as a generic concept. When the discoverer of the stress phenomenon, Hans Selye, described his remarkable work on stress, he also, inadvertently, created a ticklish problem of semantics.

Selye defined stress as "the nonspecific response of the body to any demand made upon it." You can see the problem already. Physicists define stress as "a force exerted on a body that tends to strain or deform it," and so most of us interpret stress as something that *causes* our tensions, not as Selye defined it, as our *reactions* to something demanded of us. Little wonder the semantics of stress is confusing.

Insights from Common Sense

The fact that a good many of the professional ideas about stress are confused and illogical doesn't necessarily mean that the substance and data behind the ideas are wrong. Understanding the nature of stress and how to deal with stress disturbances can literally spring from the simple operation of looking at the stress phenomenon logically and carefully.

Most stress researchers and practicing clinicians are convinced that both the emotional and physical reactions to "stress" are produced by an "arousal" of the body's physiological mechanisms, as described above. The belief is that what we call stress somehow excites the instinctual body mechanisms used to defend the physical organism (the fight-or-flight reaction). When Selye documented the precise biological and biochemical changes that occurred in (physically) stressed organisms (stimulation of the neuroendocrines, the adrenals, the autonomic nervous system), he showed what happens in the body when the alarm button is pressed, as it responds to assaults by physical elements or invasions by organisms.[6]

But what so many psychologists, psychophysiologists, and therapists interested in psychosomatic medicine *thought* he had discovered was how the body reacted to what you and I call "stress." But what you and I—as well as the experts—call "stress" today is hardly ever meant to be direct physical stress. When we say that someone's asthma or nervous breakdown or alcoholism or hypertension is caused by stress, we mean something quite different. We mean the kind of stress that comes from social tensions, from mental and emotional reactions to various kinds of situations that we label social activities or interpersonal relationships.

The big question is, How does this social kind of stress, this nontangible, *nonphysical* stress, involve the nerves and hormones and endocrines of the body to react in a general way as they do to direct physical injury or bacterial infections? If stressful social situations "activate" the body's physiological defense mechanisms, how do they do it? How can the words we fight by saying, "But words will never hurt me," really hurt, and make the heart race, the muscles tense, and breath gaspy? How indeed can unrequited love transform the body and make skin rashes out of anxieties or ulcers out of competition or sweat out of fear? One of the extraordinary curiosities of modern medicine and psychology is that they have been content to know that these things do happen, and hesitant to explore either *how* physical effects can be caused by "mental" events or *why what causes what* (why do the same social activities, such as taking exams or competing for a better job, cause such different effects in different people, such as tension headaches or insomnia or high blood pressure or neurosis)?

Most stress theorists make no real distinction between what they call physiological stress (physical, chemical, or bacteriological assaults) and other kinds of stress they call psychological, social, or economic. Lumping these different sources of stress together makes it easy to explain the effects of stress on the body by the arousal-alarm theories.

---

6. Actually, Selye's very important but often overlooked conclusion is that the endocrine, biochemical, and other physiological changes stimulated by physical assaults are innate devices that resist effects of the assaults, and that most medical and surgical procedures *assist* these intrinsic healing mechanisms. The same principle operates in psychosocial stress.

The odd part about this widely accepted concept of stress and how reactions to stress occur is that it is so obviously illogical.

We can improve vastly on the experts' theories. To start, consider the different sources of stress: physiological, psychological, social, and economic. Do you see the odd member of the series? *Physiologic* stress involves direct contact of the chemical, physical, or bacteriological agents with the body; psychologic, social, and economic stresses are causes that *never touch the body*.

So, the first distinctive quality of "stress" is that it is *nonphysical*. Chemicals penetrate the skin or other surface barriers, physical accidents assault the body, and bacteria invade the body's systems, but "stress" never physically touches us. Psychologic, social, and economic stresses are always the result of an interaction between human beings and their human environments. Except for physical stress, all stress comes from the social environment. "Stress" is, in fact, *social stress*.

What is called psychological stress, such as the stress of unhappy relationships, arises from the mind's interpretation of *social* relationships and interactions; social stress, which is chiefly the kind of stress that comes from conflicts with cultural traditions of family, religion, ethics, or love, also arises from the mind's considerations of how the self relates to its own traditions and to its own activities; and economic stress, the stress of unemployment or poverty, is a reaction to the *social* conditions one finds oneself in. Everything except direct physical stress of the body is nonphysical and of social origin.

Knowing the origins of all nonphysical stress means we can identify a second distinctive quality of stress: it is always associated with events in the social environment, i.e., it always involves the self and how one's self and one's beliefs, attitudes, feelings, and perceptions relate to social situations and circumstances. The kind of "stress" we mean is *social stress*.

A third characteristic of "stress" is a seeming contradiction: that things in the social environment are not, in themselves, inherently stressful. Mothers, fathers, bosses, lovers, colleagues at work are not stressful in themselves; it is only after we attach meaning to their behavior that they can become a source of stress. Mothers and fathers, the source of so much emotional stress, or business and work associates, the source of so many psychosomatic illnesses, are not the stress. It is only after the mind interprets their behavior that mothers, fathers, work colleagues, or other people become stressful. Nasty Aunt Polly, whose interferences in family affairs are acutely stressful, is tolerated because any day she may bequeath a tidy sum, but she is not, in herself, the source of stress although her behavior at times can be *interpreted* as stressful. Outside the family she has friends to whom she is comforting and perhaps even tranquilizing. Neither Aunt Polly nor most human beings that populate the social environment innately exude stress; for the most part friends, associates, acquaintances, and family are carriers of "stress" only in certain kinds of circumstances. Even impersonal populations like government bureaucracies or AT&T or Exxon are not in themselves the carriers of stress; it is the *relationship* between self and other people or symbols such as corporations or governments who represent still other people that is stressful.

It is clear that the interpretive mind is the intermediary between the nonphysical, social environment "out there" and the body's alarm systems. There have to be *two* elements involved in all nonphysical stress: the social activities of one's world and the personal, individual mind that interprets them.

The most important and totally unique characteristic of "stress" as a cause of illness is that it is the *only cause of illness that requires activation and energizing by mental processes.*

It is the mental processes of attaching meanings to perceptions, of associating memories with perceptions, of fitting perceptions into the traditions of one's culture and education, of imagination, and a host of other manipulations the mind makes with its experiences and memories and imagination that endow particular things in one's social environment with the qualities of stress. It is the mind that transforms the environment from something of nonmeaning into events or circumstances or relationships *with* meaning. If there are no prior bits of information, the "boss," e.g., is simply the person who makes business decisions and issues orders, and the agency to whom you are responsible. The "boss" becomes a meaningful element only after you interpret his or her intentions, motivations, and interests to have special meanings for *your* relationship with the boss.

Eyes, ears, and other sensory apparatus absorb the physical nature of the environment, but it is the resources of the intellect that give the world meaning. Modern, twentieth-century man does not, like his ancestors, live in a place teeming with hazards to the physical well-being, with thorns on the fruit trees or vipers in the grass or plagues racing through the human host. For most of us, today's world is complicated, striving, conniving, competitive, political, and a laby-rinthine network of social relationships that taxes our intellectual ingenuity for social survival and well-being. How we perceive this world is the "stress of life." Only the intellectual capacities of the mind can interpret the social dynamics that surround us and account for most of our worlds. Only the intellectual capacities can take the information the senses detect and give it wholeness and meaning and make it useful. Only the intellectual processes can interpret the social world, and only when the intelligence perceives a difficulty in one's social world does the social world become stressful.

Most often we interpret our lives as reasonably satisfactory and keep our expectations within reason and within a practical reality. But when there are disappointments, the mind reacts. It perceives the activities of the social world as unpromising to its social well-being, and when it does this the mind endows those special bits of the social environment with the qualities we call "stress." The mind detects a problem, a discomfort, or an irritation because what it perceives from the social environment is not what it expected or desired. It has an unfavorable perception of the social environ-ment.

"Stress," or more accurately, social stress, can be defined as *an unfavorable perception of the social environment and its dynamics.*

The time has come to treat man and his distresses with a good deal more sophistication than the oversimplified psychologist's thesis of disturbed emotions or emotional reactions as the cause of both emotional and physical distress.

Stress Is Manufactured by the Mind

The mind interprets its social situation as unfavorable to its social well-being when it cannot understand, accept, or rationalize the differences between its perceptions and expectations. At this point in the operations of the interpretive mind, stress is a problem to be solved. The problem is simply, Why?—why doesn't what I perceive and interpret about my social relationships match what I had hoped for or expected? The mind's detection of the problem is invariably a stimulus for an operation of mind that plagues man's mental com-

posure so completely it seems to be the original intellectual endow-
ment: searching for the answer to why.

Human beings have a compulsion to understand the why of any
problem they face, and this is especially true in our social relationships. We know this nagging compulsion to solve a problem under
the more familiar name of "worry." "Worry" is, in fact, a most appropriate term for the mental activity that comprises "stress."

We all know that a little stress can be good for us, like the stress
of athletic or musical competitions or just putting on a good party.
But we also know that too much stress can lead to emotional, even
physical, problems. I believe we can understand stress a good bit
better if we call it "worry," first, because worry is a natural event of
mind, and second, because while worry means to be uneasy or troubled in mind, the mental activity behind this mind state is the intellectual process of problem solving.

Worry can lead either to coping with life's problems or succumbing to their impact. It all depends upon whether the problem solving
of worry is productive or unproductive. In the following sections I
will elaborate on worry as the critical mental event in stress and
stress reactions, and will detail the steps in the mental processes that
can lead either to maintaining a state of well-being or to becoming
a victim of stress.

Worry is a useful term also because we all understand its broad
dimensions. It includes both conscious and unconscious worry and
can be accompanied by any or all of the emotions of apprehension,
anxiety, feelings of inadequacy, of insecurity, of uncertainty, feelings
of frustration, irritation, hostility, failure, loss of self esteem and oth
ers.

All of these emotions are rooted in an *intellectual* concern—a
concern about social activity, about adequate social performance,
about meeting social criteria, and concern about ensuring one's social
well-being and survival. The subjective sensations are, in effect, all
expressions of a disturbed intellect, a disturbance of the intellect
about the way in which social relationships are perceived and appreciated.

Take the college instructor, anxious to move up the success lad-
der. He is under mental pressures to perform well, to teach, and to
do research. His problems are intellectual concerns, and when he
thinks he may not be performing well as an instructor or that there

are obstacles to his progress, his social well-being is threatened. His churning intellectual concern can lead to ulcers or colitis or essential hypertension or headaches or an anxiety neurosis.

The executive who develops ulcers is also a victim of his own intellectual activity. His most important social activity is his work. He lives with demands to perform, to gain recognition, and he must constantly interpret every happening in his work, figure out how he can do a good job, how to behave to show he is doing well, try to meet other people's expectations. It is all mental, intellectual activity, and when he interprets his social environment as unfavorable to himself, the mind sees this as a threat to existence, for it *is* his existence, and he begins to react, first with his intellect and only later with his body.

"Stress" is manufactured by the intellectual systems of man. The only other species that shows the effects of social stress is the domesticated or captive animal. The intellect, with its internal mechanisms that accomplish perception, awareness, reasoning, judgment, direction of attention, state of consciousness, memory, experiential set, and the myriad of other mysterious functions of mind, operates to transform the extrinsic factors of one's social world into the sensations and the feelings and the recognition of the contentment and comfort of one's well-being or the worry and anxiety and discomfort of what we call "stress." And it is the product of this transformation within the mind and brain that also produces the neural change that supports equanimity or arouses the body's physiology and gives the objective expression of stress reactions.

Although psychologists define emotions in various ways, the most popular and widely accepted definition states that emotion is "an aroused state of the organism involving conscious, visceral, and behavioral changes," . . . they are "more intense than simple feelings and involve the organism as a whole." The definition is not a valid one.

The kind of emotions we and the psychologists talk about are not usually intense or acute reactions. We all generally include as well such emotions as apprehension, anxiety, depression, feelings of rejection or frustration. But more important, the "aroused state" (body, mind, or both) does not usually consume the person; changes in conscious states, in the viscera, and changes of behavior tend to be quite *specific*. We do not see stress reactions or emotions that involve the organism as a whole; all except disabling emotions allow people, including their viscera, to continue to function and to behave reasonably well.

Most people grasp the global implications preoccupation with worry has for one's own well-being. Most people know from experience that too much worry interferes not only with mental vitality and emotional balance, but also with the well-being of the body. Psychoanalysts, psychiatrists, and psychologists, however, prefer to tie very specific emotional reactions to very special disturbances of mind and body functions, such as feelings of rejection to depression, or broken homes to asthma in children. They tend to view "worry" as an emotional process and a relative of "compulsive rumination," which is the primary symptom of the obsessive patient and an abnormal mental activity.

I contend that the emotional and physical distress we call stress reactions are reactions to the stresses manufactured by the mind, and that the process all begins with reasonable worry. If we can define and isolate the mental mechanisms that cause our emotional and physical reactions to stress, then we will be able to treat stress reactions more efficiently and more intelligently.[7]

Mental Steps to Distress: (1) Expectations

How do reactions to stress start? Why should perceptions of one's social relationships ever be unfavorable? Certainly social activity is integral to human life. What happens in social activity that some part of it is perceived as unfavorable and stressful?

No perceptions can be unfavorable unless there are prior expectations of something other than that which is perceived.

The first mental event in reactions to social stress is the expectation of the person about what a social situation or a social relationship might be.

The "exam anxiety" that all students suffer at one time or another illustrates the fundamental role of expectations in stress reactions. Everyone expects something about an exam: just to pass, perhaps to do very well, or not to flunk. As exam time approaches, you the student begin to perceive many things that seem to hone right into

---

7. A concept of how the stress the mind manufactures can produce so many varieties of stress reactions (as listed in table 1) is given in Appendix B.

the exam situation: rumors the exam will be tough; the instructor seems more severe than usual; something interferes with study; and other clues and things that you put together. But in each case, for every clue you perceive, the clue is colored by your expectations or hopes. You hope the exam won't be too tough, that you have studied the right material, that you'll feel sharp. But what you perceive about the exam, those many clues, don't seem to match the expectations.

It is when there is a real difference between what you expect and what you perceive that the problem begins. You expect or hope for an easy exam, the clues say it's going to be tough; you expected to know the material, but the rumors say it's going to cover other material. And you start to worry. For good reason. You have a problem you must solve for your well-being. The problem solving of the worry may be productive and stimulate you to more study, or the problem solving may show you a way out, and you get sick on exam day. But the whole process starts with expectations.

Expectations are multidimensional subjective activities that depend upon individual history, and are determined and modified by and linked to one's aspirations, one's motives, and the various clues about a situation that can have either immediate or long-range implications. All of these influences contribute toward whether expectations can be satisfied or not. No intellectual or emotional problem arises if what one perceives is something like what one expected to perceive, or if the perceptions don't match expectations but one can develop effective mental or psychological defenses against disappointments. If people can understand the reasons for differences between their expectations and their perceptions of their social relationships, or can in some way use the experience as a learning experience and gain some satisfaction toward long-range goals of social satisfaction, well-being, and survival, then there are few personal problems.

The relationship between expectations and perceptions for any social activity is enormously complex. Expectations are shaped by past perceptions, and perceptions are shaped by expectations. The expectational "set" influences what one perceives, and what one perceives can influence what one expects to perceive.

One profound influence on expectations comes from the consensual consciousness, the effect of our beliefs and culture. Much of the way we react and our social behavior is a result of what our social consensus had decided, and we are both consciously and unconsciously aware of how our social relationships and social activities should go to meet the standards approved by the social consensus. Even when we know they are wrong, we still try to meet the expectations we have been taught by social consensus.

Mental Steps to Distress: (2) Perceptions

What is perceived in a social situation or social activity or relationship requires extremely complex mental activity. To perceive, one must observe both events and series of events; one must interpret social behavior, decipher the various ways social behavior is expressed, guess at motives, take into account various personality influences, social customs, body language, and a hundred other clues about the meaning of things and events and behavior. To perceive any social situation means observation, associations, analysis, judgments, and conceptualizations.

Perceptions are fragile and unsubstantial when it comes to deciphering the meanings behind human behavior, and the frail nature of perceptions about human social behavior poses quite serious problems for the intellect and its problem-solving activity. The first problem is that the information one can perceive about social situations and relationships is usually tenuous, incomplete, and inadequate to construct solutions to social problems or for developing understandings. The mind is called upon for greater effort to fill in the gaps. Uncertainty and frustration increase and worry becomes more intense.

A second obstacle we face in trying to understand the meanings of social events that touch us is the puzzling interplay between what we seem to recognize in conscious awareness and the unrecognized influences deep in the unconscious—a strange interplay that leaves us only "half" aware of why we behave the way we do.

Even for the just-beginning-to-reason child the perception of any social activity, relationship, or situation is difficult and a complex function of mind. When Mother slaps his hands in exasperation, he feels the sensation of the blow, the pain, but he also *perceives* a separate collection of impressions. Mother is annoyed; he did something wrong; but he may also be marginally aware that Mother seems upset about something else, that what he did was all right at some other time or some other place; and he worries about the consequences of that special confluence of events. Putting it all together, in a vague, uncertain way the child forms a perception that he stores in memory. With more experience and learning, he may become more certain of his perceptions. If not, he will worry.

Suppose a man wants to attract a certain woman. He may work with his appearance, with his conversation, and do many things to make the kind of impression he thinks will be attractive. Now he watches the woman's reactions. He is attentive to everything she says, to every gesture, every facial expression, every reaction. But he is relating all of this very specifically to what *he* has done to cause her reactions. On the other side, the woman is looking at the man as if from another world, with other ideas, other thoughts that all affect the way she reacts. She does not react directly to what he says, how he is dressed, what he wears, how he acts, but she reacts to the way all of these expressions fit into *her* world of thoughts and beliefs and desires and needs. But the poor man cannot read her inner thoughts. All he can perceive is the way she is reacting. The problem begins when the woman doesn't respond the way he hoped she would. What's wrong, he thinks, she wrinkled her nose, she tapped her foot, she looked away, my *God*, she didn't *hear what I said!*

He's reading her reactions, gathering clues, and he makes a mental construction of what he thinks her actions mean. He has more questions than answers, and he rehashes his memories and the clues, trying to find the answer to why she isn't reacting to him the way he wanted. His perceptions and expectations are in conflict. He has just taken the first two mental steps to distress.[8]

Most social happenings take place over time. That is, we observe human behavior in disconnected places and at disconnected times, and to perceive and try to understand the dynamics of our social worlds, we then weave our impressions into some kind of logical, acceptable story to ourselves. The mind must construct a reasonable image of *many events occurring through social time and social space,* and involving human behavior that is often artfully camouflaged by unknown motivations, social behavioral defenses, use of obscure sym-

---

8. And this process is the reason why new psychological counselling techniques so strongly emphasize sharing feelings—at the moment—whenever one has an awareness of an inner emotion.

bols, and a good bit of nonverbal communication that may be only subliminally perceived. The perception of human behavior and human social activities may, in fact, be the most hazardous occupation of intelligent, modern man.

Mental Steps to Distress: (3) Worry

Worry does not begin the minute the mind detects a difference between one's expectations and one's perceptions of a social situation, for there is usually a reservoir of experience the mind first calls upon to reconcile the differences and to give time for second thoughts. But when the perceptions focus and magnify the difference from expectations, the difference is seen as a problem. It is then the mind begins the furious problem-solving effort of worry. With its innate curiosity and ever present "why?" the mind initiates intense activity to try to understand the reasons for the unfavorable perception or to find some way to resolve the difference and the feelings generated by the discovery that even the most reasonable of hopes and dreams may not be fulfilled. Human beings are well aware that most expectations are like betting the short end of 50 to 1 odds and are realistic enough to call most expectations daydreams. But, like the man said, "Hope springs eternal in the human breast," and human beings have so mythologized hope and desire and dreams that nearly all of human society rides through its existence on the waves of expectancy.

Expectancy exercises man's intellect more than any other social influence. The intellect is in a life-saving race with dreams to keep the being psychologically healthy. It is the intellect that must analyze and consider reasons why the apparent reality that one perceives does not tally with expectations. The temptations to dream spiral in the modern social world. Carrots are dangled on a thousand advertising sticks, and in the carrot fields there is always another carrot to dream about. The intellect is kept dancing to the carrot tune, searching for reasons why this one or that one cannot be reached, rationalizing why this one or that one is not desirable as first thought, rejecting, denying, or withdrawing to protect the ego and to resist the imminent stress of disappointment or failure.

Only a part of this mental activity may be known to conscious awareness, for the detecting systems of the unconscious mind are often highly sensitive to the subtle signals of social interactions. As with any subliminal perception, the unconscious intellect perceives and judges complex information without conscious awareness. The person who later recalls a minor inconsistency in a friend's conversation and "discovers" a problem in their relationship has, more often than not, unconsciously appreciated the incident and begun the worry process until the increasing concentrated intensity of the problem-solving worry finally breaks through the consciousness barrier.

Mental Steps to Distress: (4) Uncertainty

In most problem solving that deals with the elusive, disconnected events of social activities, the mind swings between what it believes may be promising and unpromising solutions. During those periods when it believes the solutions are unsatisfactory, or even useless, there are two activities of mind that have profound effects on the body. First, the fear of not knowing the possible, or reasonable, answers for the future is a threat to the well-being, a threat that arouses the self to prepare for the potential dangers of the unknown. And second, the failing problem solving acts as a nagging stimulus to the imagery of the mind.

Not being able to solve a problem about a social relationship means that the social future is uncertain, and the uncertainty about the future is a distinct threat to future social well-being. Since we know that apprehension and anxiety cause the body to assume a posture of physical arousal (tension), we can only assume that under the duress of social stress the mind does not distinguish between threats to the physical well-being and threats to the social well-being, and the body reacts to social threats much as it does to physical threats. A threat to well-being evokes the most primitive of instincts, the instinct to protect and defend the being against harm and danger, the fight-or-flight reaction. The defense mechanisms of the body, excited because of a threat to future well-being, mobilize a defense posture characterized by tension that is a preparation of the body to take defensive action.

This brings up an intriguing question about the merits of the human arousal response for the well-being and survival of the human species.

I contend, as I describe elsewhere, that the instinctual physiological arousal of *physical* mechanisms, developed over eons as animal species have evolved, to defend against physical assaults is not at all an appropriate defense against assaults to *social* well-being in the social environment that man has created. It seems eminently more logical to assume that an intellectual psychological defense in man either simply hasn't evolved adequately to be the usual reaction to social threats for most people, or that intellectual resources for defense against threats to the social well-being for some reason have not been exploited adequately. This notion is supported by the successes of the newer methods of psychotherapy that give people knowledge about social realities and about social coping devices.

Mental Steps to Distress: (5) The Images of Worry

During problem solving and worry, one of the most pervasive operations of the mind is the construction of mental images. Although the imagery that accompanies worry can be useful and restorative, it also has the potential to be seriously destructive. The mind's construction of images, the extraordinary potency of mental images to alter the physical operations of the body, is an activity of mind that is remarkably undervalued.

Edmund Jacobson, the father of Progressive Relaxation and the tense-relax exercises, showed long ago that images conjured up by the mind are powerful excitants of the body's physiologic systems. But the power of the imagination over the body continues to be largely neglected by science despite the common knowledge that mental images of sour or bitter tastes stimulate saliva flow, that memory images of sad events can bring tears; that images of impending disaster can make the body tense; or that sexual fantasies can lead to almost uncontrollable biological activity.

The common use of imagery in allaying anxieties, especially with children (if you are brave at the dentist's, we'll go for ice cream afterward), has not, surprisingly, led to exploring imagery as an internal mechanism fostering the malfunctioning of physiological systems. Yet, logically, if mental images can stimulate body systems to activity to produce changes that are beneficial when appropriate, then imagery can also cause physiologic changes that are inappropriate and destructive. The child who develops a fear of a spanking and constricts his chest as the blow is struck no doubt has images when he remembers the experiences, and may be the child that develops asthma.

During the problem solving of reasonable worry, the mind—spurred by the confusion between conscious perceptions and the inner, unconscious awareness—creates a thousand images. It recreates in imagination all it can remember about the problem it believes it has, visualizing and feeling the scene over and over, making guesses about how it happened. As the mind struggles to find answers, it projects images of the possible solutions into the future as well as into the past. In the images, places and people, words and behavior are manipulated back and forth in time to find answers that can satisfy the intellect or emotions or both. If I sense that my supervisor at work is not happy with my work, but he gives me no direct comments, I will summon up images both to account for how the problem arose and how I might remedy it in the future. And for every image, for either past or future, I recreate the body postures I assume in the image. Each body posture is one of tension, the taut, expectant body waiting for the decision on whether the imagined answer is the right answer or the wrong one.

Between Reason and Unreason

Up to this point the operations of mind I've called worry are all quite normal, steps we all take in trying to solve problems we perceive to be imminent. We all become alert, feel some anxiety, try to mobilize our reason, construct mental and emotional defenses against an apparently impending trouble for our psyche.

There are at this point two outcomes possible for the problem solving of worry. It may become productive, as when we begin to understand the problem and how to handle it—the process we call coping. But when the intellect cannot find the answers it needs (with the information it has), the mind seems nonetheless compelled to keep trying to solve the problem. If there is no new information, no new insight or perspective that can help, worry degenerates into the mental activity called rumination. The sequence of mental events leading to stress and stress reactions is diagrammed in figure 2.

Normally we fluctuate between bursts of productive and unproductive worry, but when the problem solving of worry is frustrated, the mental activity and the physical changes it excites can become destructive, ending in one or another stress illness.

Destructive worry begins when the problem solving of reasonable worry is unproductive and frustrated, when no answer seems

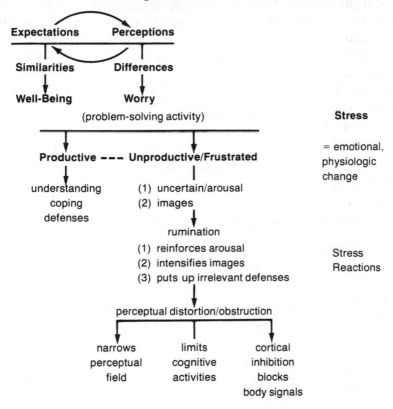

Figure 2. Flow Chart of Mental Operations Leading to States of Well-Being or Stress and Stress Reactions

right. The classic television episode in which the wife finds a slip of paper reading "Linda, 345-7756" in her husband's shirt pocket begins destructive worry after reasonable worry concludes she can't remember anyone her husband knows named Linda, or he denies knowing a Linda, or can't account for the slip of paper, or laughs it off, telling a weak story about crossed wires on a telephone call.

Destructive worry is a normal consequence of the uninformed or of the untrained and undisciplined intellect. Destructive worry occurs when the emotions escape the governing throttle of the intellect, and for a legitimate reason: the intellect lacks the information it needs to solve the problems it perceives.

Mental Steps to Distress: (6) Rumination

Rumination is that insidious, persistent preoccupation of the mind with pondering, speculating, imagining, and projecting images back and forth in time. It is a rehashing and a regurgitation of every bit of information about a problem in every conceivable combination, but without success. It is a hopeless, unproductive, destructive operation of mind so preoccupied with its problem that it cannot see *why* it cannot solve its problem.

Rumination is one of those very useful words that psychologists and psychiatrists have appropriated for an intensely parochial and pathologic use, usually reserving it to mean a compulsive or obsessive preoccupation with distressing thoughts. But before the word was invested with the overtones of neuroses, English literature cleverly used its original connection with the cud-chewing cow to describe the human inclination to ponder the same thought over and over.

Worry I suspect is that stage of problem solving where attention and thought may find answers to the problem, but once rumination starts, the attention turns to the distress the problem is causing rather than staying on the work of solving it.

So in a sense the psychologists are right, except that it is the *result,* not the *process,* that is pathological.[9] It seems quite reasonable for the mind to become preoccupied with its operations when they fail

---

9. The difficulty in finding the right words for mental activities gives an interesting insight into the propensity of the mental health sciences to label quite normal thought processes as quite abnormal, and an insight into the frustrating lack of scientific attention to what might constitute the *normal* activities of mind.

to produce urgently needed answers. It is not a failure of mind or thought that makes rumination destructive to mental and physical health; it is the lack of information the mind needs to solve the problem it detects. But even in the intense, circular worry that is rumination, some sudden insight still can penetrate the attention barrier and then, curiously enough, problems can be solved so quickly they literally seem to vanish.

Psychologists talk a good bit about problem-solving activity, but they focus exclusively on the kinds of mind-brain operations considered to be responsible for precise, decision-making human thought. Most of the mechanisms studied are patterned after computer operations: memory programs for handling different kinds of information, alternate routines for handling data under different conditions, system state (such as attention, nonattention), or cognitive strategies—even though inevitably the analysis of human thought mechanisms ends with the mystery of "higher order" controls (spirit? will? psyche?).

Human problem solving, nonetheless, is regarded scientifically as a mechanical process where all of the conditions and requirements needed for effective operations are present. The person who has a problem in his social relationships scarcely has an ideal situation for social problem solving. He lacks great quantities of important information needed to begin problem solving let alone arrive at a reasonable answer. He lacks information about the motives and intentions of the human beings he interacts with. Yet the enormously complicated process of sorting out thoughts from their original emotional accompaniments, and trying to solve problems with mere bits of valid information, has not received much attention, if any, from the mental health specialists.

As rumination continues, so do the adverse effects of worry on the body's physiology. The uncertainty about answers continues to keep the body aroused, the inability to find answers leads to frustration and intensifies apprehension and anxiety. As fears increase, the rumination tends to generate "worst case" solutions and irrelevant emotional defenses, and "loads" the thought processes, distorting the operations of mind and intellect into a tight, closed circuit of worry and fear, tension and distress.

There are two effects of rumination on the body. The first is to intensify the uncertainty about the future of one's well-being. The arousal of the body that makes the body "uptight" accompanies a growing realization that worry is unproductive and becomes intensified as rumination proceeds. There is a growing sensation that well-being is, indeed, seriously threatened, and this increasing threat to social survival generates increasing apprehension and anxiety, and this in turn excites the neural mechanisms that result, indiscriminately, in muscle, visceral, and subjective tension, the physiologic responses that are partly innate, partly learned reactions to threats to the well-being of living organisms. And because rumination involves the constant creation and re-creation of the social situation and problem as mental images, the effect of imagery on the body is intensified as well.

As rumination continues, so does the cycle of insecurity and images, each cycle reinforcing the tensions of the body. If there are no new insights or no new, helpful information for the problem-solving process, rumination begins to block out its own normal resources for productive thought, producing perceptual distortion and perceptual obstruction, including loss of awareness of body signals. These two disturbances of intellectual activity close the curtain between mind and the social reality and end in self-deception.

Mental Steps to Distress: (7) Self-Deception

Perceptual distortion is a quirk of mind that can be either a quite normal result of how one pays attention or a serious, abnormal defect of intellectual activity. It simply means that when the attention is occupied elsewhere, certain impressions detected by the sensory apparatus are not appreciated in conscious awareness. If I am engrossed in a good book, I may not hear the dog barking to get in. It is commonly believed among psychology theorists that the brain has only a certain amount of information-processing networks (I strongly disagree) and that when the attention is absorbed in intent thought, any different thought activity is limited.

It is true that when rumination becomes excessive and the attention is thoroughly absorbed by intense mental activity there is much less attention paid to other kinds of information available to the mind. In rumination, the individual becomes preoccupied with certain kinds of conclusions about the outcome of a problem and particularly with conclusions that reflect fear for the worst. Perception becomes limited to perceiving those elements of a social situation that fit a preconceived notion. The individual begins to see only what he wants to see and hear only what he wants to hear, selecting only those items that will fit the preconceived notions and solutions he has developed to the problem he believes exists between him and his social environment.

One of my own rumination episodes may explain the process better. One time, returning from India, I was more than a little annoyed by things the housesitter had done around the house in my absence. My annoyance grew daily as I discovered small, bothersome problems she had created. Finally, one day I couldn't find the new cake pans, and a bit later I couldn't find my special shampoo. Small things, but they were the proverbial last straw. I was steaming with annoyance, and the more my search for the items was fruitless, the more disturbed I became. Over and over in my mind I recreated visions of the housesitter disregarding my instructions, probably having wild parties, and on and on. In a few hours I was terribly tense and irritated, ready to explode in an almost violent reaction to the product of my own mind. Finally I remembered what I lecture about and relaxed, amused by myself. Looking in the kitchen cabinets for a cooking pot, I found —there before my eyes—the cake pans. And before I could remind myself about perceptual distortion, I went to my bathroom, and there, too, right where it should be, was the shampoo. My rumination had blinded my perceptions; I failed utterly to see what was in front of me.

The ruminator, in effect, begins to distort his social reality by extracting bits of it out of context and using them to construct an imaginary case for the problem solutions that he has, until this point, held only as tentative. He distorts his appreciations of reality because his preoccupation leaves no room for him to perceive anything that doesn't support his foregone conclusions. If I have decided that my lover is losing interest in me, without some totally convincing evidence otherwise I will pay attention to his absences and magnify them until his presence becomes nothing more than a confirmation that he has been absent.

Unconsciously but intentionally distorted perceptions continue to aggravate the effects of the perceived stress on both the subjective feelings and the physiologic functions. With problem solving limited to a distorted intake of information, it becomes unproductive, and the cycle of rumination–perceptual distortion continues. The uncertainty and insecurity about social well-being become more acute and intensify the threat to future well-being that in turn reinforces the body's physiological arousal and the posture of tension.

Hand in hand with perceptual distortion is the perceptual obstruction of important internal information. With the attention circuits occupied by rumination, the perception of information about internal activities, both cognitive and physiological, becomes blocked. No longer is the normal assortment of alternative memories easy to retrieve; access to self-correcting logic and an appreciation of internal reality diminishes, and the cognitive functions are tied up in unproductive efforts and no longer available to bring new perspectives to conscious attention. At the same time the pathways for the appreciation of sensory information are obstructed so that consciousness fails to recognize the body signs of tension. The internal physiologic signals that warn of too much tension or too active a physiology are no longer heeded. The result is that body tensions continue to build up and the failure of the cerebral circuits to appreciate the increasing tensions actively prevents the physiologic regulating mechanism from operating normally.

As these mental processes continue, the distress to the body they cause leads inevitably to emotional or physical disorders or both. The form in which the distress is expressed—in any one of the many varieties of emotional disturbances from anxiety to alcoholism or physical distresses from headache to stress-induced epileptic seizures —depends upon the constitutional makeup of the person, his store of experiences and learning and cultural influences. There are no doubt quite specific genetic differences and biochemical deviations that can account for the tendencies of different physiologic systems to be vulnerable in different ways to the effects of stress. Life experiences also determine the way reactions to social stress are expressed. Certainly each of us stores in memory different physiologic reactions to different types of traumatic or disturbing experiences that can account for why some of us react with asthma, others with hypertension, and still others with cardiac arrhythmias.

One of the most important overlooked phenomena of mind over the physical being is the fact that when an individual reacts to stress with predominantly emotional reactions, it is still the disturbance of intellectual (mental) functions causing changes in *brain* (physical) functions, which are manifest as anxiety or depression or hysteria. Mind over body.

Back to Square One

Let's look at table 1 on page 82 again, this time to see whether the definition of social stress as an unfavorable perception of the social environment (and its consequent worry) holds up for *all* stress-related problems and whether it helps us to understand how stress can cause so many very different types of problems.

The way of classifying stress-related problems and illnesses in table 1 is new, yet each of the emotional or physical distresses noted, from headache to epilepsy, has been agreed by the medical and psychological communities to be related to stress. Putting them all together in an organized fashion was mainly a matter of collecting the examples and figuring out the proper classifications.

One of the most interesting consequences of table making is the very new perspective it can give "old" data. Almost always, toting up information in different ways leads to better understanding of the information, and often it can lead to insights about the nature of the phenomena being worked with.

If it is true that elements in the social life become stressful only after the mind interprets them to be stressful, then we should find that all the stress problems and illnesses listed in table 1 begin with worry because the mind perceives the social environment as unfavorable to social well-being.

What do we find? All the distresses in the first category, emotional problems, obviously originate with social stress, and the expert consensus is that each develops because there is worry about social adequacy or social performance, or worry about social censure or about the security of one's social self. The same holds true for psychosomatic illness. And how about certain physical malfunctions, such as migraine or epilepsy or arthritis? It is almost universally believed today that experiencing stress provokes the acute episodes of such organic illnesses, and the stress is nothing more nor less than worry about social achievements, social performance, and a feeling of threat to one's social well-being. Exactly the same underlying problem is associated with each of the problems and distresses we now call stress-related disorders. They all begin with worry.

People with Stress Are 100 Percent Logical!

A good many therapists frankly deceive their patients and clients by using bad theory implying that anyone who falls prey to stress and develops emotional or psychosomatic problems is "not thinking straight." This is patently untrue. The person under stress who succumbs to drug abuse or migraine headaches is actually thinking as well as anyone else. His problem is that he doesn't have enough information or the right kind of information to make his thinking effective and productive.

If we follow the mental processes leading to stress problems, each step can be seen as eminently logical *with the information available.* It *is* reasonable to worry if I have a problem at work and the boss behaves more favorably to a competitor for my job. It *is* reasonable to become mentally and physically aroused as a way of paying attention and concentrating on trying to solve the problem. It *is* reasonable to worry and to use the imagination to keep trying to find the answers. The failure of intellectual activity to be productive is solely because the intellectual mechanisms lack the right information to produce answers that can effectively relieve the problem and the stress the intellect creates because it cannot produce effective answers. The perceptual distortion and the perceptual obstruction that follow excessive rumination are merely mental devices used to sustain attention and thought on the problem at hand, albeit they are directed toward an insoluble problem.

Most people suffering from stress are not aware that most of their problems are caused by an important lack of information. Paradoxically, this is, in itself, information important to the stress reduction process, and having *this* information (that one doesn't have important, relevant information) may be one of the most important factors in the entire psychotherapeutic process or the stress reductions procedure.

Once people understand that their stress problem is due in large part to a lack of information, they can more easily become motivated both to seek out relevant information and to be alert to the potential value of the bits of social information they acquire and of their emotional reactions, which they might otherwise ignore.[10]

There are two clear occasions when the intellect lacks the information it needs for favorable functioning of the psyche, and these occasions provide the breeding grounds for the mental distress that leads to the emotional and physical disorders we recognize as "stress related."

The first occasion is when there is a lack of information to the cognitive, perceptual, interpretive intellectual processes needed to perceive the realities of social situations, social relationships, and social dynamics of their social environments.

Information about the nature of the social reality and ways to develop effective coping devices can be obtained through many varieties of psychotherapy. For the most part, the value of psychotherapy lies in improving the understanding of the social reality and creating insights into improved ways to cope with socially derived difficulties. Whether the therapy uses aided self-analysis or focuses on the pragmatic aspects of the social reality, the psychotherapeutic process can bring to the patient a clearer idea of the true meaning of social situations and can furnish strategies for dealing with problems that distress the intellect and arouse the emotions.

The second informational deficit that contributes to developing the signs and symptoms of stress disorders is the direct result of the mind's preoccupation with problem solving and worry: failure to appreciate internal perceptions. With most of the cortical circuitry occupied with activity directed toward the problem of concern, little is left to appreciate the internal signals of increasing body tensions. Under ordinary circumstances, the interpretive cortex acts as a governor for the body's automatic physiologic functions, relating the need for physiologic change to the circumstances of the external environment. The cortical neural circuits used to appreciate the external environment apparently are also closely related to those that appreciate changes in the internal environment, and when these circuits are tied up with other activities, their sensitivity to internal signals is remarkably decreased if not blocked altogether. The net effect of the blocking is that the governor of internal physi-

---

10. See also Appendix C.

ologic activity is disabled. Without the governor, no corrective changes occur and tensions continue to mount.

Under normal circumstances the cortex is unconsciously aware of body tensions that occur during normal functions and behavior, and when tension is no longer needed, the cortex passes on signals to the muscle-control areas of the brain that allow the muscles to relax. But in stress reactions, when the cortex is preoccupied with rumination and mental images, it skews perceptions and fails to pay attention to signals of the body's tensions, and continues to send messages to the muscle-control areas to stay tense, ready for action. Then the cycle is repeated, for although the tensions are appreciated by other unconscious systems, the tensions are not corrected. This reinforces the sensations of subjective tensions, continues to skew perception, and intensifies rumination.

We still have to explain why tension states can be so persistent. If the basic reaction is arousal, then we are obliged to deduce that the arousal is persistent. But the stimuli that cause the arousal are not persistent; the stimuli are social stress situations and the cognitive-emotional reactions to them, and these persist not in fact, but only in the mind and unconscious. This must mean that some mechanism of mind exists that can maintain the stress-stimulus effect in the absence of the real stress situation. This mechanism is the continuing mental activity concerned with a problem, real or imaginary.

When worry or rumination interprets a problem in social activities as a threat to well-being, even though it is to the *social* well-being, the longer the worry continues the more the threat is generalized to include *physical* well-being as well. The interpretive cortex, alert to the threat, relays neural messages to the lower-brain muscle and visceral centers to keep the self alert, ready to take action. This cerebral preoccupation prevents (inhibits) the appreciation of proprioceptive information (signals from the body) indicating the degrees of body tension, and so the body and viscera and subjective awareness stay tense, and tensions increase until problem solving is productive of a solution or of some effective defense or way to cope.

The failure of the cortex to pay attention to and appreciate internal signals can be corrected by providing mind and awareness with information about the body's state and the body's reactions to stressful situations. Many new techniques are now available to assist the interpretive cortex to recognize internal tensions and to help to reactivate the governing function, allowing for relaxation of tensions. Information about internal states can be supplied through yoga, biofeedback, various body awareness techniques, imagery, self-suggestion, and various kinds of relaxation procedures.[11]

The Second Illness

The academic, intellectual, and therapeutic schisms between psychology and medicine have made the problem of being sick—from any cause—a hundredfold worse than it has any right to be.

The very sectarianism of these two therapeutic disciplines may be why neither of them has seen one of the most fundamental problems of being sick. The fact is that any disturbance of body or mind spawns still another, a second, very real disease. There is, I have ventured, for every illness or mental distress, a "second illness" that is the distress of just being sick, or, for that matter, the distress that comes from being out of any part of life's normal course for any reason at all.

The "second illness" is the mental and emotional reaction to being sick, to having a problem, and it is a very real illness with very real and important effects on mind and body. Almost inexplicably, both medical and psychological therapists treat illness as either a problem of the emotions or a problem of the body. Rarely, very rarely, do they treat mind and body as the inseparable whole that they are. Even exclusively emotional illnesses are often treated as if they are solely of physical, physiological origin, and just as curiously, psychotherapy itself concentrates its attention much more on the roots of raw, primitive emotions (suppressed anger, hostility, hate, fear) than on the mental apparatus of the literate, ingenious, inventive human mind that is the wellspring for emotional distress.

As we begin to understand more about the interrelationships between mind and body in health and illness, it becomes clear that problems of the mind (and emotions) can seriously affect the functioning of the body, as in psychosomatic illnesses, and in the same way the mental, emotional problems caused simply by being sick can

---

11. A more detailed discussion of techniques is given in Appendix D.

aggravate existing problems, emotional or physical, and interfere with recovery.

The prevailing tendency of the professional therapists for dividing sick people into two parts has profound consequences for the welfare of society. For when we neglect the Second Illness, we quite literally create two kinds of outcasts: the psychological outcast who becomes either neglected or is regressed to a state of pseudo-infancy by family and friends, and the social outcast who is rejected by society as a whole because his illness has removed him from the activities of a normal social life.

To appreciate the surprising scope and true virulence of the second illness, let's look at different kinds of illness in a very general way. First there are the illnesses or distresses of life that cause moderate discomfort and diminished ability to participate in life's activities. The almost infinite varieties of health problems, from recurring headaches, ulcers, or bouts of hay fever to bereavement or high blood pressure, no matter how mild or severe, all impose restrictions on both an individual's performance and on his participation in social activities. The physical distress or the emotional discomfort pushes the individual to the side of the mainstream of his normal life, often with annoying, sometimes intense psychological reactions to the strange circumstance of his inability to perform up to potential, and to being different in a society that prizes normalcy and effort and achievement.

The second main category of illness is the disabling illness, such as paralysis, loss of a critical body part, cancer, other debilitating, chronic illnesses, and even severe mental illness. Victims of these illnesses become social outcasts, set aside as permanently impaired and beyond rescue. Even with partial rehabilitation, any deficiency in ability to perform is generally considered to be a total inability to perform. The person is the eternal patient, consigned to the back corridors of life with the meagre gift of custodial care.

Both categories of illness, mild and severe, share the powerful effects of illness on emotions, mind, and spirit. As long as the mind survives, it perceives and responds; it perceives its wholeness diminished, it perceives its deprivation from social wholeness, and the mind reacts with the force of any perceiving mind, understanding the problem but none of the answers because, for the most part, our society has not been concerned with answers to the psychological and social effects and needs of the Second Illness.

Consider the psychological impact of *any* illness. Whether the illness is distress of mind or body, emotional or physical, the mind and its intellect perceive the slightest loss in capacity to perform, to participate, to behave as a normal human being. The housewife with a headache is not just uncomforable, she is also aware that the performance of her family role falls short of what she desires. For the double amputee, the *nature* of the emotional reaction to illness is basically not much different, even though the emotions are much more seriously disturbed and for much longer times. The emotional reaction to not being able to perform up to expectations, personal or public, involves a tangle of nearly every emotion known to psychology: anxiety, depression, frustration, anger. And the anxiety is multiple because of the fear of the unknown, the not-knowing if the signs of sickness herald something even more serious, the not knowing how to get by until one can perform again, the not knowing where to get help or what kind of help to get, the not knowing about how long the illness may last.

The anxiety about a diminished ability to perform is compounded by the sheer frustration of not being able to perform. The secretary with a headache, under pressure to produce work, also suffers the distress of not being able to keep up, and the very real implications of any flagging for job security. The pains and aches and physical discomforts of illness are modest troubles compared to the distresses of mind that illness brings. Whether it is high blood pressure that diminishes activity or a crippling arthritis, the emotional impact goes far beyond the anxieties and frustrations, social relationships, and outlook for the future. There is as well the uncomfortable feeling of suddenly losing one's independence and becoming dependent upon the experts and family or friends, and suffering the companion of dependence, the loss of self-esteem.

Being ill, in short, is stressful—seriously, interferingly stressful. The stress of being ill is a surprisingly large component of illness to be so neglected in the treatment of it. Typically, when the emotional symptoms are obvious or disturbing, they are treated by tranquilizers or sedatives; but while tranquilizers and sedatives are necessary to relieve obvious or acute anxiety, they are not helpful over the long haul. They have, in fact, helped medicine and psychology to create a drug society, and the second illness that accompanies drug abuse.

When the second illness, the "stress of being ill" is not treated, the first illness becomes more debilitating than need be, and recovery from the illness takes longer than it should. Even the seemingly most benign physical problem, the tension headache, has distressing emotional overtones. To lose a day to headache, and over time to lose many days to headache, is a serious disruption of life's activities, performance, social relationships, earning money, and ensuring the security of job and finances. But the headache is the symptom that receives the medical attention, and often not too successfully at that, while the patient endures the emotional problems and mental distress as best he can.

The emotional distress of the chronically ill or the handicapped bears a similar hallmark. The problems that such illnesses cause are much the same as for the less severe problems. But because the disability is obvious, these kinds of illnesses often attract enough understanding, concern, and affection to provide some measure of the needed psychological support, although official, medically sanctioned treatment is a long way away from dealing with any effectiveness with the disturbances to mind and of mind to body that engulf the handicapped.

Slowly, bit by bit, emotion by emotion, the mental and emotional torture of being ill is being recognized as part and parcel of all illness. There is no unified attack yet on the "stress of being ill" by medicine or psychology, but there is a growing awareness by professional healers that the psyche, the core of modern man, exerts a profound effect on the course of all illness. More and more the need to treat mind and emotions during illness and physical problems is being recognized. The need of the handicapped for improved self-esteem has become a part of therapy, the need of the dying for understanding and love has produced the new science of thanatology, while at the other end of the spectrum, self-help and awareness techniques are proving to be equal to drugs in the management of distresses caused by the stress of life.

The mind, it turns out, can be a master healer. The problem now is to learn more about the resources of the mind to heal its own being.

PART III

THE BRAIN CONNECTION

CHAPTER 7

Mind and Brain

An old dictionary of mine has a long list of definitions for mind. It is, in the end, an amazing exercise in obfuscation. For example, I first read that mind is "memory," then "what one thinks," then that it is "intention or wish," and still later, that mind is "that which feels, perceives, wills, thinks, etc." I particularly like the "etc.," because when an authority such as Webster's has to resort to "etc.," it is like the ultimate imprimatur confirming the helplessness that most of us have about defining the mind.

I read on to definition 7, that mind is "the perceptive and thinking part of consciousness, exclusive of will and emotion," wondering why Webster has just told me in definition 6 that the mind is "that which wills." Definition 9 increases my confusion. It gives the philosopher's definition of mind as "the conscious element or factor in the universe; spirit; intelligence:—contrasted with *matter.*" I'm confused because this is remarkably different from the psychologist's view in definition 10 that mind is "(a) the total of conscious states of an individual and (b) one's capacity for mental activity."

A newer, larger dictionary gives me pretty much the same thing, but adds more modern, perhaps colloquial definitions of mind, such as, "the intellect in its normal state; reason, sanity," and "a person having intelligence," and "a way, state or direction of thinking and feeling" along with "all of an individual's conscious experiences" and "the conscious and unconscious together as a unit; psyche."

Then, in what seems to be a try at clearing up the confusion, in another enormously long paragraph the dictionary illustrates the different things mind can be by explaining the meaning of some twenty phrases using the word mind. The phrases fill an entire column but add little except for two explanations that somehow didn't get into the original list. These are that mind can also mean "mind's eye" (the imagination) and "to pay attention to."

It is, however, the list of synonyms at the very end of the entries under mind that sketch a truer picture of the complexities of mind. Synonyms for mind include soul, spirit, intellect, understanding, opinion, sentiment, judgment, belief, choice, inclination, desire, will, liking, purpose, impetus, memory, remembrance, and recollection. These are descriptions of mind that explode with the immensity, the mystery, the ineffability, the capacities, the power, the divinity of mind. Mind is, in sum, all that man is.

The Mind-Body Problem

Early in the history of thought about the source of man's own vital energy, the internal organs were most often believed to be the fountainhead of conscious life. As philosophy became more sophisticated, wise men began to puzzle over the curious connections between the intangible essence of subjective experience that is consciousness and the substance of physical being. The question of how the physical being gives rise to consciousness and awareness of one's own being, known as the mind-body problem, baffles the most erudite of scholars.

The mind-body problem pits an indefinable, unmeasurable quality of human nature against physical qualities readily definable and measurable. Bodies have mass, can be weighed, and occupy space, all characteristics of what we define as matter. But mind has no mass, cannot be weighed, and does not occupy space. Mind is a not-thing, but a reality nonetheless when one is aware of one's own beingness and identity. Consciousness of being, of one's own thoughts, of the meaning of experience, are the nonphysical essence of man, the immeasurable, unmeasurable central nature that holds the reins of all human behavior. The core question of the mind-body problem is how this nonphysical nature evolved from its animal substrate to assume command of life.

How the Experts See Mind and Consciousness

Despite the wealth of research on brain, body and behavior, no serious effort is directed by science toward exploring the ultimate nature of mind. Psychologists study the way in which people interact with their environments, sociologists study the behavior of groups and the effect of other people on individuals, and the medical and biological sciences concern themselves only with the physical nature of man and animals. None specifically studies mind although most agree that what we call mind is a product of the brain.

It is the allied sciences of neurology, neurophysiology, and neurochemistry that have developed the most precise tools for documenting physical changes of the brain.

The complexity and richness of the neural networks that course throughout the body and the maddening enigma of how brain relates to body and behavior have attracted many of the most brilliant biological scientists. The tools they have developed to study the brain are incredible. Neurochemists and neurohistologists can tease away a hundred atomic and complex substances from within the structure of a cell of microscopic size, while neurophysiologists can impale single nerve cells with minute electrodes to record their electrical activity. Enzyme chemists can follow the minuscule chemical changes within the cells themselves.

The neurosciences have discovered many of the systematic changes in nerves that occur when information is transmitted through the neural networks of the body. We know, for example, how chemical and electrical changes occur in the nerves when visual, touch, or other sensory information is transmitted to the brain; we know something about which parts of the brain receive the information, judge it, and initiate actions appropriate to the information sensed, and we know how the action information is transmitted to the effector organs of the body.

With their extraordinary fund of knowledge about anatomy and physiology, the medical and psychological sciences find it easy to account for the effect of mind-brain on the behavior and operations of the body. Since both brain and body are physical substances and are physically connected, whatever they may produce in the way of behavior and feelings and thought are properties solely of physical reactions. Nerve receptors react to change in the environment and convey electrochemical messages about the external environment to the neural coordinating mechanisms of the central brain that make the appropriate adjustments of the physical being to the conditions in the environment.

It is on the knowledge of these elemental fragments within the nerve cells of the brain and nervous systems that most modern theories about the mind-body problem are based. The higher-order, learned reactions of complex human social life are, according to prevailing theory, merely a few steps removed from instinctual reactions and involve the physical body in a similar way. Most mind-body theorists conclude that mind and all of its integral functions of consciousness, awareness, and thought are nothing more than specialized combinations of the brain's physical activities that give rise to perceptions, memories, and the computerlike ability of nerve cells to change with experience and mechanically execute programs of behavior impressed upon the tissue of the brain.

These popular conclusions are, however, merely guesses, for what we do not know, and may never know, is how electrochemical information carried in nerves and brain is translated into thought and concept, awareness, and conscious experience.

Brain-to-Consciousness Theories

In elaborating theories about the mind and consciousness and about what the brain does, brain and behavior scientists somehow magically forget that there is no *direct* evidence that what nerves and brain cells do is the origin and substrate of the mind, although, of course, there is a great deal of indirect evidence. They try, nonetheless, to develop concepts of mind that explain mind and consciousness by the mechanical actions of nerves and colonies of nerves, building hierarchies of brain activity from the simplest reflex to the most complex mind functions. None of the theories can come near to a reasonable explanation for inner conscious experience, and the dominant theories of the century either reject or ignore the uniquely human characteristics of the conscious mind: subjective experience and free will.

The greatest stumbling block is the troublesome fact that what the whole brain produces is far different from the product of the sum of its parts. The parts are microcosms to themselves and the whole brain-mind complex is a macrocosm with the complexity of the universe. We know how the parts function; what the theories attempt to explain is how the physical parts become the intangible wholes we know as mind and consciousness.

Among modern physiologists who study brain and behavior and set the physiologic data and beliefs for psychophysiologists, the most popular theory of consciousness has been the identity theory or some variant of that theory. The identity theory states (and not too brilliantly or with any evidence at all) that mental processes and physical brain processes are identical. A variant of this concept, called psychoneural parallelism, suggests that subjective or psychic events are caused by neural activity and run parallel to them, but the subjective activity has no influence on the physical actions of the nerves. Still another variation of the identity theory is the Gestaltists' concept called isomorphism, meaning that there is a one-to-one correspondence between conscious experience and the condition of the physical substrate (the brain) but the processes are not identical.

Anyone, it seems, except neuroscientists, can see the incredible vacuousness of these "theories." They are a scientific way for saying, "Consciousness has some relationship to brain but we don't know what it is." The reductionist perspective of science that studies the mind as separate bits of sensory perception and mechanical learning stubbornly ignores the obvious fact that the totality of mental processes is unequivocally different from the collected sum of the individual processes of perception, memory, logic and judgment. Beyond the reach of science is that totality of mind with its special characteristics that cannot be explained by knowledge of brain function or any discrete analysis of behavior. Consciousness, voluntariness, intentionality, imagination, abilities to abstract, to form and synthesize concepts, to impose order on nature, are all properties of mind that are not properties of any component part of mind or brain.

There are two gigantic questions about consciousness and thought that may never be answered. The first is how the physical processes of the body, from the receptors of sensations in the toes to the labyrinthine exchange of information within the brain during thought, are translated into conscious experience. The second question that may forever defy explanation is how the electrochemical changes in the nerve cells transmit meaningful information, i.e., how information sensed by the nerve receptors of the body converge in brain substance to become the content of thought.

One of the newest and more persuasive concepts about the nature of consciousness that attempts to reconcile the two aspects of the objective and subjective mind is that proposed by Roger Sperry. Sperry's long and active experience in experimental psychology, psychophysics, and as one of the leading researchers of the "split brain" phenomenon, is a broad background far greater than the scientific experience of most scientists who spin theories of the automated brain. Possibly being more honest than political, Sperry confronted the problem of consciousness with the data of science and found the physicalists' theories lacking. Sperry notes, as I have above, that no proof exists for the behaviorist-materialist concepts of mind and consciousness.

Sperry proposes that consciousness is an emergent property of the brain, evolving from interactions of the simpler elements and properties of the brain in such a way that the nature of consciousness can not be predicted from the interactions. That is, consciousness is a property of brain with capacities that are greater than the sum of the capacities of the parts involved.[1]

Sperry's model for the way in which mind relates to brain uses the information of the neurosciences in a way that recognizes inner-conscious awareness as an integral part of brain activity. I believe that his model is not only testable, but has already been tested and found valid. All of the new awareness techniques, self-suggestion, mental imagery, and meditation show time after time the ability of mind and changing consciousness to affect the physical processes of the brain and its body.

A few quotes from Sperry give a clear statement of his thesis. "Mental phenomena built of neural events are conceived to act as dynamic entities in brain organization interacting at their own level in brain function." And, "a mutual interaction between the neural and the mental events is indicated." And, finally, "the subjective mental properties and phenomena are posited to have a top-level

---

1. Sperry's notions deal with the relationship between mind and brain. A theory proposed by Konrad Lorenz about the evolution of mind indirectly supports Sperry's concept (see chapter 9).

control as causal determinants. On these terms, mind moves matter in the brain."

These conclusions, which still astound the physicalists, are based in large part on Sperry's own dramatic research with human subjects in which communication between the two cerebral hemispheres had been interrupted at surgery for therapeutic reasons. He found that conscious experiences occurred only when information about the environment was given (visually) to the dominant hemisphere (usually the left hemisphere) and not when information was given to the nondominant hemisphere. The apparent isolation of conscious awareness in one hemisphere occurs despite the fact that the nondominant hemisphere can equally as well understand and judge perceived information and activate totally appropriate, skilled responses to a demand for action without any conscious experience at all. For example, in patients with divided hemispheres, when the nondominant (usually right) hemisphere is presented with information demanding a specific response, the patients not only make a response appropriate to the demand, but an intelligent response occurs without any conscious awareness of participating in the response.

From these kinds of experiments it was deduced that whatever brain activity (synthesizing experience) goes on in the nondominant hemisphere, it reaches consciousness only after the brain events are transmitted to the dominant hemisphere. Since the patients could not be aware of their actions, no matter how "reasonable and intelligent" the actions were, it is believed that the nondominant hemisphere does not initiate voluntary action, and that decision-making brain activity and decision-implementing activity (the will) are, in some way, carried out or controlled by neuronal activity within the dominant hemisphere.

The problem here is that awareness, intention (the "intelligent" direction of behavior) and decision making are equated with consciousness, taken to mean a consciousness of self, and the concept has been expanded by a silent consensus to mean that intelligence, consciousness, and self-awareness of behavior are dependent upon activity of the dominant hemisphere. One of the annoying mistakes that scientist-philosophers make, surprisingly, is an imprecision of definition in areas where specific definitions are mandatory. In discussing "consciousness," mind-brain scientists often neglect to inform us just what kind of consciousness they are talking about, apparently forgetting that the spectrum of consciousness ranges from a primitive unconscious to verbalizable conscious awareness.

In a discussion of Sperry's work and concepts, for example, Sir John Eccles interprets the differences in hemispheric activity to indicate that the nondominant hemisphere is pretty much like a superior animal brain, and further, that it is literally out of communication with the conscious self (no self-awareness). At the same time, unfortunately, he discusses experimental evidence to suggest the opposite.

He cites, for example, the Sperry experiments in which a task is demanded of a "split-brain" subject that must be implemented by "direction" from the minor hemisphere, and the demand to do the task is given so that it can reach only the minor hemisphere. If such subjects, taught to retrieve a dollar bill when presented with a picture of one to the minor hemisphere, are confronted with coins but no bills, they will retrieve coins. Similarly, if the subject is trained to retrieve a clock when presented with a picture of a clock to the minor hemisphere, and then no such clock is available, the subject will retrieve the most closely related object available, such as a child's toy watch. Eccles refers to this capability as the ability of "the minor hemisphere to program a refined stereognostic performance," i.e., his "superior animal brain."

I think Eccles does an injustice to both human beings and superior animals. In the study he cites, the patients lacked communication between the two hemispheres, and lacked, as well, the brain centers that allow speech; nonetheless, they not only formed concepts about what the specific task was, but when the tools to complete the tasks perfectly were absent, the "nonconscious" brain made a decision about the best-fitting approximation that could fulfill the task demand. The "unconscious" decision reflects both the decision-making and decision-implementing abilities that Eccles ascribes solely to the dominant hemisphere.

Sperry suggests there is "another mind" in the lesser hemisphere. I would agree with Sperry, especially because the *unconscious* mind can be shown to have extraordinary abilities that *never* come into conscious awareness.

I would, however, challenge Eccles' interpretation. Sperry's research seems to me to indicate a different explanation—that the two hemispheres *contribute* different kinds of mental operations to the development of self-awareness and intention, the nondominant hemisphere seeming to be able to analyze and synthesize concepts and then to direct *appropriate* behavior, while the dominant hemisphere adds the elements that relate to consensual discrimination and the relationship of the concept synthesis to individual being (the self-awareness). Neither kind of mental operation can become both conceptual and appropriate, however, without a continuous interchange of information between the hemispheres. To select a coin, for example, upon being asked to retrieve a dollar bill when no bill is available, means that the response—an approximately appropriate action—could develop only through appropriate concept formation on the one hand and some kind of awareness identified with the self on the other hand. Only by having a well-defined concept of an appropriate response *and* by having an awareness—even though not an identifiable conscious awareness—of the only self that can carry out the response could the action take place.

How much consciousness is tied up with language may never be known entirely, but if the brain structures for speech are found only in the dominant hemisphere, the failure to be self-aware of one's own actions (in the split-brain patients) could equally as well mean that speech is tied to the mechanisms for self-awareness only and not necessarily to other aspects of consciousness. Certainly an unconscious awareness of one's own body is necessary in order to produce coordinated, purposeful actions. Moreover, one might suspect, in view of the remarkable redundancy of brain circuits, that with experience the split-brain patients might eventually *learn* self-awareness, just as chimpanzees have learned human symbols.

The point is, that if the nondominant hemisphere can perceive tasks to be done and then do them, all without the benefit of the dominant hemisphere and its conscious awareness, there must be an unconscious awareness of the information perceived; a logical processing of the information, evaluations, and judgments to be made about the perceived information; and an impetus to perform. Simply because these events cannot be communicated even to the self does not mean that the organism lacks an appreciation of the events. It is obvious that the "consciousness (self-aware)-deprived" hemisphere had an awareness of how the self (the "I") was involved or the self would not have performed any purposeful actions at all. It seems clear that conscious awareness is not needed to develop sophisticated syntheses of the relationships between environmental demands and appropriate responses and that the syntheses developed are not only subjectively or biologically appreciated, but are also both put into and retrieved from memory.

A third eminent neurologist and neurophysiologist recently joined the ranks of revolutionary new science thinkers about mind. In his 1975 book *The Mystery of the Mind*, [2] published just before his death, Wilder Penfield announced his conclusions after a lifetime of scientific study of the brain. He wrote, "There is no good evidence . . . that the brain alone can carry out the work the mind does."

Penfield also adds a word of caution. He admonishes scientists that no one should pretend to draw a final conclusion in man's study of man until the nature of the energy responsible for mind action is discovered. Most other realists about the mind-brain relationship acknowledge that we may never come to know the energy responsible for mind, and if we accept this view, the only way new knowledge about the operations of the mind can be gained is by continuing to make best guesses.

So the conjectures that scientists make about the mind-body problem are just that, conjectures. But by tradition the conjectures are accepted as being more valid than they really are because they are "scientific." Creating and accepting concepts about the mind are very complex phenomena. On the one side the experts take advantage of the naïveté or inexpertness of both colleagues and the public when they extrapolate data in developing theories of mind-body. On the other side, the acceptance of unsubstantial ideas results both from the gullibility of ignorance and also, most likely, as Franz Alexander concluded about society facing the rapid advance of science, from "the longing for childish dependence and the desire to be governed by autocratic leaders and dogma."

The sad part of the phenomenon is that we are as informed and confused as we were centuries ago. When science began to develop and became the dominant authority on thought, it adopted a unitary concept of mind and body. Both were material and of one piece. The duality science intended to abolish, however, remained, but this time the division was between two factions of society. Although science is

---

2. Wilder Penfield, et al. *The Mystery of the Mind* (Princeton, N.J.: Princeton University Press, 1975).

convinced that mind is merely the product of the chemicophysical reactions of nerve cells, almost all the rest of society has retained its conviction that mind is nonmaterial, a unique intangible, supersensible energy that, although born of brain tissue, nonetheless assumes some degree of independence of action and, in fact, can change the activity of the brain. As we have seen, some of the best minds of modern science are coming perilously close to supporting this mystical view by scientific reasoning.

To Know Mind Is to Know Man

As I noted earlier, civilization may well look back at the 1970s as the time when both science and religion first began to recognize and accept mind as the supreme energy and power of the species man. There has been little in the history of science to compare with the recent discovery that mind has the power to regulate the ordinary and not-so-ordinary functions of the body.

Beyond this unveiling of the powers of mind lies still another revolutionary discovery, an understanding and an insight into the mind that is so extraordinary it has not yet been absorbed into the minds of scientists and practitioners now reveling in the applications of mind control of body. This further discovery is the inescapable conclusion that the mind possesses an ability to regulate and control its own source, the brain.

It is commonly accepted that the mind (as a product of brain activity) can regulate the activities of the mind; indeed, this is the very basis of psychotherapy, of education, of developing understanding. But the idea that the mind can control the very functions of the chemistry and electrical nature of the brain is an idea that hard science finds very difficult to accept.

The thesis that mind directs the physical activities of the brain, while evident throughout, is developed more fully in the last chapter of this book. What needs to be said at this point is that the neglect of science to acknowledge an inherent reality and far-reaching potency of the mind "beyond the brain" may be responsible for many of the difficulties in our society.

The failure of science to deal effectively with the nature of mind can be seen in the growing complaints of every segment of society about the problems of ordinary living. Crime increases steadily and becomes more violent; drugs are abused against all efforts of science to stop it; the younger generations complain of the nonrelevance of education; inquiries into the social behavior of government officials have become routine; subtle economic ripoffs are commonplace; art, whether music or painting or writing, has succumbed to commerciality; craftsmanship has turned sloppy and mediocre; people, industry and governments wantonly waste nature's resources; and mankind grows increasingly insensitive to mankind. The increasing incidence of these destructive behaviors is less and less offset by social behaviors aimed toward improving the condition of man.

The "scientific" approaches to understanding, for example, and therefore to treating, maladaptive social behavior are disturbingly inept. The relevant sciences consider only two factors in the development of disturbed social behavior: brain biochemicals that demand correcting drugs and the environment *outside* the disturbed person. They fail utterly to consider the mechanisms of the mind. It is relatively easy to catalogue the outside environmental influences: broken homes, poverty, criminal environment, poor education, bad health from environment, peer pressures, and all of the other distasteful conditions our society inflicts on the less able and the less well-off. And it is, of course, true that these devitalizing conditions render the defenseless victims confused and unstable, and that a good part of remedying the behavior of individuals is to change their social environment, as counsellors in psychology and social work do when they can.

But no amount of manipulation of social environment to change unfortunate or disturbed behavior is a successful treatment unless that new environment successfully engulfs the individual in its culture of social adjustment, and that means using the mind to understand how the self can survive. It is more a matter of how the individual self can cope with the environment he is in and learn to control his relationship with it than it is a matter of changing environments. Many a disturbed individual, reacting to a poor, impoverished environment, has, in fact, evolved behavior that allows him to survive in a deviant environment. The individual in this way reveals his mental capacity to define and understand the problems of his social survival. The fact that the rest of society, outside of his difficult-to-handle environment, may take a dim view of his solutions to his social problems is simply another sign of our ignorance of the way in which the mind operates, and a failure to recognize intelligent mental activity when its product is one that is judged to be unsuitable in quite a different social context.

This kind of ill-conceived understanding of human behavior leads to the second of the generally accepted principles about the development of maladaptive behavior: the use of drugs to reverse behavioral disturbances caused by social problems.

I have always found it virtually beyond reason that drug abusers should be treated by giving them another drug. I don't mean that this approach is not a necessary evil at this stage in our understanding of the mind, but the extraordinary persistence of using drug treatment for drug abuse and its consistent failure should have long ago given some scientist or social worker the insight that the drug abuser abuses drugs because they give his mind something that his mind has not yet learned how to create. One breed of drug abusers, for example, found complete relief when they turned to meditation, another way for exploring the wonders of one's own mind that could be socially acceptable at the same time.

Psychotherapists' and psychiatrists' offices and mental institutions are filled with drugged patients, tranquilized out of their right minds, the divine processes of the intellect violated by foreign agents intent upon cerebrocide. The unfortunate reality is that we have trained no "mind attendants"; we have created no services to assist disturbed intellects because we know so little about the workings of the mind.

We are now facing many more puzzling whimsies of the mind. The cocaine fad is attracting a new class of drug users (probably the same as those who use and abuse alcohol): the achievers, the jet set, the extroverts, the beautiful people. The new liberalism, admixed with common sense, has led the mind-changing fun and games from the relative innocuousness of moderate use of marijuana and alcohol to a mind-titillating chemical, cocaine, whose effects on mind have the experts all pretty well discombobulated. For cocaine, in the way it is used for mood changing, is not addicting in the accepted biological sense, nor does it appear to have any adverse effects except perhaps making someone feel awfully good when we think he shouldn't.

The point is that knowing so little about the operations of the mind, the community of man is not simply puzzled by the cocaine phenomenon, but is highly fearful *because it doesn't know what goes on in the mind.* The failure to study mind as mind kindles fears in society and the ignorance is the stimulus for unproductive social argument and often unreasonable restrictions on social activities. It took perhaps ten years of intensive study before the use of marijuana could be put into any kind of perspective, and even then judgments about its relative "safety" were based on its physiologic, not mental, actions.

The need to know more about the mind may in fact be a desperate need; the need to understand better how to use the mind depends upon knowing more about the mind. And perhaps the inner yearnings of man to comprehend his spirit and the powers of his mind may be satisfied if modern thinkers begin to examine the potential of mind without the bias of scientific tradition or without the politics of science.

If the specialists of medicine and psychology fight shy of the idea of mind-as-more-than-brain and pretend it doesn't exist except when they want to blame some emotional or psychosomatic problem on its unconscious actions, is there, in fact, any scientific rationale at all for the view that what we call mind may well be an attribute of man that functions semi-autonomously from the brain substance that gives it birth and life, much as a flower becomes independent of its mother seed or a human child functions separately from its parents?

And is there, also, evidence for and logic to the view that the mysteries of mind and its power lie in a superbly intelligent unconscious mind, a part of mind withheld to limit individual, *self*-awareness during an evolutionary process of species, a survival tool that is no longer an important concern for man's survival?

The answer to both questions, I am convinced, is yes. There is abundant evidence that unconscious mental activity is efficient and intellectual, and that the intellectual functions of the mind unquestionably modify the very neural substance that gives rise to mind and its actions.

What is necessary now is to formulate a reasonable structure about the status and capacities of mind that will let us work our way out of the prison where the sciences of our physical nature have held us. The great stores of information we have about mind and human nature have not been put in unifying order except as small segments of natural systems or bits of behavior. Few suggestions about how the segments make a whole human nature or mind have been made. To formulate a different idea of mind with a view to *mind,* rather than the physical brain, as the controller of man's nature, the information we already have about the mind-brain must be organized and with the data in order, the conclusions that naturally follow explored. What science needs to do now is to make a systematic, and holistic, reexamination of what we know about mind *and* brain.

CHAPTER 8

The Creation of Mind

Mind, Brain, and the Evolutionary Perspective

When I took up the challenge to see whether the data of science could be used to account for mind as an entity distinct from the functioning sum of the biological brain (although born of brain and sustained by it), I was already aware of some of the strange inconsistencies in the scientific theories claiming brain and mind to be invariably correlated precisely, if not identical in nature, but I had no idea how vulnerable the theories really are.

The most prevalent attitude throughout the sciences dealing with man and his mind is that mind is brain, and what nonscientists call mind is merely the external expression of electrochemical communication among nerve networks. The strongest support for this attitude comes from the evidence that in the evolution of life forms, increasingly complicated physiologic functions and anatomical structures developed because the new functions were successful for the survival of life under varying conditions and in changing environments. From the scientific standpoint, the remarkable similarities throughout all animal species between nerve substance and the collection of nerves that evolved to become brain have been convincing evidence that what we call mind, no matter how complex it seems, is nothing more than the result of the biological activity of the brain.

Evidence for the evolution of brain, however, usually comes from study of the evolution of individual nerve systems of the body, each organized and developed specially for specific functions, such as sensations, memory, reflexes, instincts, and other physiologic systems, each believed to be programmed by genetic chemicals. And, it is true, there is an undeniable progression of improvement and enrichment in the anatomical structures and functions of all basic components of the brain and central nervous system from the simplest to the most complex of species. The evolution of biological systems for such functions as vision, hearing, touch, muscle specialization, instincts and elemental behaviors proceeds so methodically and so orderly that any systematic study of evolution seems to demand the conclusion that behavior and intelligence proceed to develop as they do, from simple to complex, precisely because their physical substrates have evolved so methodically. The intimate and almost invariable correspondence between anatomy and behavior through millions of years of evolving life is so taut that to scientists it is inconceivable to account for behavior, intelligence, and "mind" by any influence other than the systematic, physical evolution of the nerve substance that forms the brain.

The argument that mind-is-only-brain seems logical and solid enough until one remembers that animal life is not merely a collection of biological systems, but that all life is singularly distinguished from the inanimate by an exquisitely harmonious communion among all functional parts, and by elaborate, unifying mutual interdependencies that produce an indivisible whole whose qualities transcend the physical elements of its parts. Scientists concerned only with biology and convinced that reactions of brain chemicals can account for man's psyche and consciousness and intellect have never, surprisingly, heeded such familiar observations as "DNA makes cells, not man" that caution against forming opinions about the nature of man exclusively from his physical foundations.

The addled scientific theorizing about mind-brain is so suspect it makes one wonder whether biological evidence might not attest better to mind-is-more-than-brain than it does to mind-is-brain. If one were, for example, to use better logic and a broader view of man's nature, while still using the methods and evidence of science and drawing inferences from the same physical predicates, there is as strong a likelihood for uncovering solid arguments for mind as the vital but nonmaterial principle of man as for mind-is-brain. Teilhard du Chardin has done just this, but as science has continued to buttress its case for mind-is-brain, few other science-philosophers have troubled to argue against the strength of popular scientific opinion. Yet, as today's society struggles to express its discontent with the failures of the physically based sciences to understand and deal with uniquely human problems, it is perhaps time to renew the argument. The value of such an exercise is to establish potent grounds and motives for exploring mind as an energy entity with a significant degree of independence from the material substances that produce it. If man is more than just the sum of his biological parts, then explorations of mind-stuff, apart from brain, could lead the way to a more realistic understanding of man. This is not to say that mind can be separated from brain, but that the mind the brain produces possesses an energy and a vitality that brain does not. The problem is to prove it.

While searching for critical and relevant evidence, it became clear to me that one line of historical support for the idea that mind-is-more-than-brain could indeed come from the same biological data used to support the theory of evolution and from studies examining the antecedents of man's physiology and behavior that have been used to prove that man is merely a biological animal and that mind-is-brain. If one begins with the idea that perhaps the seeds of intelligence were sown in the earliest of living forms and became progressively more critical to the evolutionary process, some digging into the facts behind evolutionary and genetic theory easily uncovers indications that nearly all the known evidence and theories of evolution are as strong grounds for the notion of mind-as-an-entity as they are for the notion that mind-is-brain. The evidence might, in fact, suggest the archetype of mind-brain (the first substance that communicated information in living tissue) as the vital principle of life and the source determining all evolutionary change. What produced the archetype, God or an accident of physical nature, can only be a matter of convictions.

There are at least half a dozen fundamental concepts formulated by science from studies of the biological origin of man that make up the essential parts of the consensus theory of evolution. These concepts explain a good bit about the sometimes obvious, sometimes obscure similarities and differences in body structure and behavioral habits among animal life, and they offer a solid accounting for what seems to be a progressive development through species to man. They are, nonetheless, still theories in large part, although a few of the fundamental propositions are substantive enough to qualify as natural laws. There is, for example, a wealth of evidence that explains reasonably well the extraordinary course of the changing physical structure of life forms from microscopic organisms to the anthropoids, and there appears to be incontrovertible evidence for the fact that survival of species depends in good part upon the genetic chemicals transmitted from generation to generation. The theories can explain *some* mechanisms of evolutionary change, and many of the physical *causes* for change, but all the theories fall short in explaining what stimulates an orderly, ecological diversification of animal life or how individual changes in genes and chromosomes can lead to complex, integrated anatomical forms with capacities for both individual and community self-regulation.

Evolutionary theory is also vague and unclear about such crucial points as how genetic messages are selected to be coded, how the capacity for memory evolved that ultimately allowed for sophisticated learning abilities, how learned changes in behavior are transmitted through generations, how increased complexity of body structure and behavior is achieved, what "energy" directs the diversity of internal systems and organs to make a smoothly operating whole, or how man developed the capacity to influence his environment rather than, like all other animal life, to be simply subordinate to it.

The "laws" discovered for the evolutionary process deal almost exclusively with biological evolution. Science has not been interested in tracing the evolution of what makes an individual intellect, a psyche, consciousness, or the inner nature of living beings. It seemed to me that someone should at least try to look at the evolutionary process to see if any evidence might exist to support the notion of an evolution of intelligence, psyche and consciousness over and beyond what could be expected from the evolving complexities of the physical foundations of body and brain. Could, for example, a continuity of "mind" (consciousness, understanding, individual psyche) be traced as legitimately and scientifically as biological evolution is traced? Could "accidents" of evolution occur in the realm of the psyche just as biological accidents produced novel surviving forms of animal life? Accidents to intellectual processes (i.e., unexpected changes in them) could account for higher levels of organized, purposeful life. Is it, perhaps, the organizing qualities of intellect, individuality, psyche, consciousness and awareness that come to direct the way in which biological life is disposed? Is there also the possibility that still another "law" of evolution exists, a peculiar force or energy, as yet undiscovered (or even looked for) that is the unifying principle of nature hovering over evolution, directing its destiny?

The seeming paradox between the inexorable order of the universe and the scientific explanation that evolution is a series of biological "accidents" has always puzzled me. For even though survival of species does indeed appear to depend upon an ability of species to adapt to the environment, and the data make it clear that this is largely a chance phenomenon, especially in lower animal life, if one looks at the *chain* of surviving forms of life, the evolutionary process appears also to be a process of getting all life ordered. This, perhaps, is the destiny of life.

Foundations of Biological Evolution

The first task in unraveling a continuity of psyche, or intellect, through life forms is to search the basic principles of biological evolution for signs and evidence that can imply intelligence as the decisive, pivotal factor in the evolution of increasingly complex animal life. The task is not an easy one, especially since before any convincing theory of mind energy and its origin can be entertained or voiced with any authority, the current, scientifically convincing theories of evolution and genetics must be understood before their flaws and shortcomings can be detected.

Let me first give a brief description of each of the major concepts of biological evolution, then later discuss each in turn for the way in which it can be interpreted to support the notion of an evolution of a mind-is-more-than-brain.

There is first, of course, the Darwinian theory of natural selection, which explains in considerable detail the mechanism of the development and diversification of life forms. The survival of species appears to occur largely by natural selection, that process by which varieties of living things modify their structure and functions over generations in a way that ultimately results in changes in the species as a whole that are favorable for survival.

To this I would add, as a separate universal principle, although curiously it is rarely described separately, the primary role of neural tissue as the medium through which the changes in anatomy and function are produced and possibly as the medium that initiates the changes. Tracing the evolution of primitive neural substance traces the evolution of the *apparatus* of the intellect.

A third basic concept of biological evolution is that the physical basis of heredity is contained in the genes and chromosomes. Paralleling this certainty, however, is the troubling uncertainty about how genetic materials are susceptible to coding of their messages by external forces and how genetic messages can be expressed quite differently in cells, tissues, and organs under different circumstances. The susceptibility of genes to external influences often escapes the attention of genetic theorists, possibly because it implies the influence of circumstances beyond our present abilities to explore. The implications are, nonetheless, provocative, and are discussed in a subsequent section. The mysterious mechanisms for programming genes may perhaps lie in the capacity of nerve tissue to transmit information.

In our list of evolutionary processes necessary to developing increasingly complex and efficient life forms is the continuing evolution of new means for communication among varieties of cells, tissues, and organs of different functions within the body as well as for communication among members of species. The improvement of internal communication systems expedites the integration of information about the environment, leading to self-regulating systems and improved interaction among body systems of different functions, and further, provides the structural basis for complex learning that in turn improves the chances for survival. Enhancing communication among members of a species and among species leads to still other ways for species self-regulation and for maintaining species well-being.

A fifth crucial process in evolution is the development of new, improved systems within the body that make operations of the vital sustaining physiological and survival systems more efficient. New, superior, and different body systems appear to evolve from the interaction between often autonomous, self-regulating systems, evolving new systems such as the eye-saving spreading of moisture over the eyeball by the blinking eyelids. The eyeballs, the system receiving visual data, and the eyelids, the system that keeps the eyes from exposure to harm, in some way seem to have interacted to stimulate the evolution of glands for moisture and the blinking reflex to distribute the moisture, the combination that contributes to the survival of the eyes.

The most potent influence in the evolutionary process may be this appearance of quite new systems that evolve from the interaction of existing, already complex and independently operating body systems. It is only with the recent understanding about the behavior of systems from systems analysis (cybernetics) that the evolutionary processes can be examined in a new perspective. Systems analysis has shown how two different and independently operating systems can give rise to new systems with new characteristics, new forms and new functions. During evolution, for example, two biological systems such as the neural and cardiovascular systems develop dynamic, functional interactions with each other and evolve quite new advanced systems, such as the neurohumoral system, the biological system in which important hormonal and endocrine substances are secreted by the neural structures and circulated by the cardiovascular system to distant sites for important actions.

A fundamental property of new systems produced by the interactions of two related and harmonious systems is that they have a good chance for survival, while new systems produced by interaction between two unrelated or even dissonant systems have much less chance for survival. Many of the latter, however, do survive and prove to be important to further evolution. But in either case, there is limited predictability about the nature of the new system from what may be known about the systems that spawned it.

Take, for example, primordial nerve stuff, the already specialized microscopic threads in one-celled organisms that transmit information from one side of the cell to the other. As the vital activity of the neural communication system is traced in evolution, it is ways to preserve the neural communication system that have fostered survival. Ultimately protective tissue developed around nerve strands, a new system that evolved from the interaction among many molecular systems of the organism. It is easy in retrospect to understand how this development of protective tissue around nerves contributed to a greater capability of organisms to survive, but not even genes themselves can predict what their offspring may be should they be mismatched. The molecular systems they direct could as well interact to evolve inefficient, permanent protective structures.

The unpredictability of what can evolve from living systems is the phenomenon that makes theorists conclude it is the environment that "selects" the species variations that survive. From the completely objective point of view, and from the information of the past, most theorists conclude that living matter spews out variations in biological form and function in myriad ways, and the survivors are those forms that by chance are suitable to the environments they find themselves in. This is, of course, Darwin's natural selection or survival of the fittest, slightly modified by newer data.

Finally, there is the unknown, undefined issue of the energy of the evolutionary process itself. There is an energy of molecules and of living cells and organisms that is sustained throughout evolution as a potential energy responding dynamically to external change, a part of which may well have become transformed into a self-actualizing energy we call mind.

Survival of the Fittest

The theory of natural selection, usually popularized as the principle of the survival of the fittest, is often misunderstood as describing an orderly, progressive evolution to the more complex forms of life. To most theorists on the contrary, and for lack of a better explanation, natural selection is a phenomenon of chance. It is generally believed that, as the physical environment changed with changes in weather, natural disasters, vegetation, invasion by other forms of life, or as species migrated to new environments, animal species survived only if their structure, functions, and behaviors were suitable to sustaining life under the new conditions. Over billions of years, animal life has undergone almost continual change in the struggle to survive, and the species that survived were those whose changes in anatomy and physiology gradually adapted to the conditions of the environment.

Researchers of the origin of man have a phrase to describe the conditions that appear to control the evolution of different life forms: environmental pressure. It simply means that for the lifetimes of species, as well as for individual animal life, the environment is inflexible. The pressure is on the species to survive, not on the environment to change to support life. But hidden in this uncompromising requirement for survival is the curious circumstance that the pressure to survive is not on individual life, but on a species *as a whole* to change and develop characteristics to sustain the *species*.

The strategic question of species adaptation is: How does the total population of a species, covering many generations, change the characteristics of its individuals so that not only the species as a whole adapts successfully to an environment, but also the many changes they evolve *are similar in all individuals?* Geneticists claim that genetic variations in life are so abundant that by chance alone some will prove suitable for surviving under the conditions of the environment. But this does not explain how the successful mutations become genetically coded (prevalent theory implies accidental processes, yet the processes are remarkably similar), nor how the successful genetic materials become integrated with existing systems or become so dominant in their transmission that all progeny are so similar.

Another problem in evolutionary theory is to explain how the millions of individual genetic changes (like those producing longer tails and those producing muscles in tails for grasping in monkeys) converge to produce effective, harmonious acting wholes. Even if producing whole parts or whole organisms that are useful and survive is also "accidental," the process of unifying very different cells and tissues so that they are always propagated together suggests that some other mechanism or genetic chemical or unknown medium operates to keep the cells and tissues organized in the right way. There must be, it seems, some "higher" mechanism to ensure effective organization of all the parts. As animal life has become more complex in the organization of its physical elements, the organizing mechanism must have evolved as well. One observation that supports the idea of a separate organizing mechanism is the relatively rapid evolution of complex animal life as compared to the slow rate of evolution of simpler animal forms. If the genes that determine which animal life survives are merely the result of chance, then it would seem that more complex animal life would take proportionately longer to evolve.

I strongly suspect, as I describe later, that precisely because animal life does evolve as orderly as it does, and because the evolutionary process is accelerated in the evolution of complex forms, that some force or operational principle has simultaneously evolved to influence the orderliness in which life is expressed. The evidence points to neural tissue as the vehicle that both communicates all survival needs and acts as the intermediary mechanism to produce the changes organisms need for adapting and survival. If neural tissue is the medium of evolution, then its organizing influence could account for the accelerated evolution of complex and successful animal forms in the face of an overabundance of genetic changes that have no survival value.

I suspect also, that as neural tissue itself became organized into brain (by a self-modifying action), that the product of neural activity (the information it transmits) became progressively more important in the self-regulation of the nervous systems, meaning that the product of the activity of the nervous system influences its *own* activity (feedback) just as all other physiologic systems of the body, all individuals, and all societies have developed "automatic" self-regulating mechanisms in which what they do also affects the way they operate. These are the mechanisms that increase the efficiency of all animal life for survival.

Anthropologists, on the other hand, emphasize the environment as the primary influence on the course of evolution, and they talk about selective forces in the environment and their effects on evolution in terms such as "transgenerational changes are directed by selective forces in the environment," as if the forces were active influences. A good part of the environment is, however, inert, inanimate, or plant life; the only active forces in an environment are creatures that feed on other creatures or occupy their space.

These—the physical and the "social"—are two quite different types of environment, and while the basic principle in evolution is no doubt the need for species to adapt to their environments to survive, the very different qualities of inorganic, plant, and animal environments suggest that adaptation to these different environments occurs in quite different ways. Obviously, the mechanisms of simple species adapting to very local physical environments would be quite different from the mechanisms by which highly evolved animal species adapt to their complex environments. In higher species, even with the presence of supergenes that maintain the coordination of special structures and functions, there are many more genetic "accidents" possible than in the lower species. But since higher species seem to have evolved fairly rapidly, one could safely guess that some influence operates to counteract the high probability for failure of the multitude of nonrelevant genes and the low probability for the reproduction of genes favorable to survival. That is, in addition to the organizing influence of the nervous system to maintain *individual* life forms, there may be communication and a sharing of experience among members and generations of species about useful biological adaptations, a communication of "success" that catalyzes evolutionary, adaptive changes.

Information that a species should not change further also seems to be communicated. There is an extraordinary uniformity in populations of animal life, indicating the endless genetic mutations that are the hallmark of evolution become limited in some way so that the integrity of a species is maintained. Since genetic theory has concluded that genetic variation accounts for the many varieties of species that do survive, it now has to account for why evolutionary changes stop and why the special characteristics of species become stable.

When environments remain relatively constant, species tend to develop greater and greater genetic specialization, and better qualities for adapting to the environment. Here again there is an apparent contradiction in the general perspective on evolutionary events. The question is, Why does specialization stop, i.e., why do species become stable if genetic variation is a continuing process? If "accidents" change genes so frequently, what is the influence that stabilizes species and *prevents* further changes? The answer simply contains another question. The accepted answer is, apparently, that at a stable stage in their development, species have not only optimized their adaptation to the total environment, but have achieved a stability within the total ecological system of their environment. Any genetic variations from the optimal development would be detrimental; the variations would fall out of the genetic pool, allowing only the stable characteristics to be transmitted.

The question this raises is, What determines an ecological balance? There is, by necessity, interaction among all life forms, plant and animal. The principal influences determining balanced ecosystems are available food and space, predator activities, species migration, territoriality, and organized social behavior. Of these, the last two are quite different kinds of influences from the others. The act of defending a territory for all members of a species population rather than for a single family, and the tendency of animal species to develop behavioral hierarchies for social and group activities are *not* involuntary, instinctive reactions to environmental conditions. They are, instead, highly sophisticated, evolved, learned, and *orga-*

nized behaviors that not only improve chances for survival of the species, but also result in species self-regulation of both animal communities and ecological interactions that is a type of "control" over the environment. There is—it is clear—more to species survival than "survival of the fittest."

While the means to produce change or no-change in species may indeed be the chemicals of genes, the source or pressure that prompts change is not any *single* factor, but the way in which the totality of life is organized and reacts both within itself and *as a whole.* If we read the process of evolution, from single-cell organisms to man, at every level of life there is a level of organization, and with the creation of new levels, earlier levels are superseded or incorporated into other more broadly encompassing organizations of life or may be relegated to extinction. Whatever the outcome, all higher levels of organization exert an important influence on the levels of organization that spawned them. It is not the specific elements of animal life or the environment that evolving life must adapt to but to be successful and survive species must adapt to *the way in which the environment is organized.* This implies the operation of some kind of intermediary between the organized qualities of an environment that influences development and the evolution of life forms that develop a correspondent organization. The most likely intermediary would be a mechanism for the communication of information that developing forms could "understand," with "understanding" ranging from primitive organic reorganizations of life substances by trial and error to the most highly evolved forms of intellect in man.

For evolution is not all genes and chemicals and the chance fitting of life to environments. The most pervasive force in evolution is the capacity to learn, regardless of how primitive the learning process may be or how sophisticated it has become. Learning, meaning to benefit by experience, changes the reactive properties of neural tissue and is the agent that changes the chemical structure of genes and changes the messages that genes carry from generation to generation.

An important concept rarely, if ever, considered in theories of evolution is *communal learning.* Learning is always thought of as learning by individual animals that is then communicated among groups, with the new knowledge spread by learning from others. There are, however, many behaviors that suggest families, communities, and even whole species of animal life do learn communally to change group behavior. In the development of anthropoids, for example, where food sharing with the young is a mechanism for survival of the species, learning from each other could scarcely precede learning together. The rise of the drug culture in youth communities is a prime example of mass learning; the same "nonverbal" behavioral sharing of experience may account for important evolutionary change as well. We don't know, simply because evolutionary change has not been analyzed from this perspective.

What species learn changes the environment (the spider's web creates an environment with better food supply), and it is the environment that is the source of the pressure to adapt and to learn. With this kind of reciprocal change, there should be a constant upward spiral in complexity of life forms and a concomitant increasing control of the environment by the more complex forms of life.

The critical role of learning to evolution, to which I will return a bit later, may account for why there is a "phylogenetic" scale, i.e., why more and more complex forms of animal life have evolved. If it is true that species survive by developing suitable characteristics, and that hundreds of species have achieved positions of both a species stability and an ecological balance, then another perplexing question in the story of evolution is why some species, the anthropoids and hominids in particular, developed characteristics that are "unnecessarily" complex? What prompted increasing complexity over and above that adequate or favorable to survival?

Evolutionary theorists tend not to deal well with this phenomenon (nor with a number of other puzzling events in evolution). They account for the increase in complexity of structure and function and behavior of species by claiming that it provides increased efficiency of survival mechanisms, particularly in the battle for food and space. This is no doubt true, but it is only a partial explanation. Certainly the lion is more *versatile* in his survival mechanisms than his feline ancestors or his equine relatives, but there are many forms of life that have a comparable *efficiency* for survival. Lizards, mice, fish, bees, and ants are enormously diverse, yet they all dwell in the same general environment, and even though some inhabit microcosms and others macrocosms of the environment, they nonetheless all have an efficiency for survival.

None of the theories of evolution so far seems to account for why complex species such as marine mammals, apes, monkeys, and man evolved more skills than those needed to survive. Not "why" in the sense of ultimate causes, but "why" as in the question, Why, if hundreds of species, from single-celled organisms to cockroaches to amphibians, have lived so long and successfully in the less complex forms, were still other species stimulated to evolve increasingly more complex forms? What stimulated the production of increasing complexity that led to man? He and other higher animals are, in comparison to other species, not very efficient in surviving in the physical way lower animal species survive. They survive only because whatever was responsible for their genesis also created completely different mechanisms for survival, one of the most important being the ability to *protect* the species. This is a mechanism for survival quite different from the limited power of lower species for slowly adapting to the environment and producing excessive offspring to sustain propagation.

The biological mechanisms that *protect* species from extinction are quite different from the biological mechanisms that merely ensure survival of species taken as wholes. This creative leap in evolution means that species endowed with protective as well as reflex survival devices began to protect the young more fully, and protection expanded to include families, troops, colonies. While the mechanisms some species use to protect their young may appear to be little more than a biochemical, programmed drive, even in primitive ways of protecting the young, as in ants or bees, not all of the protective processes can be explained in terms of biochemical communication. And in "higher" species, protection of species changed from reflex, instinctive protecting of colonies of the community's young to protecting the individual young. The behavioral implications of this activity are discussed more fully in a later section.

If survival depends upon the biological success of the species in coping with the environment, yet where rapid evolution has occurred, species are also more complex, simply increasing the chances for survival by evolving through random genetic mutations of chancy survival value seems not to be the complete answer to the process of evolution. The puzzling part of rapid evolutionary change lies in the fact that it is not *individuals* of species that change, it is *populations* of species that change. Again, there is the mysterious superindividual influence.

Here, too, as for evolving individual changes, an intermediary process is implicated, an intermediary that appears to communicate experience. At the level of complex species, the role of communication and sharing of experience is easier to understand, and if this is coupled with the effect of learning (of behavior) on genes, it can be just as easily deduced that an evolving intellect is the agent that redirects the evolutionary process from a chance, mechanical process of survival to a discriminating, information-processing, self-directing faculty. It was an "intellect" that gave rise to the mechanisms for *protecting* species from extinction and ultimately to the capacity of man to control the very process of evolution itself.

The unresolved questions in the theory of natural selection are usually believed to be answered by genetic theory. Before the contributions of other principles of evolutionary theory are examined, we should consider whether current theories about the fundamental role of genes and chromosomes in evolution contribute to a concept that a parallel evolution of intellect is equally as important in the evolution of life as are the chemical processes.

Genes and an Evolutionary Inheritance

It is by now well established that the genes making up chromosomes contain the genetic memory material DNA and its chemical servant and messenger, RNA. The DNA contains the code for directing the development of inherited characteristics in the sequences of its molecular structure and serves as a template which the messenger RNA copies and carries out into the cytoplasm where transfer RNA is formed, also by template action, which in turn becomes a factory directing the production of the body's significant proteins and cell materials in tissue development.

The scientific tales of DNA and the "determining" chemistry of genes and chromosomes, however frightening their implications, cannot even approach answering the question of how the structural-functional developments determined by a gene or gene group or polygenes are organized into functional wholes with functions integrated enough to ensure survival. While DNA indeed contains the coded instructions to replicate itself in its offspring cells and can account for some of the physical operations of heredity, i.e., for the development of structures and the functions of structures at various stages of development, and even though DNA can also account for the transmission of this information from generation to generation, *there is as yet no evidence to account for either the origin of the instructions or the mechanisms that produce the genetic codes.*

If genes are actually programmed by external forces (e.g., environmental change), and the way their messages about how anatomical and physiological elements are actually expressed is also affected by external influences, then there must be some kind of medium that communicates the external "demands" for change to the genetic chemicals and also the same or another medium that energizes the changes demanded. If, for example, the prolonged drought that created the deserts stimulated a species of rat like the kangaroo rat to alter its chemical demands for fluids and alter, too, the means the organism used to obtain fluids, then in order for an entire species to evolve these changes, the "success" of the changes for survival must be communicated to the individual genetic programs. The communicated information may or may not be the same as the agency that excites the changes in the genetic chemical code and guides its expression as appropriate for survival.

Genetic theorists account for the changes in structure and function in species that do survive from evidence that the genetic chemicals are subject to very frequent "accidental" change, and that these mutations, which presumably also "accidentally" converge and coalesce to form whole parts, are so myriad that the millions having no survival value are not propagated.

Since unsuccessful variations become extinct, those gene pools with suitable characteristics gain the upper hand and are propagated. The evidence is strong for this kind of genetic activity in species development, but exactly why genetic expression should become so uniform throughout all members of a species seems a bit at odds with the claimed unlimited potential of genes to be expressed in a variety of ways depending upon circumstances. If it is true, as geneticists say, that the genetic message can be modified by experience, but that it is population changes *as a whole* that change individuals, then isolated *individual experience* could not account for the changes in the total population of a species. Instead, the probability is that many individuals have similar experiences, suggesting the possibility that experiences may be shared (and learned) by some kind of communication. Such a sharing would make for a compatibility of the gene pools, particularly since similarities in systems favor the generation of successful new systems. Certainly the characteristics of dominance and recessiveness of genes must come to be established in some way. The effect of experience sharing might be the source of supergenes. Experience is, perhaps, the catalyst, with communication as the source of evolutionary change.

The communications medium that conveys the information about changes needed in anatomy and physiologic function and that excites the changes to occur may be neural tissue and the coordinating neural networks.

Biological Communication Systems: Their Effect on Genes

Science has only recently come to recognize one of the "operational" characteristics affecting the way genes are changed and organized. The explanation is a universal principle, but our understanding of it is far from complete. Almost from the moment of the generation of living cells, a curious phenomenon developed that does not occur when chemicals are strung together in nonliving forms. That phenomenon is communication, communication among the chemicals of living substances; communication among cells, tissues, and organs; and communication among life forms. Communication is the exchange of information, and the effect of communication is to regulate the systems communicating with each other.

The operation of all living systems depends upon communication of information about the success or failure of the system's operation. When a system, biological or mechanical, maintains its functioning by using information about how its functioning relates to other systems, it is operating by the "feedback" principle (see chapter 4).

Feedback is a two-way street of operations that, within limits, allows a system to operate automatically. The electric skillet, for example, stops heating when the heat reaches the temperature we set, and turns on again when the temperature drops below the level set. The "intelligence" lies in the relay system that has been given electronic instructions to turn on and off depending upon what the actual temperature is (detected by a sensing element) and what the setting is for turning the heat on and off. (All of this automation works properly only if something outside the system has set the code.) For the electric skillet, one side of the street is what happens inside affecting what happens outside (relay makes heat), and the other is what happens outside affecting what happens inside (heat level makes relay work).

All elements that make up living substances, whether plants, small organisms, or the most complex of animal species, become organized by the functions they perform. What is outside a cell affects what goes on inside a cell, and often, such as with the excretion of metabolic materials, what is inside the cell affects the outside. Similar exchanges go on between cells, among cells and tissues, organs and system of organs, throughout all levels of biological organization of all organisms. Operationally, each physiologic system and each subsystem, from the complex systems that integrate the functions of smaller units to the smallest units of cells, has the capacity to "feed back" information to itself. In terms of function, this is called a feedback "loop" because its chief activity is to detect information about the status of operation of the unit's functioning and feed that information back to the unit (cell or system) so that any adjustments necessary can be made. What the system detects is information about change external to itself, and it is the change that leads to action.

As physiologic functions become more complex, the extent of organization becomes more complex and develops "control" over subsystems. The cardiovascular system, for example, supplies oxygen to muscle cells and so "controls" the extent of muscle activity that utilizes the oxygen in a limited system. But the cardiovascular system has a complex organization since it must function in a relationship with the respiratory system, and so it, too, not only effects its own local control but is affected by and subject to control by other systems.

Since life first evolved, feedback regulation of all life's internal and external activities has been integral to survival. This way of functioning at all levels of biological activity is so extensive that throughout evolution feedback systems with increasingly broad dominating actions over more limited systems developed. There are hierarchies upon hierarchies of feedback systems. There is molecular control of cells with feedback control of molecules by the cells, cellular control of organs with organ control of cells, and so on throughout the organism. Each of the "higher" systems that provides for the regulation of activities among different functional parts also has the capability to intervene (supervene) in the automatic (feedback) regulation of local, more limited functions. There appears always to be another system, at a higher level of organization, that can control the control of systems lower in the hierarchy.

Genetic expression appears to be regulated through feedback information. That is, variations in the genetic code that produce functional changes in organisms favoring survival (adaptation to the environment) have a high probability for propagation. Apparently the "success" of the genetic adaptations is fed back in some way to the organism, and this information changes the message contained in the genetic chemicals.

One of the problems for genetic theory is *how* the information is fed back to the organisms and to the species as a whole. It is an intriguing question because the genetic memory material, DNA, itself apparently is not subject to feedback effects within *individual* organisms.

As species interact with the elements of the environment, those mutations of structure and function that provide improvement in chances for survival of species cannot, in fact, be propagated as individual changes. There must also be modifications of groups and series of genes arising from functional changes that *only as a whole* improve chances for survival. To live, to survive, means that all parts of the organism, and all future members of the species community, are involved in the adaptation process. The operation of multiple and varied parts of individuals and all varieties of species members represents higher levels of organized systems that affect the manufacture and division of the genetic chemicals. That is, parts of individuals, individuals as wholes, and communities of individuals are all organized systems that act back upon the unknown force that codes and designs the codes for genetic chemicals to transmit to following generations, and these organized parts, individuals, and communities affect the expression of the genetic messages as well, i.e., the way the genetic messages are consummated in the structures and functions that are produced.

Genetic materials are passive; the designers and writers of the codes do not reside within the organism at all, but within a *population* of individuals. This is the unmentionable void in genetic theory: how the community action of groups of any species can prevail upon the chemical structure of genetic material of individuals to alter their biological constitution. The very fact that evolutionary development appears to depend upon a level of organization of life that is super-individual, i.e., that depends upon life forms *as groups* to determine individual development, strongly suggests that, as species evolve, their individual members also evolve abilities to sense influences operating on the population as a whole as well as on the individual itself, a super-individual intelligence.

The crucial problem for understanding the nature of life is to understand how the controls are set. The fact that genetic chemicals contain the memory to direct *how* cells develop does not explain how the chemicals came to be programmed to do what they do. Where does the intelligence that "programs" the memories come from? Not feedback, for of all the elements of living systems, DNA is not subject to feedback effects *within individuals.* The feedback, the setting of the controls, is external to the physical substance of the individual.

The fact that community action of species populations is primarily responsible for the development of similar individuals within a species is baffling indeed. It is also one of the best-kept secrets of the evolutionary theorists. Yet the bottom line of genetics and natural selection is that whatever is evolved depends in good part upon an energy or level of organization (colonies, families, species) of individuals in groups or cells in groups or organs in groups. Some force, energy, chemical, or supreme entity endows the individual with the special ability to direct its development toward a goal or standard that the population (of the species or group) *as a whole* finds useful for survival.

Is this an "intelligence," and a kind of intelligence we have overlooked in our preoccupation in science with reducing systems for study into bits and pieces, and which ignores the importance of the new and unique effects of systems *as wholes?* I believe it is. Look at the marvelous cooperation among organs and physiologic systems of the body. Enzymes of the stomach, pancreas, and liver work in the distant organs to perform life-sustaining functions for the muscles and skin and brain. Is there a DNA system that programmed this relationship? I am not aware that any has been found, nor for any other complex interactions by which the total organism functions and develops its elaborate integration of tissues, organs and systems.

It appears, in fact, to be a bit of the other way around, especially for the most important cells of the body, nerve cells. As with all other developing cells, nerves appear to contain intrinsic chemicals that direct their connections to quite precise areas of the nervous system; but when nerve cells make connections with the tissue cells they service (by communicating information), the available evidence suggests that other kinds of cells in their turn transmit some kind of information back to the developing neuron crucial to the ultimate specialization it develops. The same "external" information apparently also directs the nerve cell in making the connections within the nervous system that form reflex arcs.

Two great unknowns in genetic theory, and in the theory of natural selection as well, are not only how the molecular mutations are put into an order that makes the result an effective whole, but how the template for that whole is transmitted to create a new species. It is not terribly difficult to imagine that genetic molecules can be rearranged in single-cell organisms, especially since there are billions of such organisms and hundreds of physical forces that can stir up the chemicals. But it is quite a different situation to understand how a genetic memory molecule for skin, say, joins with genetic molecules that determine the development of claws and suddenly produces special muscles for the retractile claw. The versatility of the retractile claw, used at one time for successful hunting and at another time for batting the offspring to teach him a lesson, is only one of a million examples of the extraordinary process in evolution in which a multitude of molecules are "ordered" in a way to work together to produce a totality of structure and operation that performs diverse survival functions.

There would seem to be some kind of "intelligence" that directs all the very different genes and cells and organs to become unified into a meaningful or useful whole. Evolution, after all, is not a molecular event, nor is the natural selection of the species that survive concentrated on single genes. Whatever determines the way in which genetic chemicals themselves are organized, and is responsible for the orderly way in which they come together, resides in the power of a still higher level of organization and its communication systems.

The Communication Systems

The theories that rely on infinite varieties of genes and "chance" arrangements and amalgams so that anatomy and physiology become more and more suitable for survival in physical environments are theories, I believe, that slight some of the important consequences of the developing complexity of animal life. The evolution of life forms more able to survive also means that these same life forms gain increasing "control" *over* the environment, not simply that they are better able to respond to the peculiarities of the environment. Much of what higher animal forms do both helps to regulate the environment (using lower forms as food or living in mutually helping arrangements, such as the birds that eat pesky insects from the backs of wild animals) and at the same time ensures their own survival. Again, this seems to be a function of populations of species as a whole, not of individuals. There are hundreds of examples of symbiotic relationships among animal forms, a phenomenon that aids both species involved to survive. What we call an ecological balance is really a phenomenon of populations interacting *as wholes.*

Thus the environment that shapes evolution changes dramatically with every new increment in complexity of animal life. New species must not only accommodate to the physical environment but to a variety of life activities as well. The environment becomes more complex. Perhaps this does spawn more and more genetic mutations, but the primary demand of a complex environment is that, if an organism is to survive in it, masses of information need to be digested and integrated, "understood," and acted upon. The genetic rearrangements needed for organisms to adapt to complex environments would have to be those that could foster improved sensory apparatus, improved internal communication systems, and improved coordination of the body and its functions. The burden for improvement seems to have fallen on the nervous system.

If the principle of natural selection—that species and genes are "selected" to survive because through trial-and-error change they develop characteristics allowing them to survive—holds, then the more complex environments become the more survival of species would depend on developing specialized internal systems to deal with the environmental complexity. The systems that answer this need are internal communication systems, sensory information integration systems, memory systems, data comparison systems, and self-regulation systems. These kinds of internal systems that perceive and judge and act upon information about the environment are the tools of the intellect.

It is not known what prompted the evolutionary leap from the complex brains of the highest animal species able to meet the environmental demands for survival with some ingenuity to the completely unique intellectualizing capacities of human beings. It is, in fact, scarcely speculated upon. "Accidents" to prehistoric man, such as the discovery of fire, or recognition of the relationships between seeds and food crops, or collective hunting, or later the effectiveness of joining in groups to defend against marauders no doubt changed the environment, and the changes demanded a different kind of adaptation by the human organism if survival were to keep pace with these shifts in environmental elements. The changes also favored group action; the group fared better when information and knowledge about things not immediately in the physical environment could be communicated, and this perhaps inspired the development of language. In any event, a social culture developed, and with it developed minds that could cope with the new environmental demands that were more social and less physical. But here the evolutionary story that environment triggers changes in living things shifts completely, for beginning with the first "accidental" change from eating fruits to planting seeds or using tools, man began to control and create his environments.

Effective, useful control of the physical environment, from agriculture and hunting to protecting groups of his species from predators, stimulated new forms of communication. As communication by behavior changed to communication by sounds and then by symbols, and the physical environment became more and more controlled, the environment critical to survival became predominantly an environment of social activities.

The evolution of specialized internal communications and community integration systems has continued to change the environment. Animal species developed community life, and that developed into social life, until, with man, the "environment" became one dominated by culture. At each phylogenetic stage, the ability for communication, both internal and external, and the ability for self-regulation, both internal and external, created an environment more of intangibles than of tangibles.

Expanding Communications

The "need" to extend the coordinating activities of the nervous system also brought about a still higher level of the organization of neural tissue. While reflexes manifest a primitive kind of memory within small neural circuits, a further survival advantage was gained when organisms developed the necessary neural circuits and chemicals to store information for different periods of time, and developed neural circuits that could compare information about different aspects of the environment, make associations and decisions.

Another characteristic of life in evolution for expanding and developing more flexible abilities to maintain existence is the evolution of increasingly complex communications systems among the cells and internal organs of different functions. The expansion and specialization of these communication systems is exclusively a function of evolving neural tissue. More abundant information about events in the environment can be sensed, and the information can be conveyed to varieties of organs to react to environmental changes. The enrichment of internal communications is also related to the way in which species propagate themselves. Compare the fly and the cat. The fly, although its visual sense is highly developed and its nerves make sophisticated connections with feet and wings, nonetheless has a primitive nervous system compared to the cat, and its options for surviving are limited. Mainly it flies, for food and to escape danger. It also propagates itself in endless millions. The cat, on the other hand, with its well-organized, abundant, even surplus, nervous system, has the ability for many kinds of survival activities, such as learning through exploration and remembering favorable vs. unfavorable circumstances. And the cat, although it may seem to multiply inconsiderately, in fact procreates at an infinitely slower and lower rate than the fly.

It is the evolution of internal communication systems, the neural networks, that fosters the evolution of different ways in which the nerve networks themselves are organized. As more sensory information is available and there is more traffic in the neural networks, survival also depends upon a more efficient handling of the sensory information. Presumably this was the stimulus for the development of neural systems organized to judge the relative importance of incoming information, integrate it, and effectively distribute the information for the most effective outcomes, and all of this increased the versatility with which species interact with their environments and survive.

From Neural Substance to Brain

If we accept the evolutionary principle that organisms become modified in structure and function through a long process of adapting to their environments, and if we accept the fairly obvious evidence for a continuity of anatomical elements and physiologic functions through changes as phylogenetic evolution proceeds, then the communications function of neural tissue emerges as the prime mover and catalyst of the evolution of all living beings. It is the *messages,* the information communicated among body parts, not the physical substance, that produce *functions* that survive.

There are, in fact, two weighty lines of evidence. When neural tissues are compared successively from single-cell organisms through increasingly complex animals to man, one can see an orderly development in the *number* and arrangement and structure of nerve cells, but little change in their function. From the barely discernible strands of special intracellular tissues, the neuremes, of the single-celled paramecium, which transmit messages from one part of the cell to another part, to the meter-long neurones that chain endlessly in vertebrates, the function of nerve cells is to communicate information vital to the organism's survival. The *form* of nerve cells has adapted progressively to changing needs of the organisms and species, developing special receptors for sensing different kinds of information, branching their parts to distribute information and receive information from many sources, and developing a one-way transmitting part to distribute information in an orderly way to cells and tissues to excite them to react to care for the organism as a whole, but all nerves in all species transmit information in exactly the same way.

Nerves transmit information by the simplest of codes. The degree of significance of any specific kind of information (heat, pressure) is transmitted by varying the number of nerve impulses, while the kind of information is determined by the kind of nerve receptor that is stimulated. It is up to the neurons of the central nervous system to distribute and associate information. Exactly how pooled, composite aggregates of complex information are communicated is unknown. Although research has not been able to capture the transfer of complex kinds of information, the suggestion is strong that packages of related information are communicated through the brain as patterns of neuronal activity. The implications of this concept are enormous, for in order for patterns of nerve impulses to be generated, conducted, and received as a unit of meaningful information, some capability must exist for transferring information in this way. And since the elements comprising the patterns are communicated along with the pattern of information, the capability of communicating patterns must include the ability to communicate, simultaneously, discrete bits of information as well. The challenge to any theory of nerve and brain is to explain how the summed, integrated meaning of a pattern can be communicated and still communicate critical information about individual elements of the pattern.

Another remarkable step in the evolution of nerve tissue has been the expansion of communication among the nerves themselves. As the "need" for more nerves increased, nerves continued to specialize and to forge new connections, and to organize themselves into communities, i.e., into groups of similar nerve cells that we call nerves and brain, an adaptation that allowed cooperative action among the neurons, increasing their efficiency and range of influence. Sometimes, as new adaptive forms developed, older forms contracted rather than expanded, and became either more efficient or vestigial.

One development that fostered further efficiency, energy saving, and life saving was the development of reflexes and self-regulating systems. The extraordinary response of developing organisms to environmental conditions, and the success of their neural systems in coordinating life-preserving activities, led to the development of two quite different kinds of reflexes. The amorphous neural network of the autonomic nervous system split off as the service mechanism to maintain a fairly automatic functioning of the body's vital organs and systems. Another type of reflex developed to translate data sensed from the environment and to service prompt action that could favor survival, such as in the fight-or-flight reaction.

Even in their earliest evolutionary state, it was the nerves that supplied the intelligence of living beings; without them communication between the organisms and the environment did not take place. As they continued to adapt to the changing environments, their expanded communications and developing capacities to store information gave organisms options for different kinds of responses.

In every case in the further evolution of living things, it is the neural substance of the organism's being that has expanded *itself* (and sometimes contracted as it increased in efficiency) as higher forms developed. It has been the neural tissue that has *invented* new activities and new forms for the organism in order to continue life. Finally, when it created the human mind, that miraculous ability of nerve substance to provide infinite ways to continue life (for some ways failed), performed perhaps the ultimate miracle, the creation of the ability of mind to look at itself and discover the keys that could shape its own destiny.

Learning and the Evolution of Behavior

One of the amazing abilities of nerve tissue, however primitive, is its ability to "learn." The simple neural tube of the earthworm can somehow store in memory enough information to "learn" how to distinguish one artificial signal from another. The scarcely differentiated cells of minute marine animals can be easily demonstrated to show "learning" in a primitive sense, as for example, when they fail to react by their usual body contractions to pressure stimuli after the stimuli are repeated at frequent intervals. Technically called habituation, the curious process of temporarily decreasing an innate response (reflex) when the stimulus has been repeated for some time, it represents the earliest evidence of the ability of cells, and particularly neural tissues, to "learn" how to adapt to the environment. Curiously, the opposite kind of "learned behavior," where the organism comes to increase innate reactions to environmental changes (by rate or magnitude of response) emerges at a later evolutionary level.

The prevalence of these simple, primitive forms of learning through the evolution of increasingly higher forms of life illustrates both the unpredictability of behavioral mechanisms in evolving forms and the remarkable variability in ways in which behavior itself evolves by retaining phylogenetically old combinations for new adaptive purposes and the development of more efficient behaviors. Habituation, the primitive ability to depress reactivity temporarily in the presence of repeated stimuli usually harmless for survival, is maintained throughout evolutionary history; sensitization, that reaction of increasing reactivity to repeated stimulation, is, for the most part, lost as higher organic forms are developed, and is superseded by more efficient behavioral reactions.

These antecedents of learning in lower forms of life are local reactions within the peripheral tissues of organisms, i.e., reactions occurring locally between receptors registering environmental changes and the effectors which reflexly alter the activity of the peripheral tissues. As neural tissue evolved its capacities for memory (storing information) and neural networks advanced in function to make associations among bits of experience, to compare patterns of experience and thought and use its information to change behavior, the neural tissue of the brain was performing a new function: adding meaning and a sense of beingness to the physical events it had to work with.

The scientific evidence we have about the physical evolution of the anatomy and physiology of life forms is convincing. It is when we try to account for the evolution of behavior that we run into trouble with evolutionary theory. The problem can perhaps be summarized by noting two major events in evolution. First, it is agreed that function determines structure, that is, in order for different forms of life to survive, their functions must be appropriate to the conditions of the environment, so it is the function (nourishing the organism, locomotion) that influences the structural development (mouth, intestine, fins, legs). The second, and probably the greatest, influence on the course of evolution is the evolution of social life, meaning not simply cooperation among individuals of a species for the survival of a species, but a social life that emphasizes the survival of individuals.

As I noted earlier, some species developed ways to protect themselves from extinction, a survival technique that contrasts sharply with the process of adapting physiologic functions in order to survive in an existing environment. While the social activities of ants or bees are devices that cope with environmental demands in a highly specialized way, and do protect the species from extinction, this kind of survival mechanism differs from the devices of "higher" species that actively protect *individual* young and organize to take offensive action against potentially hazardous elements of the environment. The great apes, the closest structural and behavioral relatives of man, evolved a spectacular new system for survival, an amalgam of behavioral devices used by communities or groups of individuals for the benefit of both individuals and the group as a whole, and perhaps not quite so much benefit for the species.

One of the principal ways in which the apes differ from their animal relatives is in their social and community and especially family activities. It seems reasonable that at some point in evolution, community action among individuals of a species operated to improve the chances for survival. Ants, bees, lions, elephants and many other species function by group or family action, but it is almost exclusively in man and in his apelike cousins (and pre-man) that social action is directed more toward the survival of individuals than of groups of young or herds or colonies or species. In some way, members of a group or species have become individuals, each with readily identifiable characteristics.

One supposes, if evolutionary theory is correct, that the new interactions between the environment and the ever-changing structure and function of the great apes and pre-man, along with the sudden shift to group and social activities, led to the development in man of quite new functional equipment. The new equipment (different bits of which can be seen in the great ape cousins), includes different neural organization and the expanding brain, which could give rise to systems of social and conceptual functioning divorced from the need to perceive and understand and react to the immediate physical environment.

As social activities became more and more important ways to cope with the physical environment, social activity itself demanded refinements if it were to be more and more effective as a survival device. As family life emerged, dramatic endocrine changes occurred, lengthening sex cycles and perhaps making individual life more precious. Certainly, as endocrine functions changed and offspring were longer and longer in gaining their maturity, the need to educate the young became a definite environmental and social need.

With increasing social organization in the great apes, the need for improved communication increased, and varieties of communications signals developed. The exhibitionism of monkeys and apes, where for no apparent reason they pound their chests, emit shrieks, and stand erect, seems to be mainly a sign to indicate their dominance over others, but frequently their behavior is directed toward nothing at all, apparently a purely social ventilation. The great apes also have a great repertoire of facial expressions and vocal intonations that are information signals.

Based on this kind of behavioral evidence, I would disagree with the popular scientific conclusion that only man possesses the capacity to transmit learning, behavior, and culture over generations when the objects of the learning and culture are not within physical reach of the senses. It is claimed that only man can pass on symbolic information to subsequent generations, but certainly the calls and gestures of many wild species do stand for things not in the immediate environment, and while many of the calls and gestures are learned when the object is in the environment, many species also have ways to communicate the meaning of quite new elements in the environment; even though these may be quite general, they are nonetheless concepts.

Evolution of the Social Mentality

There are implications even more esoteric of the way social activities have affected the course of evolution. The young, going through lengthy periods of immaturity, show trust, not just of their parents, but of other members of the community, and a similar trust is seen among members of a troop where the troop seems to rely implicitly upon the wisdom of the elders to sense danger or find food and shelter.

So much of what is popularly known about evolution and the place of man in the animal scheme of life dwells on strictly biological determinants and reduces the behavior of man to the more primitive behaviors of animals. The animal behavior scientist S. A. Barnett wrote, "The human brain and human behavior evolved in savagery." The notion that man's biologic predecessors were characterized principally by savagery may be a popular notion, but it is also archaic, and the product of tunnel vision and a hysterical immunity to logic about historic behavioral evidence.

There are, instead, a hundred more signs of human-like qualities in animals than there are animal-like qualities in man. This suggests, in fact, that these qualities were those evolutionary developments that were more successful in preserving species than the qualities that have been interpreted as instincts. The behavioral characteristics of aggression, territorial defense, nesting, etc., are more often species specific than not, and certainly are not characteristics universally distributed among animals. On the other hand, family care, care of the community, education of the young, food sharing, sophisticated forms of communication, trust, restraint, planning ahead and other "intelligent" activities are characteristics that mark increasingly complex species. This fact suggests that the tendency to develop behavior directed more and more toward coping with social environments was an adaptive mechanism of greater power for determining the evolution of higher species than primitive animal behaviors that answer demands of the physical environment.

From an accident during experiments with the behavior of macaque monkeys, a species loathing water, the monkeys not only discovered that the salt from washing food in sea water improved its taste, but that scattered food grains could be salvaged by putting them in water and collecting the floating grains. These two related discoveries produced profound changes in the culture of these monkeys. The use of water led to swimming, and eventually the juveniles of the troop found that water was a delightful playground.

While the theorists conjecture that this kind of learning is imitation or accidental, I think they miss the point. The real trigger for changing behavior—actually a changing life-style—was that for once, man was *interacting* with the monkeys, not just studying them and using them as objects in experiments.

The failure of monkey or ape minds to evolve in more sophisticated ways than they have would seem to be solely a function of their social environment. Once they enter an environment of concepts and thought, they evolve new operations of mind, presumably by reorganizing strictly mental processes. This is strikingly shown in recent studies on the intelligence of chimpanzees. It has been found that chimpanzees, without any change in brain structure, but with a new perspective that comes from *interacting* with human beings, have an extensive ability to abstract information provided solely through communication (not by example or teaching or imitation), and can modify language, translate languages, transfer concepts among things for descriptive purposes, and transfer their learned communication skills to the "uneducated" of their own species.

When a chimpanzee learns, at different times, the hand-signs for "cry" and "hurt" among a hundred other signs, then bites into a radish and signs "cry-hurt-food," he is inventing new symbols. Or when he is given a watermelon for the first time and calls (signs) it "candy-fruit-drink," not only is he forming new concepts, he is also communicating as efficiently and as appropriately as his education allows. These are intellectual skills we have attributed to man alone.

There is also the evidence that "enriched" environments (handling, helping) increase the size of rats' brains, indicating that perhaps symbolic behavior does, in fact, change material structure. It is just as easy (and correct) to think in terms of living matter having to catch up with nonmaterial evolutions, as in the case of the rats, as it is to believe that sophistication of intellectual activity needs to catch up with advances of physical change, as in the case of the chimpanzees.

The point is that the functions of neural tissue can be changed by using the existing brain substrate. Since the function of brain is mind, the suggestion is strong that mind directs brain.

It is, in the retrospective of evolutionary history, fascinating to speculate on what changes in the structure and function of animal life were prompted by expanding social activities. It was long accepted by scientists studying evolution that hunting fostered the earliest hominid social activities. Obviously there were times when survival depended upon cooperative hunting. Over the millennia, the *effect* of group hunting on survival was improved by changing behavior. Hunting meant division of labor, then food sharing, and these in turn meant planning ahead for the hunt, restraint in eating, and at least temporarily giving up individual roles in the pecking order.

The great break in the evolutionary scheme that produced increasingly complex animals and the antecedents of the human mind are likely to be found in the implications of even primitive community action. When true social activity evolved, animal life was no longer life to be molded exclusively by the demands of the physical environment. By some "chance" circumstance of evolution the power of the physical environment to dictate the directions of evolutionary change began to diminish until, with man, the physical environment is (if it stays the same) no longer the controller, but is well under control.

It is, of course, as true as we can ever be sure of truth, that the powers of mind are carried out by means of chemical and physical changes within the brain and the nerves that serve the brain. We can trace the *physical* evolution of brains through related animal life, from lower to higher (amount of knowledge in the living system), and science can supply weighty evidence to show how the increasing knowledge and sophistication of organisms is quite precisely linked with changing behavior. But what science cannot prove, nor has scarcely a grain of physical evidence for, is a physical mechanism that can account for the abilities of human beings to transmit symbolic, conceptual information, and the ultimate puzzle of the mind, the paradoxical unity-duality of a brain looking at itself. "I know I know" is the subjective appreciation of personal and supraindividual experience and knowledge, the carrier of the nonmaterial culture of human beings that epitomizes man's two levels of existence: biological and intellectual.

Whether mind is a new creation, a nonmaterial entity spawned from the material world, or whether it is merely an inevitable offshoot of the successful evolution of species more and more capable of living and surviving in a contracting universe is a question that cannot be answered on the basis of present knowledge. Some scientists seem not to understand the deficiencies of the evidence, but the most knowledgeable do reluctantly admit that mind is indeed beyond the knowable of the brain. If it, indeed, is, we may have missed the antecedents of mind and consciousness in the overzealous attention we have paid to the more obvious evidence for physical evolution.

The attitude of the physicalist scientists is intolerantly inhibitory to understanding the mind and to exploring the mind for the supermind capabilities that unquestionably exist but are neither studied nor nurtured. If chimpanzees can extend their mental abilities far beyond those ever exhibited before, simply by being put into a different culture and given a cultural heritage that they can transmit just as do human beings, then human beings, with far greater capacities, may indeed be extending their intellect and psyche toward a new form of life from the synthesis of intellect.

Best-Fitting Hypothesis?

One of the greatest problems in the sciences that conjecture about the origin of man is the lack of communication among the many different branches of science that contribute information about evolutionary phenomena. There are zoologists, anthropologists, paleontologists, psychologists, physiologists, sociologists, and so on, and each separate discipline tends to theorize around the material of its specialty. As I have reviewed the scientific data and the various theories and ideas about the origin and nature of man, I have been struck by how parochial even the experts are when they theorize about man's beginnings. The geneticist concentrates on the molecular transformations of the genetic memory materials; the ethologists concentrate on the way species respond to their environments; anthropologists concentrate on either the physical or the cultural characteristics of the human species; and other specialists promote the importance of their special scientific interests. Occasionally an expert does attempt to bridge the knowledge from two specialties, but for the most part these efforts are prejudiced in favor of the primary specialty.

If there are any unifying themes within the collections of expert opinion on evolution, it is the concept of natural selection and the genetics of inheritability of physical characteristics. Yet, despite the prevailing consensus, there are more unanswered questions about the origin of man than there are answers; there are more exceptions to the rules than expected cases; there are more gaps in the theory than evidence. This is not to say that overall theory is wrong, for I doubt that it is, but the omissions and discrepancies argue for serious consideration of other perspectives, other logic, and most important, for acknowledging the role of the cooperation of systems that seem too diffuse simply because they have not been studied in perspective. And there are hundreds of cooperating systems that have profound effects in evolution. Such systems are community and intercommunity organization; the way in which the wholes of organisms, species, and even internal systems modify the structure and function of the parts and are functionally different from what could be expected from the sum of the parts; the systems that make for individuality and personality in species; exploratory behavior; and the "controlling" system that pulls together the thousands of DNAs to make a whole man.

Too often we accept theory as fact. Nor is it the average person, depending upon science for guidelines about the nature of life, who is deceived into important misconceptions. The majority of scientists themselves not only tend to rely on someone else's theorizing, but they, too, uncritically expand theories far beyond reason. Psychologists, for example, depend upon research theorists' concepts about the origins of behavior, and the research psychologists in turn depend upon sociologists or neurophysiologists, who in turn often depend upon anthropologists or neuroanatomists or microbiologists. So when the theorist about the nature of life or the origins of behavior begins to fabricate his concepts, he runs the risk of relying on incomplete data or undeveloped logic or limited concepts.

Those who guide our conjectures about life and being become so engrossed in their revelations about how bits of chemistry or biology fit together that they usually neglect to tell us about the bits of chemistry or biology that don't fit together. They glide over the giant open spaces of theory and logic as if they didn't exist.

Theorists about the origin and nature of human behavior become ecstatic when they find similarities between man and animals, such as aggressive behavior, or courtship behavior, parental "instincts," or hunting or play behavior. They pounce upon these characteristics as if man had no mind, only hormones and body/brain chemicals. The argument that, since evolution demonstrates a continuity of biology, evolution should also imply a continuity of behavior is oversimplified. It is, of course, apparently true—in part. The part of the story that students of human behavior fail to note is the most fundamental characteristic of all development: that when new forms and new systems develop out of old ones, the elements that characterize the new forms and systems are not only new, but cannot be fully predicted on the basis of knowing the characteristics of the old forms and systems.

When new systems evolve, often it is a rearrangement of the component parts of old systems that produces the new systems. If, in the evolution of life forms, it is function that is necessary for survival, then we do not always have to look for obvious changes in structure. Certainly, in the complex organization of the brain, changing functions may not always be accompanied by obvious change in brain structure, but may occur by a reorganization of the functioning of the existing structures. It is only when species evolved highly specialized structures for surviving in their particular environments that major changes in brain structure occurred as well.

The new system in the evolution of species that became mind would seem to represent primarily a reorganization of the neural connections within brain, evolving functions that could not be predicted from the functions of the neural systems that interacted to produce it. It is the unpredictableness of the functions of new systems in biological life that Konrad Lorenz calls the "creative flash." The creation of the new system of neural activity that produced consciousness and the ability of mind to look at itself changed, if only by a reorganization of the brain's neural systems, forever the course of evolution.

For with man the nature of life is much different. With his capacity to abstract meanings and to think in symbols and create new arrangements of elements in the environment, man has learned to control much of the physical environment. No longer does his species, or any species for that matter, need to adapt to the physical environment; man can adapt the environment not only for himself but for all other animal life as well.

Man's survival, instead, depends upon shaping the social environment that man himself created. For, on the one side, to survive means to gain control of the social elements as man has come to control the physical elements; while on the other side, to survive means to create a society better suited to the exercise and use of the abilities of mind that have evolved and can perhaps evolve further by mere reorganization of existing neural capabilities.

The essential part of the evolutionary process that seems to have escaped the speculation about man's future is the determining role of his mental apparatus for his own mental growth. There can be no question but that the next phase of man's evolution, a phase in progress, can be the evolution of a supermentality. The logic is clear. There is, first, the natural order of all events in the universe, and, second, there is the contemporaneous change in the functional capacities of living things as the environment changes. Man has evolved the capacity to effect changes in his own environment, and has changed the environment from mainly physical to mainly social. The more sophisticated man's society, the more the intellectual factors determine man's behavior and the future nature of man himself. Man has transformed his environment into a predominantly mental environment. It is the nonmaterial environment to which he must adapt to survive, and as he continues to adapt to the world he created, he will undergo changes in the mind's capacities and functions.

PART IV

THE UNCONSCIOUS CONNECTION

CHAPTER 9

Tracking the Unconscious Mind

The Invisible Fabric of Mind

Brain and behavior scientists have skirted the idea of any intellect below conscious awareness for so long, they rarely use terms such as unconscious or subconscious. Psychotherapists and psychiatrists who do use these terms also have difficulty with them, using them interchangeably without ever so much as being concerned about the makeup and nature of the subconscious or unconscious parts of the mind, except, as we noted, when they attribute emotional or psychosomatic problems to unconscious defenses and conflicts, or to people worrying subconsciously. In psychology the word subconscious is used exclusively as an adjective (subconscious content, subconscious desires), even though the dictionary allows that it surely is a noun, meaning "that portion of mental activity of which the individual has little or no conscious perception." The behavioral scientists, unsure that a subconscious exists, discount its existence by making only occasional and vague references to subconscious activity. For the most part, the psychological sciences disallow the possibility for any serious intellectual activity in the subconscious-unconscious by calling any unsophisticated or deleterious activity of mind the work of the unconscious. But because it is the most commonly used, we, too, may as well settle on the term unconscious.

Psychologists and psychiatrists fix their research focus on the behavioral results of abnormal mind activity, the unconscious struggles and unconscious conflicts that distress the emotions, rather than on the compartments of the *normal* unconscious mind and how they function. Nor, inexplicably, do the sciences that study the nature of man show any interest in the endless examples from both research and from everyday life that confirm the extraordinary nature of the normally efficient operations of the unconscious mind.

For example, since it is widely agreed that unconscious conflicts cause personality disorders, one could reasonably infer that when there are no disorders of personality, the unconscious mind operates most admirably. Yet despite the consensus on the role of the unconscious in emotional disorders, scientific reviews that discuss neuroses painstakingly define the characteristics of neurotic reactions, categorize neuroses, list conditions arousing anxieties, but rarely, if ever, mention the unconscious mind. Even in psychotherapy, away from science and into practice, less than one-eighth of accepted psychotherapeutic techniques are based on any presupposition of discrete and identifiable unconscious mechanisms.

Or take problem-solving dreams. The unconscious mind in dreams can solve many a problem that the conscious mind cannot, especially these days when we are learning how to direct the contents of dreams. Dreams and fantasy are experiences of mind that literally illuminate the extraordinary activities of the unconscious mind. They can manufacture bizarre or beautiful or introspective dramas by unconscious direction alone. Or think about perfect performances, mental or physical, in which there is demonstrated an uncanny unconscious ability to unify and sequence every mental and body activity needed to meet what the mind's eye projects as the perfect performance.

There are, as well, physical changes in the body caused by unconscious mental activity that hard science, if it wished, could measure. The effect of imagination is such an obvious example it is surprising it has not received more scientific attention than it has. Consider what happens when you imagine sucking on a sour lemon. The salivary juices flow, and sometimes you can even feel a change in gut motility—the same effects that physically sucking the lemon can produce. Or imagine a creepy, crawly, slimy bug suddenly landing on your arm. Even the image makes the body recoil, the heart race, and the breath may gasp, the face grimace, and the arm may reach up to wipe the nasty thing away—exactly what happens when a really icky bug attacks.

It is the mental image the mind conjures up that excites the salivary glands, or sends shivers down the spine, or rouses the other body activities. A conscious thought musters a hundred different memories from the unconscious storehouse, constructs the image requested; and it is the mental image recruited from the storehouse of the unconscious that directs how brain and body respond.

Although psychologic study concedes the unique faculties of mind for forming abstract concepts, generating and projecting images, and ordering events around us as important functions of man, research has found no reliable ways to document such obscure and cryptic interior performances. These acts of intelligence are carried out by the unconscious part of mind with little, often no, conscious awareness. Unconscious mental functions are so elegant that it is surprising there has been so little effort to understand their operations or trace their origins.

The Unconscious Reality

The first time I became aware of the power of unconscious thought was so dramatic I will never forget it. It happened on the final day of my first year in medical school. My mother had driven some five hundred miles to fetch me and my belongings back home, and there were only a few things to do before we left the medical complex. At lunch with some of my friends, we had gone through the cafeteria line delighted with the prospect of watercress and shrimp sandwiches and cold soup on that summer day. We sat at the table, and as I started to eat I suddenly became convulsed by an overwhelming nausea. Simultaneously I excused myself and ran hell-bent to the nearest restroom. With stomach in reverse peristalsis, and mouth filled with acid flow, I threw up just as I reached the closest basin. A bit later, white and weak, I rejoined my mother and my friends. I whispered to her what had happened, and she whispered back, "Is it because your grades are being posted now?"

In the euphoria of the moment I had completely forgotten the crucial ritual of public posting of the semester's grades. What they revealed would determine my future. My unconscious mind, though, had not forgotten. Without a sign to my conscious awareness, the unconscious mind had reviewed my difficulties of the past semester.

I had had a soul-searing year, from a philosophic disillusionment with medicine to a long siege of migraine headaches. I was indeed unsure of what my grades would be, and I was uncertain about continuing in this highly regarded profession even if my grades would let me, worrying, too, about what failure would mean to my family. It was enough to make anyone sick. Consciousness had refused to understand even when confronted by the misery of body sickness. But as Mother spoke, I knew she was right. I suddenly became fully aware that my acute body distress came from a simmering worry below conscious recognition.

Although my mother believed my anxieties were uppermost in my mind, there had been not a single clue in my own conscious awareness. I was, instead, stunned by the way in which some very serious considerations in one part of the mind had been so successfully hidden from the part of mind I believed could give me conscious understanding, and I was baffled by how this unconscious worry could have been so intense that it had sent my body into uncontrollable spasms. There was also another enigmatic effect of the hidden mind, for as soon as my mother made me understand, the churning of my insides began to subside—long before I saw my passing grades.

Nearly everyone has had similar kinds of experiences. The friend who develops persistent insomnia may know she is worrying about how life will be after the impending divorce, but cannot understand why, after an evening's diversion, with her head filled with enjoyable, encouraging ideas, she still can't sleep. Or the pathos of the ten-year-old fifth-grader who develops very real stomach pains the day or so before school opens in the fall. Shadowy images of the demands of school have floated unrecognized through his head and aroused the gut but not the conscious mind.

Psychologists usually interpret such episodes as signs of unconscious anxieties, but they are not merely emotional reactions. What appears to occur in the unconscious is much more like a mental struggle that involves accurate observations and reasonable logic. It is not so much the emotion of anxiety as it is the mental wrestling with a very real and knotty problem that poses a real threat to one's social and emotional well-being.

It is not enough, I think, to say unconscious anxiety occurs and can distress the body without trying to understand the nature of an unconscious that can also erect a barrier to conscious understanding, yet carries out intelligent, logical thought. The most cursory inspection of such experiences reveals the rational operations of an active mind apart from conscious awareness. It perceives and appraises information, searches for answers, creates images of past and future, and makes judgments, all beyond the reach of conscious awareness.

If unconscious worry can distress mind and body, is it not possible that the unconscious mind may also function actively to ensure well-being? While most theorists confine their speculations to disturbed unconscious mechanisms, I believe there are other qualities of unconscious mind operations in disturbed conditions that can be identified and can also yield insights into the qualities and abilities of the normally functioning unconscious.

My experience described above illustrates a number of extraordinary features of unconscious mental activity that are frequent in human experience. Such experiences differ from the serious episodes of emotional and physical stress in several ways. They deal with fairly accurate information rather than struggling with a lack of information, as in stress problems, and they are generally acute and temporary. Perhaps for these reasons such intense unconscious activity can be brought much more easily and rapidly to conscious attention so that both the content of the unconscious thoughts and their association with physiologic reactions are recognized and confirmed by conscious awareness. Such experiences clearly show the capacity of unconscious thought for complex and reasonable appraisals, judgments, and decisions about ideas and circumstances. They show also that there is often no recognition in conscious awareness of imminent, real threats to one's emotional well-being, even though the unconscious activity is so intense it arouses (alerts) the primitive body yet, strangely, without disturbing the intelligence that directs social behavior.

Although I described the mental operations that lead to disturbed mind and body functions in chapter 6, and in part II suggested that cognition, awareness, and unconscious mechanisms are new systems in the evolution of life forms, we still have not discussed the qualities or capabilities of the unconscious.

We still need to explore what we can reasonably assume about how the unconscious has acquired its remarkable capabilities for sophisticated thought (do, e.g., cognition and intelligence reside wholly in the unconscious?). In our scientific lore are there indicators we have missed that can suggest the emergence of a new level of evolutionary change—a level in which the powerful resources of the unconscious intellect are emerging to become the dominant influence on human nature?

These are not easy questions to deal with. There are many misconceptions about the facts, theories, and opinions held by the experts in relevant fields of study. Moreover, there has not been, to my knowledge, any serious attempt to develop a comprehensive synthesis of the available psychologic and biologic evidence to support the notion of an emergent consciousness.

As a way of beginning our explorations of the nature of the unconscious mind, it is important first to have an understanding of how the relevant sciences view the unconscious. For this I will review briefly the history of interest in the unconscious and the present state of knowledge. Examining the history of explorations of the unconscious mind reveals the surprising extent of the unexplored territory of mind and opens the door for bringing together a series of observations about the origin, composition, and capabilities of the unconscious.

It is not possible, of course, to cover more than a few critical opinions about the origins of our mental capabilities or to explore completely whether the unconscious intellect may have undergone evolutionary change much as physical characteristics have evolved. But by pointing out new questions, I hope to encourage a more systematic consideration of the nature of the unconscious mind than exists today.

I would like to make it clear at this point that I do not intend to fortify my suggestions by citing authoritative support and lengthy lists of references. That could be a lifetime effort, but it is also a chore that, by its very nature, amounts to little more than rehashing old ideas. My interests are chiefly to stimulate considerations of different perspectives on the nature of man.

Historical Insights

Long after my school experience, I remember trying to convince my two-generations-ago mother that hidden far from conscious appreciations was a complicated world of real thoughts we called the unconscious. She rejected the idea violently, believing instead that what wasn't in conscious awareness was just temporarily misplaced or screened from recognition because consciousness was occupied by more relevant things. She had scarcely heard of Freud, but her concept was much like his idea that "below" conscious awareness is a preconscious storehouse from which human minds can easily retrieve information when they need it, and beyond that mind is but a dark abyss of nothingness, the unconscious.

It was not always this way. In the late 1880s, when dynamic psychiatry began to be formalized, there was enormous excitement about the depth and importance of unconscious (subconscious) life, and the problems for consciousness that disordered unconscious mental activities could cause. J. M. Charcot, the neurologist, entranced the medical communities of the 1890s with his clinical exploits with hypnotism and an artful extraction of powerful "unconscious" causes for abnormal behavior. Charcot and others recognized the existence of fully developed, autonomous ideas in the unconscious mind. Hypnotism became "the royal road to the unknown mind," a mental tool that could be used to understand the unknown, secret mind and circumvent the prohibitions of consciousness. And it was found, too, that the unconscious mind possessed a power to command, by mental action alone, the physiologic processes of the body. Henry Ellenberger writes in his massive tone, *Discovery of the Unconscious*[1]: "it would seem that Récamier was the first to perform a surgical operation under magnetic anesthesia (hypnosis) in 1821. It is surprising that so little attention has been given to findings that could have avoided much suffering."

In spite of the remarkable power of hypnosis to reveal the inner mind and to direct both mind and body by the commands of a will obedient to thought alone, the unparalleled potential of hypnosis

---

1. New York: Basic Books, 1970.

melted into the archives of psychiatry as scientific attention turned elsewhere. It was, instead, the age of technology that claimed the interest of scientist-physicians, and both medicine and psychology turned from the unknown promise of the wispy, inaccessible unconscious mind to the more secure and ready promise that understanding physical nature held for understanding and remedying the more urgent woes of man. Dynamic psychiatry settled down to refine its methods for probing the *disturbed* unconscious, while more and more of medicine and psychology chose the apparent certainties of therapeutic chemicals and psychological methods that could deal more immediately with emotional problems rather than work with the long process of raising memories deeply entrenched in the unconscious for conscious examination.

The extraordinary insights of the first psychodynamic theorists were, with probably a single exception, never turned toward understanding the normal mind *not* wracked with internal unconscious turmoil. The scientists were mainly physicians, concerned with healing sick minds. To heal, their first need was to understand the "errors" the mind had made, not how the unconscious mind functioned normally.

It was principally the French physician Pierre Janet, in the late 1890s and early 1900s, who sustained interest in the normal unconscious mind. He speculated on the behavior and forces of unconscious mental activity and provided the first, and perhaps only, real synthesis of the functions of unconscious mind. It was Janet who created the word "subconscious," and Jung's ideas about mind being comprised of a number of subpersonalities came from Janet's idea that mind contains "simultaneous psychological existences." No doubt Janet's "renaissance" background as philosopher, businessman, editor, and psychologist prevented him from confining his thoughts and efforts to explaining the pathologies of mind. These same influences on his thinking seem also to have led to his virtual disappearance from the mainstream of dynamic psychiatry he had been so largely responsible for founding.

In concluding an extensive discussion of Janet's life and contributions, Dr. Ellenberger writes, "Thus, Janet's works can be compared to a vast city buried beneath ashes, like Pompeii . . . it may remain buried forever, it may remain concealed while plundered by others, but it may also perhaps be unearthed some day and brought back to life." We are now, I think, on the threshold of rediscovering what Janet discovered so long ago.

Freud, as a student of the physicalist school dedicated to the belief that "no other forces than common physical-chemical ones are active within the organism," brought an unparalleled respectability to the mysterious inner sources of the human mind by using scientific methodology to describe and categorize and test his ideas about the causes of mental disturbance. Few, if any, advocates of the role of the unconscious have been so definitive. Freud's spectacular accomplishments were, however, focused on how the unconscious mind could destroy personality, not on the normal operations of mind and consciousness. In retrospect, Freud's concept of the mind was certainly not tidy, nor, as a matter of fact, very brilliant. He "described" the three aspects of mind as the conscious content, that is, what a person is momentarily aware of (e.g., you are now paying attention to the words I've written). The preconscious content consists of those events *not* in a person's consciousness at the moment, but which can come into conscious awareness without difficulty or can bring appropriate memories into consciousness. (You may be reading but can bring up from memory the idea that it's time to make a certain phone call.) Finally, the unconscious of a person's mind is what he is unaware of, even when trying to recall.

From Freud's time until now psychiatry has devoted itself almost exclusively to the practice of the mental healing arts and to theorizing about how the unconscious mind escapes its bonds of harmony to distress the conscious self (or perhaps it is the other way around). Systematic exploration of mind fell to the newly born science of psychology.

The Approach of Psychology

The experimental psychologists who labored in those same years as Freud came mainly from physiology laboratories where scientific rigor was a prevailing research doctrine. There was keen academic pressure on research psychologists to prove their ideas about human behavior by easily verifiable observations. This left no room to explore the activities of mind and consciousness implied by Freud's studies.

A small flurry of authoritative interest in mind did develop in psychology in the 1880s, when Wilhelm Wundt, a physiological psychologist, proposed that psychology should be defined as the study of "conscious experience." Wundt undertook to dissect experience as a way to identify and characterize its elemental properties, and then, by systematically reassembling the properties, discover how experience is synthesized. A realist, Wundt knew that introspection and subjective reports were the only way conscious experience could be scientifically investigated.

But for the rest of the world of experimental psychology, the idea of resting a science on the unreliability of reporting subjective experience was much too risky for a young science trying to be a science. The resulting disregard for the territory of the subjective world by psychology is an extraordinary commentary on the course that psychology has taken since the 1880s and Wundt's strong argument for the study of consciousness. Until the most recent times, subjective experience reporting has been rejected as unscientific, and, with it, the most direct route to the study of the mind. Committed to the scientific method as the sole acceptable and primary technique of science, psychologists considered introspection and quantification of subjective experience and human behavior to be mutually exclusive. There seemed to be no way to validate subjective experience because there were no physical changes to measure.

It was decided instead that the important elements of psychology were how man functioned as an organism, not how he *felt* when he was functioning. It became accepted that the proper study of psychology was the study of functions involved in human behavior, not feelings and thoughts. So psychology in large part became a science in which functions such as sensations, memory, learning, perceiving, and behavior were all characterized in terms of how organisms responded to changes in the environment, changes researchers could isolate and measure and call stimuli.

This is not to say that there are not other schools of psychology that rely much less on the need to establish physical correlates of behavior. The Gestalt view of human behavior, for example, emphasizes the organization of the perceptual field from the standpoint of the wholeness, studying the patterns of both the events in the environment and the events within the reacting organs. It is, in a sense, the analogue of the field theory in physics which concerns itself with the dynamics of all component elements interacting with all other elements, and the properties and behavior of the whole. But studying how the mind can organize and reorganize what it perceives is difficult at best, and most such approaches have yielded to the more expedient techniques that measure the objective aspects of behavior. There are, nowadays, many ideas about mind, consciousness and awareness contributed by descriptive psychologists, but none has yet been confirmed by the Scientific Method. This ogre of research may, fortunately, be losing its vitality as new ways of communicating experience and subjectively appreciated states of consciousness evolve. But until now psychology has contributed little to an understanding of the mind.

It is still impossible, as it was when psychology began, to describe thoughts or states of consciousness, or most mental activities, by their physical consequences. There are still no physically definable biological changes in the brain that can be related to thought activity, to conceptualizing, to decision-making, or to the functioning of the unconscious. What the mind does and where consciousness is stays elusive, wary of capture. In the age of science, the inability to measure and weigh or toy with internal gears should be an embarrassment.

The Roots of Consciousness

A favorite ploy used to explain human behavior is to compare data from different species of animals. Bits of animal behavior, neatly defined in laboratory experiments, or bits of neurophysiologic activity recorded from anesthetized or caged, socially deprived animals, are rather grandly compared to bits of human behavior, and especially those bits of human behavior that have got deranged for one reason or another. The fact that the reactions of certain brain tissues in a person mentally or emotionally deranged enough to require experimental surgery seem to bear some resemblance to data from experiments in animals with a comparable reaction of brain tissue appears to be enough to justify the conclusion that the normal human brain functions just like the comparable animal brain and serves the same purposes.

Much the same kind of reasoning lies behind our accepted concepts about more complicated human behavior. In searching for the origins of human behavior, research has concentrated a disproportionate amount of its attention on animal behavior, looking at bits and pieces that resemble bits and pieces of human behavior. There are some obvious difficulties in this approach, particularly when the bits and pieces come from an animal's milieu, yet it is suggested that they function in a similar way in the very different circumstances of human environments. In a way the anti-creationist prejudice that man is superior to animals only in being a more advanced animal model has resulted in a remarkable overstudy of the more primitive and obviously animal behaviors. At the same time, a great deal of animal behavior has been understudied and undervalued. Almost invariably the intelligence of animals has been reduced to sets of unflatteringly stereotyped behaviors. Pleading lack of objective evidence, students of behavior spurn the idea of examining the likelihood that the abilities for abstract conceptualizing and planning for the future using mental images can occur in animal minds.

I remember, for example, how the scientific community was swept up in Lorenz's notion, or at least their interpretation of his notion, that "aggression" is an innate instinct of all animal creatures and a primary and innate characteristic of man. A scientific society on aggression was even formed. It was believed, and still is by many scientists, that aggression is necessary for survival of all species. The instinct for aggression was blamed for huge chunks of man's behavior, from childhood play to football to riots. Only gradually did a few science scholars argue and logically show that much aggression even in animals springs from frustration in achieving behavioral goals. Later they also learned that Lorenz and others claimed evidence that animals also possess seemingly innate anti-violence, anti-aggression instincts. Perhaps this is how the oppossum's playing-dead behavior arose—certainly this peculiar "anti-violence" behavior belies the potential harm the possum can cause with his great mouth loaded with fine, cutting teeth.

Sometimes one can observe what might be interpreted as an anti-aggression instinct in the meeting of two dogs who are strangers to each other. Depending upon dogs and circumstances, one dog may quickly fall to his knees (quite literally), then roll over with the head back and the legs half bent. He submits *before* the fight, although he retains a posture from which he can quickly rise and fight or flee, should the other dog not accept his gesture.

The aggression-nonaggression explanation may, however, be one of the many explanations of animal behavior that are so oversimplified as to be flagrantly misleading. I recall a dramatic example of such behavior. When I was visiting a friend who had a dog notorious for fighting and severely injuring other dogs, my gentle dog, who always ran away from any possible fight, escaped from the car, leaped directly toward the vicious dog, and in an instant the war-dog was lying down on his back, my cowardly dog standing over him in victory.

Instincts the experts say? (Actually the experts now talk about instincts as species-specific behavior.) Perhaps, but I doubt that the behavioral process can be explained on so simple a basis as the idea of instinct implies to behavioral scientists. The experts would explain the dogs' behavior by citing the dogma that certain stereotyped behaviors occur in many animal species, or are species-specific, or that the behavior was learned, mainly through the animals' trial-and-error reactions in different situations. In the case of *my* dog, all such explanations can be ruled out; and we are left with no explanation except that he and the other dog reversed their usual behaviors because of complex perceptions and communications that we human beings may never understand. But what we can understand, and the question for the behavioral experts is, How could a situation seemingly identical in most respects to the kind believed to invariably precipitate aggression-submission behavior (two dogs meet, the vicious one in his home territory) contain imperceptible clues so rapidly significant as to reverse the characteristic behavior of both dogs?

Shouldn't we finally concede that many kinds of animals "think"? When they communicate behaviorally by reacting appropriately and usefully to circumstances they have never encountered before, doesn't this suggest use of images and concepts, planning and decision-making abilities?

Does "Primitive" Behavior Mean "Primitive" Mind?

In the course of developing higher animal life, shaped in diverse ways by the supplies and demands of the physical environment, the need for animals to survive against the potential hazards of their environment was met by the brain developing more and more coordinating nerve networks. It ultimately became possible for animal life to anticipate danger, presumably through a simultaneously evolving property of nerve tissue, i.e., the ability to learn—to learn by associating information from previous experience, from parental teaching, and from senses keenly tuned to detect shifting patterns, all tempering biological genetic predispositions. The ability to *anticipate* danger no doubt marks one of the most crucial developments of the evolving brain, for it means that the information from many sources and many signals not only must be detected and given appraisal, but also that some decision is made about the relative difference between the degree and immediacy of the danger and the ability of the physical organism to avoid or escape the danger.

Watching wildlife react to potential danger is revealing. A gazelle, for example, may pick up the scent of an approaching lion. He lifts his head, all attention, and after a bit he may do one of three things. He may casually lope off to a safer place, or he may break into a desperate run, or he may seem to shrug his shoulders and lower his head to resume grazing. Students of animal behavior too often write off these behaviors as instinctive, stereotyped. The animal is reacting to impending danger to be sure, but his behavior is, in fact, a reaction of the intellect, however "primitive" that intellect may be, and demonstrates the existence of the intellectual building blocks for the further evolution of higher animal species. If the intellect is a mechanical comparator system (such as comparing a set of known types of danger with a set of available responses), as is postulated, it is much more sophisticated than is generally recognized. The animal appraises the nearness of the danger, the magnitude of the danger, and has an appreciation, literally, of the mathematical product of the time-space factors of the immanent danger *and* of his own time-space potential, i.e., how fast and how soon and what distance the danger will travel to reach him as well as how fast and how soon and what distance he must cover to escape the danger.

That in itself is an amazing integration of data, but the animal also considers many other elements of the situation that further modify his behavior. He may sense, as it often seems, that the lion is well fed and on a lazy stroll as lions often are, or that a nearby gully offers suitable cover so that the need to escape is less critical than if he were on a great plain without cover. At other times the animal may consider the need to protect the young of the group, and so take his action sooner than if he were alone. What the computer analogy of perceptions and decisions does not consider is that external behavior is limited by the anatomy of the animal and may not be at all a true reflection of subjective activity.

Scientific explanations for such animal behavior are weak and incomplete. Scientific study dissects behavior, it does not synthesize. There are few students of behavior with enough cross-discipline experience to be able to weave the observations of bits of animal behavior in sterile laboratory experiments with observations of animal life in the natural environment. For the gazelle responding to impending danger, the authoritative expert discusses the behavior as a simple product of genetic characteristics and experience that molds patterns of behavior into repertoires of fairly automated reactions. This means that, depending upon the way in which different patterns of information about a particular environmental situation are sensed, there are patterns of nerve excitation specifically related to the situation that can put into effect one or another of the few alternatives for response. This may be true, but it certainly does not explain why a sick gazelle, who has never experienced sickness before, reacts to danger by lying down and succumbing to it. The sick gazelle may have witnessed the fate of other sick gazelles, but relating another's experience to solely internal sensations is a most complex thought process. Nor can the data of biologists explain why a mother rhino who has watched her baby mauled and killed by a lion is enraged and long after the baby's death will stalk the lion for a chance for retaliation. I have watched exactly this situation, and was deeply touched by the remarkable change in the face and eyes of the mother rhino. If I may be permitted a bit of anthropomorphizing, it was as if the mother rhino was expressing grief and anger and the intent to retaliate all at the same time. What a turmoil must have been in her primitive brain, yet the behavior she chose next, which *seemed* instinctive, that is, charging the lion, was actually not so instinctive because, armed with the fore-knowledge that the lion would disdain a chase just after eating, she charged the lion only after it had eaten, and then she ran off. The decision certainly seemed to be dictated more by intelligent appraisal of circumstances than by raw desire and instinct. I doubt very seriously that the rhino had ever before experienced a newborn lost to lions, nor had her genes endowed her with a "behavioral pattern" to cope with a trauma to some maternal hormonal system science calls maternal instinct.

What I think the scientists forget to explain is that animals, too, are often faced with "new" situations definitely not in their experience-behavior repertoire, and that these situations forge new nerve connections in the brain. This is, of course, experience, but neither the animal nor the neurophysiologist ever gives us a clue about how the brain behaves when it is *making* new connections, what kinds of behavior these new connections evolve, and why one past situation is put into the memory bank in one way and another situation can be put into memory in quite a different way, yet there may be associations between these two different types of experience that actually synthesize or initiate a new behavior in quite a new situation.

Any dog owner knows the extraordinary sensitivity of his dog to sets of circumstances that almost defy definition. The owner who occasionally travels invariably becomes aware that his dog is aware of the fact that he is going on A TRIP, not just an excursion to the local shopping center. The dog senses the approaching event long before his owner begins to pack a suitcase. I have tried keeping my dogs out of the house on such occasions (to satisfy my scientific curiosity), yet they invariably sense the forthcoming trip and begin to mope. They huddle together on my bed or tag after me around the house and yard, activities distinctly different from their usual behavior of drowsing under the trees and listening for sounds on the road. And the behavior is also in sharp contrast with the way they act when I am about to leave on an errand that may take only an hour or a day. Then they waggle and jump, hoping for a ride in the car.

I know, as any dog owner knows, that the dog knows pretty much what my plans are. At least he has a darned good general concept that I will be gone for either a short time or a long time. He, as any dog can, is able to select out of his owner's behavior and activities exactly those special characteristics that relate to "house leaving," and is able further to discriminate among the most subtle of clues to determine which kind of "house leaving" is coming up. And while I am quite familiar with every scientific explanation about animal behavior, from John Paul Scott to Robert Ardrey, Tinbergen and all, there is none yet that can explain this rather ordinary ability of domestic animals.

The unexplained, unstudied everyday miracles of much animal behavior reflect a private, subjective universe, unknown and re-

jected because most behavior study denies animals a creative intellect. New attitudes about the nature of life are, however, promising.
Researchers are discovering the porpoise's ability for communication, and if the communication is as sophisticated as believed, we are
forced to recognize how sophisticated the intellect must be to need
and use such a complex language. The newly discovered ability of
chimpanzees to use human language signs—and even invent new
expressions with them—is another revelation about the roots of consciousness that should make us think twice about our arrogance in
denying such animals a complex mental life simply because we cannot understand their language.

The evolution of an animal intellect appropriate to new, intangible demands of its environment is evident in the domesticated animal. The closer and longer the relationship to man, the more obvious
the evolving intellect becomes.

Sometimes domesticated animals show evidence of surprisingly
advanced intellectual processes. Often they can be observed to display an ability to form concepts and symbols for those concepts, then
communicate them in a way that human beings can understand.
Many years ago I owned a magnificent squirrel-colored German
shepherd named Geire. For perhaps four years after a Siamese cat
joined the family, he must have been aware of an occasionally occurring sequence of events between myself and the cat. This had to do
with the cat's persistent hunting activity. Every day and sometimes
twice a day the cat brought to one of the doors her catch to show her
prowess. More often than not, her prize was a writhing snake, for
which she received a scolding and a few screams of disgust and fear.
At other times she brought a gopher or mole, and then she received
as much praise as I could give under the circumstances of seeing her
eat a newly dead small critter of the wild.

One day at dusk I heard Geire rustling the ivy and brush in the
terraces below the house, and presently he bounded up the steps
with a large object in his mouth. He came to me quite slowly, stopped
in front of me as if I had said "sit," and carefully deposited the object
at my feet. It was a large possum. I examined it, and except for great
globs of saliva around its neck, it was unharmed. In the meantime
Geire had sauntered off, never being interested in hunting or wild
animals of any kind. Some time later the possum roused from his
"playing possum" catatonic state and loped off. Geire had proved his

point. He too could make a catch and bring it home. He hadn't wanted the praise, but it certainly seemed that he wanted to prove a point.

I doubt that any learning theory ever devised by biological or behavioral science can explain this kind of behavior, or similar intellectual behavior that the animal lover so often sees and the behavioral scientists so often reduce to an unflattering sequence of responses to stimuli. In Geire's case, if we grant him the ability to extract and abstract somewhat complex information from the environment and associate it with something particularly meaningful to him *and* to me, we also have to conclude that he was capable of forming a concept (hunting can be rewarded), a symbol (some suitable animal), projecting it (developing a plan), and translating the symbol into highly appropriate activity by which he communicated the essence of an idea, as well as *finding the right occasion* for effective communication. It was a symbolic gesture, requiring a very special type of behavior on his part to ensure my understanding.

Geire's intellectual feat, and the blurred understanding of the rhino species-generations before him, can tell us a good deal about how the antecedents of concepts and symbols are formed in the mind and most important, how superior intellectual systems arise from these very animal capabilities.

What the study of animal behavior has failed to recognize, I think, is that the expressions of thought and emotion of animals are limited by their physiologic structures and capabilities (stalking, turning the head, physically submitting, running away, barking, fighting, etc.) but that this in no way can be used as evidence that "intelligent" brain activities do not occur. Certainly, without my knowledge of my dog Geire's history and of my relationship with the cat, whatever the dog might have expressed would have been unperceived and unobserved.

It is asserted by the behavioral scientists that animals build up behavioral repertoires through experience, and that these repertoires constitute their only alternatives for expressing their needs and desires. This, of course, is theory, not fact. The dog who persists in wearying travels across half the country to find its owner who left him behind or lost him on the road has no prior experience to guide his behavior. Nonetheless, he must have a pretty clear concept of his family, his need for their companionship, and most curious of all, some good idea about where they are. And he must know too that he is faced with a difficult search and a difficult journey. Just as human beings, he has nonphysical goals, the desire for social companionship.

It may be difficult for animal behavior scientists to observe these kinds of intelligent activities in animals, especially under the kinds of conditions that science imposes for rigorous study and documentation and analysis. For too long such scientists have dissected animal behavior in the artificially created situations of the laboratory, interpreting the behavior observed to fit into explanations based on the way animals react to very specific and usually artificial circumstances. Incredibly, it is only now after a century of intensive research that animal behavioral science is realizing that the behavior of animals depends in large part upon their *social* environment. The behavior of animals in zoos, for example, upon which was built a great deal of theory about animal behavior, was finally discovered to be not at all like the behavior of those same animals in their natural, wild environment, and that insight led to the realization that the behavior of domestic animals is different from that of "wild" animals.

Communicating by Time-Space Patterns

In fact, I believe that a good bit of animal behavior can be interpreted as evidence of how identifiable antecedents of the extraordinary mind activity we call subconscious or unconscious developed. What we know of animal behavior and cognition is, for scientific purposes, based exclusively on what and how animals communicate to human beings with their limited communications abilities, or what can be interpreted to be communicated among animals when observed from the outside. What we human beings have done is to improve upon animal communication abilities, first by language, then by travel and commerce, and finally by electronics, but all of this marvelous communications ability can convey but a minute fraction of what human beings truly feel, nor how they have arrived at what they do communicate. I should think that scientific honesty would acknowledge also that not all of an animal's cognitive activity is communicated. Yet science seems to take it for granted that animals have no complex awarenesses, nor conceptual concerns, nor images of the future.

I remember a broadcast by Msgr. Fulton Sheen, who likened the difficulties Jesus had in communicating his font of knowledge to the inability of the family dog to express his concerns for his family and his understanding of their behavior.

There is a vast chasm between what nonscientific observers of animal behavior observe and what scientists observe, a chasm created because the scientist insists upon objectivizing all behavior. The nonscience observers on the other hand relate feelings and subjective experience to the behaviors they observe, that is, they *identify* certain inexpressible, nonobjectively communicable sensations and perceptions of animals, perceptions that can be understood only from observations made over time and through animal space. These are the subjective aspects of behavior that cannot be measured by the crude tools we have today.

There is reason to believe that nonscientist observers might well be more correct in their ideas about animal behavior because they do pay attention to patterns and the time and space dimensions of animal behavior. The nonscientific observer might, for example, as the Chinese have done, note a subtle change in the behavior of their animals and come to recognize it as a special behavior that signals an imminent earthquake. Western scientists typically abjure this kind of conclusion. They will not accept the relationship between unspecified "idiosyncratic" bits of animal behavior and an approaching disruption of the earth's physical structure. The key in science is to know relationships so precisely that any prediction has a high probability for being correct. With animal behavior and earthquakes, the animal behavior can't be neatly measured. It is only a mild deviation from normal behavior, perhaps a change in the bearing of the animal, or a diminished interest in usual things, that suggests the attention is elsewhere. The animal does all the normal things, but he does them only slightly differently and only slightly out of his usual routine. This could just as well indicate a tummy ache or a bit of sulking, but it is the *pattern* of behavior, the patterned bits of behavior in space-time together, that contains the important information.

The impression communicated is a Gestalt perception, the result of a highly integrated process of perceiving the nature of the total behavior as distinct from its components, and communicating the meaning of the whole. About as much as we, as human beings, can communicate about our perceptions of the animal's behavior (before earthquakes) is, "Something is a little different, I can't quite put my finger on it. I thought he was looking at the ground funny, and he usually naps over there, not here by me."

Complexly, the pattern exceeds the ability to be perceived by any single sense, yet the information is nonetheless communicated and perceived and understood. What the cognitive processes have done is integrate tiny bits of information from many sources and received by many senses, and compare the constructed whole picture with what memory recalls from other patterns. Other cognitive processes then recognize the small differences that make the new pattern a question in attention that needs the answer: what does it mean? And still other cognitive processes are required to associate the patterns of collective, abstracted understanding before the Gestalt perceived is united with the product of the internal cognitive activity that brings relevance and meaning to the perception.

If we human beings can perceive the meanings of patterns of the behavior of animals, as we are now learning how to do in observing behavior in natural habitats, this means that the animal is expressing a *pattern of mind-brain activity* that directs the coherence and appropriateness of the behavior pattern. The mind-brain activity includes as well subjective appraisals and awarenesses, and thus the pattern of behavior includes these antecedents of overt behavior.

It would seem reasonable to speculate that some, perhaps many, of the qualities and abilities of the unconscious mind have evolved over time and species, and that the intimate relationship of much mental activity to the physical mechanisms of survival makes self-awareness of these activities—no matter how sophisticated or evolved they may seem—remote from detection. In contrast, the awarenesses of self and being (self-appraisal, detection of threats to social well-being), are more newly developed or in the process of evolving and in this case would be an active state, attracting attention (awareness).

The Evolution of Awareness

Earlier in this book I referred to the conclusions of several of the world's most expert neurophysiologists who, to generalize a bit, believe that mind is indeed more than any sum of the brain's activities that can be projected by applying known laws of physics or chemistry or neural function. Their conclusions are based almost exclusively on findings from neurophysiology involving surgery and electrical stimulation and recording, interventions that cannot help but disturb and distort normal functions. The neurophysiologists theorize from these data and have not considered the evidence from studies of normal behavior.

Surprisingly, or perhaps not so surprisingly for a natural scientist, the man most closely identified with comparing the behavior of man to behaviors of animals, Konrad Lorenz, has recently written a summary of his conclusions about the evolution of complex brains and behaviors through the phylogenetic systems.[1]

From his long lifetime of observing animal behavior, Lorenz has isolated behavioral characteristics that clearly demonstrate not simply the cognitive, intellectual activity of various animal species, but the fact that some of these activities are innate properties of the mind-brain complex. Take curiosity and exploratory behavior, for example. These are internally generated behaviors, apparently unrelated to genes or experience or learning. Exploratory behavior is self-motivated learning and not, as is often thought, motivated by some drive such as hunger. Exploratory behavior *creates* motivations. It is, as Lorenz notes, a cognitive process, and he suggests it has distinct similarities to the drive in certain scientists to pursue research.

At another stage in evolution, some species have become *self-exploratory*, a new evolutionary step in cognition and awareness that gives the developed animal an awareness of the self in relation to the universe. The kitty that grooms itself has an awareness of its own being; when monkeys groom each other, they reveal an awareness of self as others see them.

From thousands of such observations, Lorenz also concludes that mind may be as different from brain as inorganic matter is from organic life. I interpret the analogy to be that while organic life contains the very same inorganic elements as inorganic matter, life forms possess a different organization of the inorganic elements that gives them the peculiar properties of a self-regulating metabolism and the ability to duplicate their organization by self-reproduction. Mind is made up of the living functions of the brain, but it, too,

---

1. *Behind the Mirror* (London: Methuen & Co., 1977).

represents a different organization of the brain functions from that simply sustaining the organism and providing the means for physical reactions. Brain functions detect, transmit, and translate physically related information; mind is characterized by intangible yet subjectively known and communicable events, ideas, and abstract knowledge.

Lorenz argues that intellect is a new creation in the evolution of life forms. His reasoning is similar to my argument (chapter 3), based on cybernetics principles, that new, unexpected systems with new functions and characteristics can emerge from the interaction of two or more existing systems. The physical structures of living forms develop successive and successful modifications from interactions among existing systems. As the physical structure of evolving animal species became more and more complex, the elements of the older physical systems of animal bodies, and particularly the clustering of nerve cells that became brain, also evolved new systems and new structures and with them new characteristics and new functions. Lorenz suggests that, at one point in evolutionary development, older physical, physiologic systems of the brain, independent for the most part and independently functioning, interacted and fed back information to each other and created an interacting system with the new characteristic we call the cognitive mind. The new system that became mind evolved with the completely new abilities to appreciate itself, to have an intellect, *and to assume a supremacy* over its antecedents, the physical systems of the body.

This last quality of mind is my own addition, and discussing the evidence for this most important characteristic and capability of mind is a good part of the objective of this book. But to view mind as a new evolutionary form, it is first necessary to establish the probability that what brain has evolved (mind) is of a completely different order of nature because of the properties of the many different systems that comprise it (systems that keep other systems active, systems that mediate emotion, systems that process sensory information, etc.).

Lorenz believes, totally, that the unique characteristics of man we call mind characteristics are of a completely different order than those of what we might call the mind or intellect of animals. This does not mean at all that man differs from any lower animal in the nature of his physical apparatus or in the ways he may use brain and neural systems, nor that behavioral characteristics of animals do not exist in man. What it *does* mean is that with the evolution of man came another new system for dealing with the information of the environment. Lorenz talks about the "creative flash," meaning a "creative" integration of existing biological systems that form a new entity, the "flash" or surprise that comes from different systems interacting by chance or need, first in the emergence of life from inorganic matter, and second in the emergence of the human mind. As Lorenz puts it, "The second great gulf, that between the highest of the animals and man, was produced by another 'creative flash,' which, like the first, produced a new cognitive apparatus."

It is not clear from Lorenz's argument whether this wholly new system that is the unique cognitive apparatus of man is one that nonetheless operates *only* via physical mechanisms or whether his notion of the cognitive apparatus might resemble Sperry's emergent consciousness. Truthfully, none of us seems able to envision a purely nonmaterial functional milieu for mind, but neither can such a conclusion be avoided. The best we can do, I imagine, is to suggest that the totality of electrical charges of brain transmitting complex information can—as a pattern—exist briefly in an independent state. Logically then, if the pattern of information is to have any meaning or use, it must exert its effects on neural tissue, the only means human beings have for appreciating the world, themselves, and their thoughts.

My discussion of the unrecognized roots of intellect in the animal world was to stress the basic, operational influence in evolution that is only now being understood: that new systems evolving from the interaction of existing systems can be *new creations*, with actions and properties unrelated to the actions and properties of the systems that generated them. This does not mean the loss of the old systems, although this can occur over time, only that quite new, added systems can evolve from old ones. The "old" systems, such as the olfactory system, may be partly retained in structure while their neural activity becomes reorganized to serve more complex functions.

If physical systems can evolve, why not mental systems? Certainly, if the functions of brain that underlie thought, memory, perceptions, and images reorganize and evolve, it is not unreasonable to consider that, as abilities to abstract information, create symbols, expand images and form concepts, and for self-learning and self-awareness develop, they, too, can undergo reorganizations of their interactions to form new, even more highly evolved, systems of intellectual operations.

In a discussion of the human mind Lorenz says, "The autonomy of personal experience and its laws cannot in principle be explained in terms of chemical and physical laws or of neurophysiological structure, however complex." I agree with Lorenz that the operations of subjective experience arising from mind and intellect are of a different order from what could be predicted from the biological and behavioral nature of animals. But I would go much further, and suggest that the cognitive apparatus that is unique to man also evolves.

CHAPTER 10

The Nature of Exceptional
Mind States

Dissociations of Consciousness:
Unexplored Resources of Mind

The most puzzling adventures of human minds occur when they split off unusual and very private segments of consciousness. When a microcosm of mind activity becomes isolated from the social reality and has no features in it valuable to society, the mind state is brushed aside as mental illness. But when a unit of consciousness is isolated from social realities and is redeemed by insights illuminating the desires of man, that state may be called mystical experience or insight.

One of the miracles of our evolving mind may, in fact, be its ability to partition itself into sophisticated, logical, seemingly autonomous unitary bits of consciousness.

The ability has always resided in the mind, as we know from the baffling enigmas of mental issness. There are, however, more benign and more socially tolerated states of "altered consciousness" that we are just beginning to recognize: the intriguing dissociations of consciousness that occur during meditation, religious experiences, peak experiences, with the therapeutic use of hallucinogens and hypnosis; during dreaming and moments of depersonalization; and even during episodes of neuroses. Labeling these experiences "altered states of consciousness" is meant to distinguish insightful kinds of mind

196

states from the diagnostic label of "dissociated states of consciousness" that implies pathology. As I have examined the characteristics of nonordinary mind states and probed the mental processes involved in all varieties of altered states of consciousness, the data have convinced me that we are at the edge of new discoveries about the extraordinary processes of mind hidden from conscious awareness. I also believe that as intellect becomes more sophisticated, so too does the ability of mind to create more and increasingly complex states of mind.

As new ways of "raising consciousness" and "expanding awareness" confirm the validity of nonordinary mind states in everyone, the potential of human beings to manipulate consciousness becomes clear. I suggest, in fact, that the fundamental processes of mind may be similar for both useful and harmful states of consciousness. In this chapter I explore some qualities of altered (dissociated) states of consciousness as a way of organizing what we can deduce about them for the ultimate goal of establishing a more reasonable basis for understanding and using effectively the ability to alter consciousness to fulfill the human potential.

Nonordinary Mind States

The general public first became aware of the phenomena of *nonpathological* states of dissociated consciousness when the street use of LSD became popular. Since then we have become aware of more and more nonordinary states of mind. We have discovered not only that a dozen different kinds of drugs cause a dozen different kinds of altered states, but that different kinds of meditation, self-awareness, self-actualizing techniques also can produce different kinds of altered states of consciousness. We are beginning to learn that the mind can be contortionist or chameleon, assuming different shapes or different shades of functioning.

The ability of the mind to slip into different modes of operation suggests that dissociations of units of consciousness activity are more common than we have been led to believe. I suspect we do not recognize the wide range of mind behaviors we call altered states simply because we label some pathological and others inspirational or mystical.

Traditionally we analyze human behavior in terms of learning and emotions, with very little attention to processes of the intellect. Our notions of the role of intellect in behavior and activities of the mind are generally limited to consideration of I.Q. levels, learning, experience, attention, motivation, and other easily identified influences. I would suggest that there are, as well, complex processes of the unconscious intellect that are fundamental determinants of behavior and cognition, which we have failed to recognize simply because they operate clandestinely, beyond perception and measurement.

I propose we look at examples of many different kinds of unusual, nonpathological mind states, from everyday episodes of unusual behavior to the most occult of human experience, to discover whether or not some—perhaps the most important part—of human behavior can be explained on the basis of mental, "intellectual" operations.

Currently, there is an awe of altered mind states that makes many people shiver with fear when, for example, they realize the totality of mind conversions to Jim Jones, the Reverend Moon or to one or another of the more spectacular Indian swamis. What appears to happen in these instances is the separation of groups of glued-together vital bits of mind processes, processes trained to follow each other according to rituals of thinking set down by custom and social consensus. That is, we perceive our worlds pretty much alike because we have been taught that certain objects fit certain classifications, such as red is red, or a shaft of light is a shaft of light. But if we personally endow red or a shaft of light with extra qualities, we become either poets or crazy people. Our safety and security lies in perceiving by consensus.

When the processing faculties of the mind spin cocoons around a microuniverse of related thought and perception and anchor the threads to pillars that consensus believes to be illusion, then mind is believed to be lost to reason. The splitting off of a great global unit of consciousness that makes the Moonie devotee and divorces him from his parents' world shows how completely separate units of consciousness can be and the impenetrability of the mental wall that is constructed around a specific belief.

Roughly the same splits and walls occur in hypnosis, conversion hysteria, total dedication to any cause, total involvement, and a hundred other puzzling states of the human mind.

Less socially disturbing (although often irritating) altered mind states in fact occur frequently in everyday life. They occur when the complex interactions of belief, emotion, and personality that identify an individual conjoin to produce extreme but still tolerated departures from the ordinary course of human behavior.

I recently participated in a symposium on stress, and as a parting shot, I noted that the mind was emerging as a new tool of medicine (after all, everyone knows how effective placebos are, and what faith can do). A research antagonist who is also a practicing physician was incensed, and roared to the audience, "Talking about the mind will set medicine back fifty years!"

His violent emotion was a perfect illustration of how completely one set of associated beliefs, experiences, thoughts and emotions can become dissociated and isolated from all other intelligent activities of mind. His intellectual and economic security was bound to the consensual consciousness of the scientific community, to which unknown mysteries of the mind are threatening. His outburst was, perhaps, the splitting away of a unit of consciousness, separating one functioning section of intellect and emotion from a consciousness of the full reality of knowledge and experience.

While psychologists explain such behavioral episodes mainly as escaping emotions, I think it is a mistake not to consider that the emotion may have developed from an intellectual integration of cognitive and experiential information, and that the escape of emotion comes out of the depths of unconscious mental operations. It is, in effect, the escape of a self-contained, functioning unit of consciousness.

The strong emotions and dedicated behavior of zealots are not, I think, operationally or causally so very different from the altered states of mind we call neurotic or psychotic or from those we value as insightful and enlightening. While we disapprove of altered states induced by drugs or those which end in terrorism or cult behavior or neuroses, we often judge other altered states to be favorable. The hypnotic state, creative flashes, the ecstasy of meditation, and even "good" hallucinogenic experiences are all examples of altered mind states that can be esteemed, coveted, aspired to, or pursued. There are differences, to be sure, between altered states we discredit and those we accept, but the differences are mainly differences in the values society places on the way altered states are expressed. Society can understand total religious devotion when the beliefs are ortho-

dox (priests, swamis, ayatollahs), but society rejects such total devotion when beliefs deviate from the traditional. The same is true for
traditional politics and political extremists. Regardless, the intensity
and single-mindedness of believing and the behavior appropriate to
the beliefs are the same whether the beliefs are accepted or rejected
by society in general.

There are, in fact, many kinds of altered mind states that can be
beneficial to both the individual and society. These are altered states
that do not threaten the consensual being but hint instead at the
depths of undeveloped mind resources.

There is, for example, the dissociation of intelligent behavior
(although sometimes not appropriate) from self-direction, as in hypnosis; or the dissociation of learned logic from the logic of imagery
as in dreams, when units of the unconscious mind dissociate from
each other and one unit weaves a fairy tale while the other stands at
a distance, watching, interpreting, and sometimes commenting on
the dream in progress. There is also daydreaming, when awareness
of mind separates from the awareness of relating self to environment,
or the dissociation of thought awareness from body sensations as in
depersonalization, or the dissociation of unconscious mental activity
from consciousness as in subliminal perception or creative thought,
and the dissociation of consciousness found in meditation and con-
templation. In each case, a remarkable complex of intelligent operations of mind is dissociated from the direction of conscious awareness
that conforms itself to the social consensus about what the behavior
of mind should be.

The Nature of Altered States

There has been a great deal written in recent years about "altered
states of consciousness," and about meditation and imagery and
dreams and hypnosis, but to the best of my knowledge no one has yet
attempted to discover whether these diverse states of mind and
consciousness might have common mechanisms. Nor has anyone yet
attempted to systemize observations about unusual states of mind as
a way of characterizing them for subsequent classification and analysis. I suspect, from my own cursory analyses, that what we now
believe to be different states of mind and consciousness can be found
to break down into identifiable categories that share certain charac-

teristics. I suspect, too, that organizing our knowledge about unusual mind states may uncover strategies for reproducing unusual states that can be used for the benefit of mankind as well as lead to the development of new techniques to guide the intelligent unconscious, much as we are now using new techniques to direct the content of dreams.

A long-standing problem in observing and analyzing unusual states of mind and consciousness is the tendency for such states to be estranged from the normal stream of consciousness through which we describe or analyze events within the altered consciousness. The feebleness of ordinary language in communicating altered states justifies the scientist's wariness of the accuracy and reliability of subjective reports about such experiences. Most perceptive scientists agree, for example, that the distortions of perceptions and sensations caused by hallucinogens cannot be fully appreciated from someone else's reports, so the competent scientist nearly always uses his own hallucinogenic experiences as the avenue to understanding the nature of the altered state.

The same difficulty of communicating the total experience exists for other altered states of consciousness. As a scientist I always feel there is something missing when I hear other people's reports of their altered states, something I feel unsure about interpreting, and so I become unwilling to chance misinterpretation. Fortunately for my penchant for analysis, I have another choice. My own mind has taken many adventures on its own, as if it were impelled to explore the potential of mind without ever so much as asking permission of my conscious awareness. It is these unexpectedly visited dimensions of consciousness that so chill and frighten the systematic scientist. I suppose that when the mind adventures on its own, rupturing the grip of consensual consciousness to unveil its nonordinary capacities, then science feels it loses its anchor to physical reality. Without the physical anchor science is hesitant to probe the unknown or even admit to useful and visionary mind adventures. But when it is *you* who has the mind adventures, you can feel their relationship to the whole you, body and mind. So it is with my own experiences.

Mobilizing the Unconscious Resource

The most extraordinary nonordinary state of consciousness I've ever experienced happened a few years ago when I was a principal speaker at a UCLA symposium on alpha brain wave biofeedback. Because the subject was so familiar, I put off preparing until the day before, which unfortunately turned out to be the beginning of a prolonged storm. I happen to be "allergic" to low atmospheric pressure (the barometric headache), and the pain was too excruciating for me to work. I thought I would prepare the next morning, but the storm continued and so did my headache. By the time I reached the auditorium, the headache was screeching, but I was determined to go through with the lecture.

As I began to speak my consciousness split completely. Part of my mind-consciousness, my perceptions and all conscious sensations, found themselves occupied with a pastoral image, where I was resting on a great green lawn under a tree. I became intensely identified with the nature of the place, and felt beautifully calm and totally relaxed. Occasionally I was faintly aware that something related to me was on a platform and was speaking with words and thoughts as if inspired. The separated "I" had no idea about what the other "I" was talking about. It was as if there was someone speaking far away, and I was far too content to bother listening. At the end of a ninety-minute speech the split consciousness rejoined. I left the platform to considerable applause and was almost immediately seized with the returning pain of the headache, unable to talk to the few reporters following me. At home, I collapsed with the pain that had miraculously disappeared during my lecture. Later, listening to tapes of the talk, I was amazed by the continuity of ideas and the phrasing. It was quite possibly one of the best talks of my life.

This is not, surprisingly, an uncommon experience. It was the circumstances that made it notable. Actors, painters, teachers, business people, moms and dads must often perform mentally and emotionally on levels they ordinarily feel are out of reach. The spectacular results of splitting consciousness are easy enough to recognize in acting, or in masterpieces of art or literature. Somehow it seems to be expected that artists of all kinds can mobilize interior resources to express the inexpressible.

The average person, however, who has similar experiences rarely gets credit for them being unusual states of mind. When my neighbor, for example, who faints at the sight of blood, one day heard screeching brakes and, running, found her huge dog gushing blood into the street, she moved with great strength of mind and muscle, hoisted the dog into the station wagon and rushed him to the vet. That, too, was an achievement of mind over both mind and body. What experiences of these kinds reveal is the remarkable capacity of isolated units of mind for full intellectual activity—operating without any conscious awareness at all—to produce behavior valuable both to individual well-being and for the conscious appreciation of others.

Using my experience as a model, we can make observations about such nonordinary mind states: (1) the intellect was used much more efficiently than is often possible under such circumstances; (2) in the unconscious mode of operation all conscious appreciation of pain sensations was successfully blocked; (3) the dissociation of consciousness served at least two useful social purposes—fulfilling an obligation in a social relationship and meeting the social demands of the situation. A fourth observation may apply only in special cases, such as mine: the unconscious mental processes appear to operate on two levels, one organizing and verbalizing conceptual information and the other creating imagery to provide a composed, recollected medium for expression of that mental activity.

Visions of Hidden Intellect

I doubt that anyone ever born has not experienced some unusual turns of mind activity. The problem for most people is that there are no truly satisfying explanations for extraordinary feats of mind or for remarkable adventures of consciousness. For some, of course, spiritual answers are enough. But probably for all of us, there is the haunting notion that the mind could achieve undreamed prowess if we only knew how to use it. While the experience I described above revealed an ability of the unconscious mind to function appropriately in a difficult situation, the following episode illustrates another capability of the unconscious mind—the ability to solve problems and forge new insights.

This remarkable mind excursion occurred while I was trying to write a scientific paper. For nearly two years I had struggled to explain the actions of a new drug. Given to animals, the drug obviously affected the brain, but the changes in the animals' behavior were subtle and difficult to define exactly. When I had exhausted the repertoire of critical experiments, there came that inevitable phase of research—writing a report for publication in which, to be scientifically acceptable, it is necessary to have some theory to account for any exceptional results, in this case to propose an explanation of how the new drug produced its effects. For six months I labored at writing a discussion of how the drug might affect the central nervous system, trying to develop some suitable theory, but there was none I could apply. No known mechanism seemed to fit its peculiarities. Then one day I sat down to the typewriter for still another attempt to explain the new drug.

I began to type, and suddenly words were racing across the page. I was scarcely aware of anything except typing as fast as possible, and there was no conscious recognition at all of the words or thoughts. Finally there was an end, and more than twenty pages for the theoretical discussion alone. The time was less than three hours, a typing speed almost beyond my capacity. I read what was written. It was a perfect, logical, flowing exposition of a theory about the new drug's action, written in the provincial language of my (then) profession of pharmacology. I was astounded and exhilarated, but half dazed by the intense mental experience.

Even later, as I read the words published verbatim in the leading scientific journal of my specialty, I was filled with wonder at what my "unconscious" mind had produced. The near perfect order of the thoughts particularly astonished me, as did the completeness of the discussion. There had been no conscious organization, although of course I had been over the data hundreds of times before. But on earlier attempts it had been impossible to arrange the data and thoughts in logical order, and any possible theory to account consciously for the drug's actions had always eluded me. Yet here it was, all the answers in precise order and complete, and all organized and written without the help of conscious awareness.

The outstanding features of my "unconscious" burst of analytical, creative writing for the scientific paper can be listed as follows: (1) it was a spontaneous, "accidental," nonconsciously directed episode of productive, logical mental activity; (2) both the physical and mental performances were accomplished with no conscious awareness;

(3) the performance reflected sophisticated thought, i.e., the mental processes were highly organized; (4) the act was intelligent, purposeful, and the result enhanced my social well-being and survival; and (5) there was no recall of any part of the experience except a vague awareness of the typing.

This experience, too, is much more common than one might think. Not too many people have such complex and definitive problems to solve for such specific purposes, nor do they have so much potentially related material stored in their heads to work with to solve their problems as was the case in my experience. But many people do recognize that the unconscious mind can solve problems, that they can think remarkably clearly when conscious mental activity is occupied elsewhere, and many people intentionally develop habits to facilitate the process. This may be why the mother, distressed by problems with her offspring, abandons a direct confrontation with those problems for the humdrum monotony of the dust cloth and vacuum.

Many people observe that they think much more easily and logically when they are busy doing some routine task, although they fear taking leave of intentional, concentrated thought because they have been educated to believe that thinking takes conscious effort. It doesn't. Many business people enjoy their commuting drives to work. Being occupied by the routine of driving in familiar traffic but alert to possible problems seems to create a balance of mind activities between a curious state of relaxed alertness and a state of the mind-body running on semiautomatic. I myself keep a note pad on the car seat alongside because this balance of relaxed consciousness and alert subconsciousness often releases a fountain of new, creative thought. Many people like to work on plane or train trips, feeling freed by the mild occupation of conscious awareness with the activity of traveling. There seems to be something about this particular state of mind-body balance that frees the hard-working subconscious from the worries and fears of the conscious mind. Other rewarding and productive splits or dissociations of conscious from subconscious activities of the mind are discussed in several following sections.

Glimpses of the Caring Unconscious

I often wonder whether the peripatetic nature of my own willful unconscious mind has not in some way influenced the activities of my conscious mind and life's activities. I seem to have accumulated enough experience of altered states to illustrate a score or more ways the unconscious mind behaves. The following story illustrates still other capacities of the sophisticated unconscious mind: a concern for the welfare of others, the richness of unconscious imagery, and the paradox of unconscious sensations of body behavior when body activity is impossible.

As a sophomore medical student I experienced a lengthy siege of excruciating headaches that attracted the attention of some of the faculty. Succumbing to the weight of medical authority, I found myself in the hospital undergoing a radical and not well proved diagnostic procedure in which the cerebrospinal fluid from brain and cord was drained, replaced with oxygen, and x-rays made. Owing to some fault in the procedure, I lay unconscious for three days. On one of those days my parents visited me, having driven more than five hundred miles.

I was aware of the fear and worry my parents must be feeling about their only child in a strange hospital, undergoing a rigorous procedure to see whether she had a brain tumor. Waiting for them, I told myself to be bright and cheerful in spite of the discomfort and pain, not to do anything that might worry them and to pass the whole thing off as nothing very serious. My parents came into the room. Not able to lift my head, I nonetheless embraced them with my arms, gave a cheery smile, asked them about their long trip, how the dog was, and even recounted a funny story about a friend of mine who had, earlier that day, eaten my hospital lunch. After they left, I congratulated myself for being such a good actor, and I was more than pleased because I hadn't given a sign of my discomfort. I even remember chuckling about it.

The following weekend my parents visited me again. The worry on my mother's aging face disappeared when she saw me. Although I was still flat on my back, I was grinning ear to ear, my face was relaxed, and my eyes alert.

"Thank God," she said, "you can't imagine what a week it's been, worrying whether you'd pull through."

"Oh, come on!" I said, surprised. "Didn't you think I acted pretty chipper last weekend?"

"Chipper! Oh my darling, you never moved. Dr. Mako [the surgical resident] was stationed outside your door, two nurses were here with you, and everyone was so worried. You were unconscious for so long!"

I had, they told me, not recovered consciousness for another thirty-six hours after their visit, and I was hard pressed to believe it. After all, I had not just been aware of their visit the weekend before, I had known they were coming. We also verified that my friend had indeed eaten my lunch that day, so I had been aware of that, too.

I had imagined a wish-fulfilling fantasy, but, inexplicably, I had had an awareness of at least two bits of reality, the visit and the lunch. And most confusing of all, I could recall my performance totally. I could remember what (I thought) I had said, I could remember (what I thought were) their reactions, and I could even remember a second (un)conscious awareness of being pleased that I had carried out my deception so successfully. It was as if one unconsciousness had looked at what another part of the unconscious had done and applauded in appreciation.

Medical experts seem to want to explain unusual states of consciousness as tricks of the brain's biochemistry, so they might suggest in this case that some medication given at the time of my hospital experience may have acted to block muscle activity so I couldn't talk or move. But of course if that were so, the trauma of being conscious yet unable to communicate at a critical time would certainly have been impressed into memory. At any rate, only supportive, biological materials are usually given when a patient is unconscious, and it is doubtful that any drug with any kind of muscle or central nervous system action would have been given. (Sometimes it pays to have been trained as a pharmacologist!)

The only reasonable explanation of my experience seems to be that a self-contained unit of complex, intelligent mental activity became separated from the total spectrum of conscious awareness. This separate unit, remarkably, retained the capacities for intelligent perception (awareness of the presence of my friend and of my parents) and equally as surprising the ability to project highly relevant fancy and illusion from within the mind. The "altered consciousness" also retained the ability for sensitive awareness of personal, altruistic concern; the ability for analysis, valid appraisal, evaluation of personal relationships; the ability to synthesize and plan and execute a relevant, appropriate plan of behavior, at least within the mind; and, equally as surprising, considering the unconscious state, an ability for self-analysis. The dissociated consciousness, like the consciousness within dream states, apparently also never completely lost contact with the memory files that conscious awareness uses in its mental considerations.

There are several other thought-provoking features about this incident. One is that the emotions I assigned to myself during the fantasy were exclusively of an altruistic nature. Although there was intelligent analysis of the various emotions involved, there were absolutely no subjective sensations about my own state, my own stress, or my own discomfort. My mental activity, and hence the illusion, was directed totally toward a concern about other people's feelings and reactions. Furthermore, even though there was an awareness of the "I," it was not my personal "I," but an intellectually objective "I" divorced from all of most of the learned appreciations about the self we call ego. This kind of concern is largely an intellectually derived concern, one that stems from serious consideration of the many influences on human behavior. The presence of this sophisticated understanding of human relationships and nonemotional, intellectual appreciation of the self in the absence of any sign of conscious awareness must mean that the mental activities of the unconscious mind are capable of a superior kind of intellectual activity. I will discuss other examples of this phenomenon in the following section on perceptual distortions.

Another observation about this experience also has considerable significance for medical and psychological theory. During the episode, while I was projecting an entire script highly relevant to a critical, in-progress situation, I was also mentally projecting all of the appropriate gestures and facial signs that are usually used in conversation. There was, however, a complete dissociation between mind and body. I was under the illusion that my body was automatically carrying out the expressions of my mind as it usually does, but even though the mind supplied all the necessary ingredients for action by the body, apparently not one single nerve impulse was sent from the brain to the muscles of the body.

Other theorists might suggest that brain operations under these circumstances could "inhibit" the sending of nerve impulses to activate the muscles, as seems to happen when we decide not to do something or, as under hypnosis, the instructions are not to react to something that generally causes an innate or normal reaction. I doubt this theory holds for my experience for the obvious reason that a strong drive was present, a determined will to perform all the right movements to convey a specific impression.

The ability to remember purely imagined events related specifically to real people and real situations, as in my experience, is reminiscent of the memory ability of certain paranoid schizophrenics, who appear to have few if any links between their imagined worlds and the other "real" worlds and their real reactions.

In these instances too, there can be a curious disseverance between emotions and intellect. I once hired a technician who had suffered one of the worst kinds of war neuroses in World War II. He had developed a severe paranoid schizophrenic reaction and had been hospitalized for nearly two years during which time he rarely had a lucid moment. Yet he could recall both his illusions and virtually every event that took place around him during his illness. One of the most fascinating aspects of his stories about his illness was the way in which his emotions separated. All his feelings, sensations, and impressions were associated almost exclusively with his illusions, and while he was aware of the reactions of fellow patients, nurses, doctors, and caretakers, he had attached little personal meaning to them.

While my technician's act of attaching meanings and feelings to himself in his illusions differed from my attaching meanings and feelings only to other people during my illusions, I suspect that the basic mechanism of mind was similar in both cases. The conclusion would seem to be that the capacity to create and to construct either relevant or nonrelevant illusions is so willful, so intentional that the mental activity also has the capacity to direct the brain mechanisms that underlie feelings and emotions. The significance of this observation is that mental activity alone, unconscious mental activity, can control activity of the brain as well as of the body.

Sleep Walking

It isn't necessary to use examples of rare or pathological states of mind to illustrate the complexity and self-determination of the non-conscious intellect. Sleep walking occurs in the absence of conscious awareness, yet the sleep walker formulates and projects a specific intention and usually doesn't stop his performance until it is completed or frustrated.

Sleep walking is still another curious form of dissociation of forms of consciousness. The sleep walker rarely if ever remembers either what he did or intended to do; nonetheless, the inference is obvious that the sleep walker not only actively devises an intention to do something, but also develops a strong conviction about the need to do it and then directs a marvelously coordinated mobilization of every body function needed to carry out the act. Possibly most interesting of all, when the sleep walker is allowed to complete his performance, he usually returns to bed. This suggests he has an awareness, albeit unconscious, that the intention has been fulfilled and, further, that he can return to exactly the state he was in before.

Sleep research has shown that sleep walking is not necessarily related to any personality or behavior disorder, although forms of sleep walking can be precipitated by severe neuroses. It is unfortunate that the behavioral sciences tend to study abnormally behaving human beings. Based on a study of severe anxiety neuroses, it was believed for some time that sleep walking was merely an "acting out" of repressed, frustrated emotions, and indeed chronic anxiety patients do often exhibit quite extraordinary, sometimes violent anxiety episodes during sleep walking. Later studies showed, however, what most of us already knew, that quite normal people, with perhaps only a slightly greater sensitivity to the stress of life than most of us, sleep walk. Obviously, researchers never were counsellors at camp or had friends who were quite normal people and also sleep walkers.

Sleep walking occurs usually in the deepest stage of sleep, a bit of evidence that rather complex mental activity occurs at even the lowest point on the consciousness scale. This is confirmed by the fact that, in certain sleep studies, when people are aroused from the deepest stages of sleep they can report recall of complex thinking.

Sleep talking, in contrast to sleep walking, generally occurs in the lightest stages of sleep, which explains why a sleep talker can be "talked to." The problem is that even though the sleep is extremely light, verging on wakefulness, sleep talkers also rarely have any memory of their behavior. Logically it would seem that sleep talking involves reasonable complex mental activity, i.e., imagining a situation, participating in it, interpreting behavior, thinking of responses, and other related mental activities, yet under the special conditions of light sleep apparently none of the experience is put into memory, at least in such a way that it is available for recall.

Such are the paradoxes of relationships among consciousness, experience, imagery, thought, and physical activity that veil the infinite capacities of mind.

Thoughts on Out-of-the-Body Experiences

The puzzling way the unconscious intellect can split away from conscious awareness, yet retain so many other critical capacities of mind, has led me to wonder whether at least some unexplained phenomena may not also be the creations of minds that can split, like holograms, into self-contained universes complete unto themselves.

For the few readers uninitiated in the propositions of modern spiritualists, out-of-the-body or astral projection experiences simply mean that the individual's spirit can slip out from the body and journey anywhere. Anywhere may be the next room, the next country, the next planet, or unknown worlds. It seems to be generally agreed that an out-of-the-body ability refers mainly to an ability that emerges only during sleep or near-sleep states, while true astral projection occurs when individuals have learned the technique so well that they can go on spirit excursions at will no matter what their state of consciousness.

One of the most delightful accounts of out-of-the-body experiences was recorded by Robert Monroe in his book, *Journeys Out of the Body.* [1] Mr. Monroe not only makes the coming and going of the spirit from the body so realistic it sends shivers down the spine, he recounts his own fears of the experiences and how he came to under-

---

1. New York: Doubleday, 1971.

stand the phenomenon so well that he ultimately learned to exert voluntary control over them. But despite his rather thoroughgoing account, there aren't many clues about how the uninitiated might develop the same power.

To be very truthful, my own fantasies are just like everyone else's, and I would adore being able to slip the bonds of body and soar invisibly to a luxurious harem in old Persia or to a secret room of the KGB in Moscow. I have often wondered why teleporters insist upon transporting themselves either to relatively ordinary places or to Star Trekian galaxies rather than to exotic places that hold real secrets. The out-of-the-body experts usually say they don't have much choice, although the astral projectionists insist they have control over where their spirits journey; yet only once have I heard of a useful journey, and this was second-hand.

My first acquaintance with astral projection came during a visit with a psychiatrist with whom I had a long-standing friendship. She had, in fact, been my college advisor, and was quite an extraordinary woman. Not satisfied with psychology, where she had been a straight A student through the Ph.D., she straight A'd herself through an M.D. and Boards in neurology and psychiatry. As the years passed, I discovered that she was also making straight A's in theosophy, spiritualism, and clairvoyance.

On this particular occasion, my double-doctor friend had, by some obscure logic, invited an itinerant peddler to share the luncheon she had prepared for me. Before I could mobilize any conversational tidbit about peddling, my friend brought me up sharply by announcing that our peddler-guest had just returned from a visit to Darjeeling in North India. I was immediately intrigued, having dreamed of visiting there for years. And how long did you spend there, I asked. The peddler was amused. Only a few hours, he smiled. I went yesterday morning and returned by three.

Suppressing a vulgarism such as "Jeez, what a crazy creep," I managed to ask questions about the looks of the countryside and the native dress and customs, even though I hadn't the faintest idea of what Darjeeling or its people looked like. The answers verged on the exotic, and now, in later life, having become a frequent visitor to Darjeeling, I know the answers were the fabrications of daydreams. But I did learn about what was then, so many years ago, called teleportation and is now called astral projection.

Beginning some ten or so years ago, the experimental psychologist Charles Tart revealed scientific studies that were widely interpreted as providing solid scientific support for the out-of-the-body phenomenon. As I remember one lecture, he described experiments in which he hid bits of information in inaccessible places, then wired the subjects for all-night sleep recordings, and particularly EEGs. On one or two occasions the sleeping person later reported moving out of the body and gave a reasonable account of the hidden information. The physiologic records appeared to show rather unusual changes at the times when the out-of-the-body experience was said to have occurred.

As a fairly well qualified expert in EEG analysis, I confess I was not in the least impressed by the brain wave recordings, failing to see any changes that could not be interpreted as more normal events in the sleeping subject. And, as I remember, the proof that the subject's ethereal self had really seen the hidden information was also somewhat weak.

But Charlie Tart's lecture shed new light on some unusual experiences of my own. As a child, I had often, during early evening sleep, become aware that my perceiving self was a tiny dot high in the furthest corner of my room, and I could look down on the bed with my body in it, sometimes witnessing my mother coming into the room quietly to kiss me goodnight. At other times my "vision" was so broad as to see the entire house from on high, sometimes to glimpse the entire neighborhood, and once or twice to see scenes of my favorite picnic places or a relative's farm.

As I remember these experiences, they were not in the least frightening, even during the time I lay near death with German measles and my grandmother, watching over me night after night, pulled me back to life when my respiration seemed to fail. I watched the whole thing from above, as a neutral observer, with remarkable detachment. This split between observing and the emotions of participating existed also the night my beloved aunt died in the next room. I had been observing the silent sorrow from my ceiling corner in the next room; I "came down" when mother woke me to say goodbye to dear Aunt Ruth, and "returned" to my observer's nook after going back to bed. Even at age seven, I experienced clinical observation, unresponding. But awake the next morning, I was flooded with the emotions of losing my dearest friend.

I have since discovered that such experiences are not uncommon in childhood, and are believed by some scientists interested in the tricks of consciousness to be simply a peculiar state of awareness-cognition that happens when the active mental processes of the unconscious mind create a complete, organized, self-involving perception and project it out of the self.

The key support for this notion may be the unnatural separation of the observer from the interpreter. It is the interpreter of events that stirs the emotions, at least in the normally functioning human being. Most reports of "out-of-the-body" experiences that I've heard or read about seem peculiarly devoid of the emotions that normally accompany any experience. When emotion is attached to the out-of-the-body experience, it generally seems to stem from wishful thinking or post-facto subjective appraisal rather than from objective interpretation or analysis.

It is unfortunate that the role of different mental processes in these states has not been examined more thoroughly. If we do nothing more than describe some of the outstanding characteristics of the out-of-the-body experience, we find some exciting differences from the way in which mental activities are normally related. The special differences are first, that the observation of the experience by the observer-participant is objective, i.e., the feelings, attitudes, and beliefs of the observer (the "I") are absent and there are no associated subjective feeling states; and second, that there is no interpretation of the experience while it is occurring.

In my own and in many other "out-of-the-body" experiences I've heard or read about, the individual's perception of the experience (when retrieved from memory) is like that of a detached, uninvolved neutral observer. That is, scenes and actions are observed, but they are not generally interpreted in relation to the self, and the experiences are peculiarly devoid of emotional reactions *during* the experience. It is, of course, interpretation that stirs the emotion.

From this standpoint, out-of-the-body and astral projection experiences are quite different from dream experiences. Few dreamers stay emotionally uninvolved in their dreams, regardless of whether they are participant or observer. If one is the observer of oneself in dreams, the dream observer almost always interprets, and can remember his emotions of the dream. Even when the emotions of the dream are minimal, the dreamer almost always has some kind of subjective impression, meaning that he interpreted the scenes and action of the dream in some relationship to himself.

So it appears that during out-of-the-body states of consciousness, perception is limited to objective observation and is *dissociated entirely from self-perception*. This effect is reminiscent of the great divide between subjective experience and physiological events that marks the special characteristic of man so impossible to explain, i.e., how the physical events of brain become the intangible events of mind. The fact that a subjective-objective dissociation occurs in out-of-the-body experiences may indicate a blocking out of all those "higher order" processes of mind that relate the "I" to the objective universe. (This way of viewing the world shares qualities of the way certain animals are believed to view their environment.)

I consider both out-of-the-body experiences and dreaming to be well-defined isolated units of associated mental events, differing only slightly in the degree of isolation of the entire complex of relevant mental activity from the perception of awareness one usually has of one's own everyday mental activity. In conscious awareness, I know I am observing, I know I am interpreting, and I know the events I observe are exciting certain intellectual or emotional reactions. In deep sleep, on the other hand, I am aware of none of these activities of my mind.

To explain the dissociation of consciousness that might account for phenomena such as out-of-the-body experiences or dreaming (or life-after-death reports), let us briefly examine some characteristics of memory. Whether spontaneous or induced, memories emerge as big chunks of associated material—visual perceptions, emotions, even judgments—and hidden behind the most immediately relevant or useful memories are clusters and loose aggregates of related memories. Every memory unit contains not only objective data such as the height of trees or the characteristics of different faces, but associated impressions, reactions, emotions, intellectual analysis, and clues to other memory units. A memory unit is a mini-world in itself; moreover, it can undergo a process of accretion, gathering into itself colorings from desire or hate or fear or love.

The most fascinating examples of isolated memory-consciousness units occur in certain forms of paranoia and schizophrenia. Years ago, for example, I knew a patient at a mental hospital who was a normally behaving, intelligent human being in every respect save one. The mere mention of the U.S. Navy sent him into the most extraordinarily compact, isolated state of dissociated consciousness I have ever heard described. He had become convinced that his father owned the U.S. Navy, and he would brook no criticism of the Navy. His focus of attention, intellect, and emotions on a single, isolated universe of associated memories and ideas was so complete that his usual good common sense could not penetrate this unit of consciousness.

I suppose that the phenomenon of déjà vu can be explained in a similar way. Many people have the experience of being in a strange, new situation they feel they have lived through before, "recognizing" every element of the physical environment, people, and feelings. What this means is that a memory unit can be so complete that it is a totally vivid, accurate contruction of an entire atmosphere and environment. With the human propensity for embroidering experience, it is not unreasonable to expect that most memory units can expand as well as contract, because every memory, every observation is associated with a host of both relevant and inappropriate facts.

We have also, I believe, what could be called a "logic template," a system of putting observations into memory in certain systematic orders that our training and experience have shown to be useful. This does not mean that the logic is correct; it is as often as not biased by emotional attachments or intellectual prejudices or simple expediency. But it is the way we build expectations, the way we conjecture about what should be, the way we fill in the things we feel are missing from a scene.

If, for example, I come to believe in astral projection, and feel that I could learn to transport my ethereal self, my "logic template" could easily project and construct a complete journey, filling in all of the details of people and places based on a selected assortment of information in memory from past experience, past reactions, future hopes, and concerns. With enough attention, my intentions, with a large unconscious component, can become so discrete as to form a fully functioning unit of consciousness, eminently logical internally, that is separated and isolated from all other conscious experience of subjective experience.

This isolated memory-consciousness unit can be connected with the rest of the consciousness domain in such a way as to *exclude* specific mental functions such as interpretation, as in the case of my own consciousness projection experiences as a child, or can *include* interpretation and judgment or emotional reaction, as in the case of dreaming, or *exclude* all appreciation of social reaction, as in the case of certain paranoid or schizophrenic reactions.

One element that distinguishes dreaming and mental illness from out-of-the-body experiences is the relative prevalence of the former compared to the rarity of the latter. All dissociations of consciousness have fundamental differences, one from another. Dreaming is a naturally occurring phenomenon; mental illness strikes only those who, for one reason or another, are intellectually-emotionally unable to endure the stress of living in a complex, expecting society, while déjà vu, experiencing life after death, and astral projection are still other ways mind processes can dissociate to break the bonds of conscious awareness. The spirit rising bears kinship with every spiritual belief since man first tried to account for the unexplained by endowing nature with spirits that moved unseen through earth and sky and man himself.

Life After Death

A good many accounts of life after death are being given these days, and books recount experience after experience of people who regained life after all vital signs declared them dead. These tales have fascinated thousands of people, especially, I would guess, those whose beliefs convince them of an eternal living happiness.

Death being what it is, and communication with the dead chancy if possible at all, the probabilities for proving life after death are remote at best. The psychical quality of life-after-death experiences is enough to dissuade most qualified researchers from the task of finding proof. The lay reader may believe that signed and witnessed reports from the living–briefly-dead are validation enough, but science prefers good physical evidence, such as the briefly-dead later reporting a real event during their deadness that can be adequately verified as a real event and never subsequently discussed with the revived person. Nevertheless, it is not to the credit of science that its inability to prove the *existence* of life after death has prevented it from exploring the qualities of mind that produce the experience.

Again, my own personal experiences are relevant to this particular phenomenon. Once, during a physical exam, I was administered a weak solution of a local anesthetic. In less than ten minutes the waves of a hypersensitivity (anaphylactic) reaction began. I lost consciousness and, I was told later, the physician decided that I was dying and, in fact, dead. When I regained consciousness I found myself lying on an examining table while what seemed to be monstrous arms with hands waved huge syringes over my chest. Apparently, this sight jiggled important memories and I aroused to a clear consciousness, seeing the doctor and nurse standing on each side, each with a large syringe poised over my chest.

"What's that for?" I asked with some vigor.

"Well," the doctor began to explain, knowing I was an experienced pharmacologist, "the nurse has Coramine and I have adrenaline. We are going to inject it into your heart to try to save your life."

"Oh my God," I said, with rising vigor, "don't do that. They don't work. No matter what the textbooks say, Coramine and adrenaline simply can't restore cardiovascular or pulmonary function. I'll have to do it myself."

Obviously the physician recognized that I was quite lucid once more, and waving the nurse away, began checking me over again.

In retrospect, the ending is rather humorous. But the important point is that the sudden return of consciousness with full reasoning power was not only helpful to recovery, but it somehow allowed me to recall instantly my sensations during the experience.

During the unconscious or dying state, there was nothing. If any description can be made, it was like not-being and a black void of nothingness. Only the blackness had any relationship to ordinary sensations.

A second experience occurred when I had the great fortune to revive a lovely lady from a coronary attack during an air trip. Afterwards I talked to her briefly, and her sole sensations and thoughts were those of pain (while changing oxygen supplies) and of her family. She, too, had had no delicious visions of an eternal heaven.

My own experiences do not dispose me toward accepting the existence of life after death. I prefer to entertain another explanation: that the phenomenon is another example of partitioning and dissociating units of mind-consciousness memories; and that the kind of experience, i.e., the subjective sensations reported to occur, depends, almost exclusively, on the kinds of information, knowledge, experiences, beliefs, and motivations the person has. Certainly in my own case, my knowledge, experiences, beliefs, and motives were all wrapped up in medicine, body functions, and how to save lives.

For other people there is often a different reality, an island of mind that contains beliefs in everlasting happiness after death, beliefs that allay the fear of death, each fed by selecting perceptions and memories and learnings during life. Most spiritual people construct their visions of life after death long before death, and it seems possible that these constructed realities can split away from the consensual reality just as easily as other dissociations of mind and consciousness do.

On the other hand, the recent excitement about life-after-death experiences has created its own consensual consciousness, making the identity of self with the beatific vision a good deal more comfortable, and an "altered" state of consciousness more acceptable to our society.

Flying Saucers

I am less certain about classifying flying saucer sightings as specialized dissociations of consciousness. By this time it will come as no surprise to the reader that I have also had flying saucer experiences. Mine were of the sighting kind only. The most convincing sighting occurred as I stood in front of my house on the hillside looking down and across the San Fernando Valley. Suddenly, in the early dusk, I saw an enormous saucer-shaped object flying low across the near valley and coming up the hill. It was, not surprisingly, the typical flying saucer, described and drawn a thousand times, with one distinctive tier of what looked like huge windows of a round stadium lighted in reds and yellows and blues. As it almost leisurely approached my hill, it suddenly partially reversed direction and angled off, flying back across the valley, but now with blazing speed.

It was so real I hung over the radio, sure that hundreds of people had seen the monstrous flying object. Breathless, I heard an announcer say that a reporter was calling in from his home, near mine, to report what he had just seen. The reporter described exactly what I had seen!

All evening I tuned in radio station after station, and the TV news, and in the morning I scoured the newspaper. There was never another report.

I am hard put to explain this experience. I was never thoroughly convinced that I didn't see the object, but then I was never convinced that I really could have. And the confirmation by the radio reporter was no help either, because as far as the news was concerned, it was as if his report had never existed.

I suspect we both saw something and by some curious circumstance we both interpreted it as a flying saucer when it actually may have been some new and unfamiliar experimental aircraft. We have lots of these flying around southern California. We may well have projected onto the flying object our memories of the now familiar drawings of saucers rather than taking the trouble to absorb its new and strange and frightening shape.

The Idiot Savant

Nothing perhaps is more revealing of the awesome abilities and mysterious nature of mind than when fragments of the whole mind separate unexpectedly into strange yet powerful caricatures of man's intellectual beingness.

Our greatest embarrassment of mind is the mind we call insane, the insanity of schizophrenia or paranoia or mania. Whether the cause is a defect in the brain's biochemistry or a defect in the intelligence that fails to cope with the pressures of life, the hallmark of the insane, we too often forget, is that the disseverances of mind *rarely encompass the total intellect,* and do not impair functions of the intellect *all* the time. A manic merely carries impulse to excess sometimes, the paranoid simply fails to discriminate reality in some, but not all, areas of life and living, and even chronic schizophrenics may have a good many lucid moments. The fractures in the mental machinery that split off these self-contained globules of mind or that can be so deep as to give one person multiple *whole* personalities reveal the power of mind to divide itself into an infinitude of parts, and like a hologram, mirror the nature of everything that makes up human beings.

Sanity lies forgotten behind all the pathologies of mind. But in every instance where the mind alone twists and warps the threads of thought, intellect survives. The operations of mind that can be obscured by mental illness or by sleep and dreams or mystical experience are simply operations of mind put to a different purpose. The mystery is how the mind can pull itself into unknown realms that challenge the understanding of conscious and consensual thought.

There is no better example of the marvels of the fractured mind than the idiot savant.

An acquaintance of mine was once the hired guardian for an aging mental defective. From time to time she would bring Nora along to small, quiet functions, generally warning everyone that Nora would drift off to the piano and play for a while, and that we shouldn't try to dissuade her. The first time I saw Nora, I'm afraid I stared a bit rudely. She was a comic book caricature of the puffy little old lady. She appeared in a subduedly flowered mauve-puce crepe de Chine dress, an antique lavalier, pointed, low-heel strap pumps out of the early 1900s, and a dull cloth coat with worn fur trim. She looked like a museum piece moldering in a corner. My acquaintance helped put down her coat and purse, and without a word Nora slid onto the piano bench while the rest of us began chatting.

Suddenly we stopped. Nora's hands were flowing across the keyboard, making the piano sing with a Mendelssohn concerto. The tones were bright, then soft, the cascades brilliant and dynamic. I was entranced. We were listening to a pianist of extraordinary accomplishment. The melodic meaning was clear, the harmonies intriguing, and the phrasing perfect.

Nora was an idiot savant. What a remarkable contradiction this psychological-medical term encompasses. How can an idiot also be a savant? I pondered this every time I heard Nora play. Her repertoire was considerable, and each composition was interpreted with understanding and great sophistication of feeling. Her muscle coordination, which at other times was uneasy, was magnificent at the piano. How had she learned?

She had, I was told, been given piano lessons in her teens, but nothing so extensive as to explain the concertizing she displayed. It seemed inconceivable that her mangled mind could so unerringly shade the complex patterns of musical phrases to interpret what philosopher-musicians had created so many centuries before.

There are two very important observations to make concerning the clear dissociation in idiot savants between the superior development of one very specific kind of intellect on the one side and the rudimentary, undeveloped state of the rest of intellect on the other side. First, a facility for music seems to be a skill that not only involves sophisticated coordination of the fine muscles of fingers, hands, arms, and shoulders, but involves as well an ability to store in memory long and sometimes unrelated sequences of phrases, and what is perhaps the most crucial and complicated mind-brain function, the ability to recall all phrases, all muscial colorings, all muscle-coordinating functions in precisely the most appropriate way. We have to remember that the musical forms we use today are intellectually developed forms, mathematical, intricate, and meaningful particularly to the musically educated. These are all high levels of intellectual development, and for a mental defective to attain excellence in performing the intricacies of musically communicated thought is a stunning feat —a stunning feat for anyone, let alone the mentally defective.

Idiot savants have also performed remarkable feats in fields of mechanics, handcrafts, art and mathematics. Their abilities stand in isolation from the rest of their undeveloped mind-brain-body. The question of *how* such isolated intellectual specialization occurs is a question of such physiologic-psychologic magnitude that virtually no one has ever attempted an answer.

The other observation about the split intellect of idiot savants is one that I have never heard discussed: that there are perhaps frequent unrecognized examples of less clearly split intellects wandering about in our society, in whom one talent may be beautifully developed without development of other parts of the intellect. This does not mean that most artists, musicians, writers, mathematicians and mechanics have some kind of intellectual deficiency in other areas, but it does seem that there are not a few artists and musicians —not to mention scientists—with specialized talents who *are* intellectually deficient in other areas.

The most common intellectual split is between the emotions of social interactions and the abstract intellect. Most people use the intellect to help control the emotions, and they mature; but there are, as a matter of fact, some striking intellects who were never able to achieve a socially acceptable intellect-emotion integration. I personally knew two such men, one a mathematician, the other a philosopher-writer, both world authorities in their fields, yet emotionally they functioned on a ten-year-old level. My own father was

an intellectual genius (he could, for example, read one of my specialized medical texts in one sitting and understand it perfectly) who was
little more than an adolescent boy in his social relationships. This is
different from the personality disorders recognized by psychologists
and psychiatrists, and does not qualify as a neurosis or a behavioral
problem. Although it should qualify as a personality defect, it is not
"recognized" chiefly because the "disorder" is difficult to detect
under the ordinary circumstances of living, which do not require
much in the way of emotional maturity.

What systematic study of the idiot savant and particularly the less
obviously specialized intellectual talents might tell us is how to maxi-
mize the development of the intellectual potential of human beings.
Most often we and the mind specialists simply sit back and take the
easy course, assuming that talent or intellectual specialization is a
matter of genetics or environment or motivation or special kinds of
encouragement. But the idiot savant's existence denies these facile
explanations. It is generally agreed that no amount of good genes or
enriched environments can produce a musician or a mathematician
or a scientist out of a child who has no such "inclination." So, if the
talent or ability to specialize an intellectual pursuit is not primarily
determined by genes nor remarkably affected by the environment,
what *is* the influence in human life that so dramatically asserts its
existence? Is it chance alone, the chance that special combinations
of chromosomes and genes are fertilized by very special friendly
environments and flower as genius or insanity or floating curiosities
of a half or a tenth of mind? Is it an "accident of consciousness," a
set of circumstances that makes comprehensible, albeit subconsciously and beyond direct communication, some patterns of orderliness, or harmonies, or identity with the inexorable logic of all nature?
How unlikely it would be—as science likes to suggest—that a particular body chemical or a special variant of a normal chemical could
predetermine complicated sequences of thought, emotion, and behavior and shape talent and desire and the focus of the mind's implements into an intellectually acceptable unusual expertise.

What is curious is that the superior intellect we associate with
genius can bloom in a kind of desperate isolation from the consensual
awareness, that awareness of life and its contents human beings share
in understanding. For the idiot savant, isolated genius exists in the
fractured mind accompanied by little if any of its social significance.

Hypnosis

The idiot savant is an extreme example of the extraordinary ability of mind to split itself into autonomous fractional units, often with superior intellect. In a way, hypnosis may be a closely related common phenomenon, for it, too, is a dissociated state. Of all the thousands of research studies on hypnosis, none offers us a usable theory.

One of the spectacular mental feats possible under hypnosis is enhancing the imaging process, i.e., creating mental images so complete, so three-dimensional, so animated, and so faithful to physical reality that the hypnotized subject accepts the imagined environment as real.[2]

Other mental feats possible under hypnosis are amnesia, age regression, hallucination, dreaming about specific events, blanking out of vision or hearing, limb rigidity, time distortion, and posthypnotic suggestion. All of these unusual mental activities under hypnosis are directed, intentional manipulations, differing from similar ordinary abilities mainly in their specificity and their intensity. Yet, except for somnambulistic states, little attention has been paid to exploring the mental activities that produce and sustain trance states. Instead, much hypnosis research concentrates on cataloguing various personality, emotional, and behavioral features of hypnotizable and nonhypnotizable people. It is difficult indeed to understand the inner operations of the mind by looking only at its external expressions. The fact that so little is understood about the causes of hypnotic trance after more than a hundred years of active "research" should be an indictment of the dominant research approaches.

One of the impediments to productive exploration of trance phenomena seems to me to be the tendency of researchers to explain hypnosis on the basis of accepted concepts of the *nonhypnotic* behavior of human beings. For example, one small but very vocal coterie of hypnosis researchers has, for some two decades, contended that

---

2. Number or letter substitution illustrates a special intellect. The hypnotist tells the subject that, e.g., there are no longer any 5s, but that all 5s are now 7s, then he asks the subject to do arithmetic problems. The hypnotized subject will write a 7 for every 5 he hears, so that 1,2,3,4,5,6,7, looks like 1,2,3,4,7,6,7. But the striking mental behavior of the subject is that he calculates equally well when the 5s are replaced by 7s, seeming to forget easily that 5s ever existed.

hypnosis is no special state, but simply a phenomenon that can be elicited easily in certain individuals because they combine high levels of attitudes, motivations, and expectations. The theorists make an analogy between the readily hypnotizable person and people in an audience who react intensely to an emotional performance by actors, and conclude that people who respond to hypnosis have different experiences, "not because they are in different 'states' but because they are receiving different communications."

I personally cannot imagine concluding that people react differently to the same situation because the information in the situation is being communicated to them differently. The information in *any* situation, in any movie or play or in real life, is the same for every individual. It is the *receiving* mind of the individual that determines which information he will receive, which information he likes, expects, or desires, or will direct his attention to. Obviously, in any situation directed by human beings, whether a movie or a hypnotist, elements of the situation may be highlighted in different ways to draw attention to them differently in different people. But it is the way the information is received that spells the difference in its effect on different people.

Another scientific put-down of trance phenomena is the argument of certain researchers that a good many people are a lot more suggestible than we think and simply follow the hypnotists' suggestions very easily. They believe that many hypnotic suggestions such as forgetting one's name, getting drunk on a glass of water, etc., can be induced by mere suggestion in a nonhypnotic state. I seriously doubt that most people are as suggestible as the academicians seem to believe, or else advertisers would have an easier and cheaper time of it. If I suggest that you forget your name, you'll probably laugh at me; but if you *try* to forget your name, the effort of trying makes you remember it all the more, and the effort of trying is easily detected. When you respond to a hypnotic suggestion to forget your name, your face, body, and voice all clearly reveal that for the moment you simply don't *have* a name. There is obviously some very fundamental difference between the way the mind reacts to the hypnotic kind of suggestion and the way the mind reacts to suggestions in everyday life.

Another research explanation of trance phenomena claims that when you make it clear to a person you *expect* a high level of response to suggestions and commands, it raises an already high innate level of suggestibility. Not necessarily. Have you ever tried to suggest substitute activities to a group of teenagers? Or to adults for that matter? Here again general observations show a clear and important difference between highly specific hypnotic suggestion and ordinary suggestion and persuasion.

There are two extremely important phenomena that can occur in the hypnotic trance that have scarcely been explored by research.

One concerns mind-over-body feats, the ability of an individual in a hypnotic trance to exert what is ordinarily impossible control over the physiologic activities of his body. Although hypnosis is used in surgery mainly to block conscious awareness of pain, it can also be a means to reduce bleeding. The old stage trick of telling the subject not to bleed when a needle is thrust through the hand—and he doesn't—is a much more remarkable feat than hypnosis researchers seem to have realized. *Not* bleeding involves a far different physiologic activity than *stopping* bleeding. (My own experience of not bleeding during surgery as discussed in chapter 3 is an example of self-hypnosis.)

The other phenomenon that hypnosis researchers fail utterly to deal with is the posthypnotic suggestion. This alone, I think, defeats all of the arguments that hypnosis is not a special state. I have witnessed this process repeatedly. The hypnotist makes a posthypnotic suggestion by saying something such as, "The next time you hear the word 'sex' you will kiss the person nearest to you," and the subject does exactly that. If you ask the person why he did it, he will say, usually with some embarrassment, "I don't know. I can't imagine why." The point here is that often a number of hours may elapse, but the subject still performs, almost impetuously, on cue, and without conscious awareness of the act until it is done.

The fact that an instruction and cue word given in one state of consciousness can trigger the precise reaction demanded during an entirely different state of consciousness is cause for considerable wonder. The first thing that comes to mind is that if the posthypnotic task is something that is ordinarily a rather foolish act, as it often is, then it is surprising that it is tackled with such alacrity and so spontaneously and without inhibition.

Most academic hypnotists, and many stage hypnotists as well, claim that suggestions to perform in a certain way will fail if the person's beliefs are opposed to the act. The usual example is that you cannot get a hypnotized person to commit a crime because personal and cultural morals are too deeply engrained in the person's unconscious. Poppycock. How does the hypnotized person, occupied with creating suggested performances, discriminate between one belief and another? A person may be willing to kill another for his country in wartime because of his beliefs, but if an hypnotic experience is successful, with the subject believing the hypnotist enough to carry out his commands to do anything from nursing a pair of shoes to turning off the pain of the surgeon's knife (certainly contrary to social belief), then it follows that under hypnotic circumstances beliefs can indeed be dramatically manipulated.

In hypnosis the suggested environment is a mental image so powerful that the entire organism reacts to the mental image, not to the reality that is neurophysiologically perceived as usual, nor to the reality agreed upon by social custom.

It is this perfectly obvious, first-order deduction that scientists studying hypnosis seem to have missed completely: that during the hypnotic state there is a dissociation of one complete universe-unit of consciousness, functionally isolated from nearly all other units of consciousness and their constituent elements of associated perceptions, memories, judgment and logic associations. Hypnosis illustrates *an ability to manipulate consciousness intentionally.* Recognizing this remarkable capacity of mind means we can use the hypnotic phenomenon to observe various compartments of mind and consciousness and learn how different levels of units of consciousness operate, whether singly, simultaneously, or sequentially. And the first thing we learn is that nothing more than suggestion, as in hypnosis, contains the potential to trigger the dissociation of quite specific units of consciousness and cause them to function very efficiently in response to the suggestion while denying the consensual consciousness that otherwise controls conscious behavior.

Sorting Out Altered States

While discussing the various kinds of dissociated states of consciousness in this chapter, I have noted some of the characteristics that distinguish one from another. I noted, for example, that some altered states can be harmful to the individual while others can be beneficial, that some dissociate perception from emotional associations while others do not, and several other significant differences. I have not found any similar analysis in the scientific literature. The different characteristics of the different kinds of altered states appear nonetheless clear cut enough to use as the basis for a more systematic study of the extraordinary nature of consciousness than has yet been proposed.

I have not made, nor do I intend to offer, an in-depth analysis of "altered" states of consciousness or unusual abilities of mind of the kind that could give a fundamental understanding of the ways mind and consciousness produce their unusual states. I do contend, however, that we scientists can gain quite valid insights into the nature of consciousness by using the descriptive approach to scientific study. Despite the fact that the greatest advances in the understanding of human nature came from descriptive scientists such as Freud, Jung, and Janet and from the observations of animal behavior by Lorenz, Tinbergen, and others, for most of this century and especially in the West, descriptive science has been replaced by the Scientific Method, the stereotyped procedure in which an hypothesis is formulated and tested. The obvious shortcoming of the Scientific Method is that the hypothesis must be amenable to testing, and testing means there must be "standard conditions," "controls," the manipulating of "variables," and getting numbers in terms of measurable physical changes.

None of that applies directly to studies of mind and consciousness. The best we can do is to scrounge the literature, collecting reports of distinctive, unusual states of consciousness that are beneficial for man's welfare, then analyze these systematically and discerningly. When the analyses bring to light similarities and differences among unusual mind states, these are the data that can be used to classify states of consciousness, and the classification then serves as a starting point for conjecture about the operations of mind that might produce such states.

One classification that comes to mind is suggested by what I noted earlier: that some altered states of consciousness are pathological, while just as many other altered states are quite the opposite, providing valuable insights into the nature of self and society and man.

It occurred to me that we could characterize altered states of consciousness according to the nature of their effects on the well-being of people. That is, some states, as in severe mental illness or those produced by excessive use of drugs like LSD or PCP, are distressing to society at large and at the same time are detrimental to individual well-being. In contrast, altered states such as samadhi or creative flashes or perfect performances on stage or in sports or in the arts are admired and even venerated by society as a whole and also benefit the individual.

Altered states that distress principally the individual are the changes in the mind-emotion-consciousness complex during anxiety attacks, in phobias, or in strange, uncomfortable dissociations of perception such as the synesthesias (mixing of sensory images, as in "colored" hearing). In contrast to this category are those altered states that are enlightening and useful to the individual only and rarely touch society, such as personal imagery, mind-over-body feats, body awarenesses, or flashes of intuition.

Table 2   Some characteristics for describing altered mind states.

1. Produces distress
   a. for society   drug abuse
   b. for the individual   phobias
   c. for both   mental illness
2. Produces benefits
   a. for society   perfect performances
   b. for the individual   body awareness
   c. for both   creative flashes
3. How induced
   a. spontaneously   revelation
   b. intentionally   drugs
   c. spontaneous after intentional effort   meditation
4. Types of mind activities dissociated
   a. emotion and intellect from consensual reality   dreams
   b. emotion from intellect   out-of-the-body experiences
   c. intellect from will   hypnosis
   d. intellect from emotions and self-image etc.   samadhi
5. Emotionality
   a. emotion present   dreams
   b. emotion absent   out-of-the-body experiences

There are, then, at least four factors to consider initially. We can classify altered states of consciousness into, first, the major categories of (1) distressing and (2) beneficial, and for each of these major categories we can have subdivisions indicating whether the distress or benefit affects primarily society in general or primarily the individual.

Still other characteristics of altered mind states can be labeled and organized. Some, for example, occur spontaneously (like phobias or dreams), while others are induced or aided by intentionality (LSD states, mind-over-body feats), and still others, such as states of samadhi or perfect performances, may occur spontaneously but only after effort to achieve the state is made. This distinction may seem trivial at first, but one of the important contributions of the process of classification is that it makes it easier to extract properties or characteristics that identify distinctive classes of phenomena.

Our analysis has already yielded two distinctive, identifying properties for altered states of consciousness: they can be either distressing or beneficial, spontaneous or induced. To these we can add a third characteristic: the presence or absence of emotion. Altered states such as drug-induced states, anxiety, and most altered states that cause stress to society are accompanied by strong emotions. But, to the best of my knowledge, the altered states that benefit man, as either a society or individual, are virtually devoid of any accompanying emotional reaction. And, in fact, any emotion associated with altered states beneficial to man occurs long after the fact and is the appreciation rather than emotion of joy or peace or understanding.

As a tentative last category in this approach to systematic description, we can develop terms for the kinds of mind activity that are dominant or absent *during* altered states. During dreaming, for example, intellectual activity (dream logic), imagery and emotions are dissociated from conscious awareness, while during LSD hallucinations active perceptual activity and imagery generally dominate the field of consciousness (i.e., perceptions, images, their associated emotions) and a tad of conscious awareness dissociates from the constellation of mind activities we identify as normal and appropriate. During the hypnotic state, in contrast, normally functioning mental processes separate from the willful "I" and all mental processes except the personal will function normally. A still different kind of dissociation occurs during samadhi, or other depersonalizations, in which, it is said, the mind splits away from the personal "I."

These differences certainly should tell us something about the nature of altered consciousness. I hope we listen.

CHAPTER 11

Quintessential Consciousness

Among the many ways fully functioning compartments of consciousness can separate themselves from the whole and come to dominate the sentient being, there are two that appear to display the essential, magical nature of mind. In their qualities they are as different from each other as sight and sound, yet both may be expressions of the way mind uses mind to know itself. One is the mysterious conversion of a workaday consciousness into an awareness of insights and understandings that transcends all ordinary knowledge, a state we describe as mystical experience. The other is the inescapable, psyche-sustaining state created by the script-writing inner self we call imagination or imagery. Both states reveal the extraordinary ability of mind to muster its inner intelligence and reorganize relationships between self and not-self, being and not-being, old and new, experience and concept, and use the information of the world, its logic and order, to create the psychic roots of human life. A completely interior faculty of mind-brain makes sweeping surveys of things and events not simply not present but never existing, and weaves them into visions, enlightenment, fantasies, allegories or journeys of self-discovery. Little is known about the operations of mind and consciousness that create the mind-state of images or the mind-state of mystical experience. The following may be a beginning.

Mystical States

Mystical states, such as samadhi or satori, are usually regarded by searchers for the meaning of life as the penultimate experience. As it is usually described, the state of mind during mystical experience is one of awareness of the unity of all elements, natural and contrived, a "knowing" or understanding of the essence of life flooding the spaces that once were mind and feeling and thought. There are, we are told by some who try to explain, no physical sensations, no feelings, no interpretations from ordinary human experience. The observer and what is observed seem to be the same.

It is curious that no one has tried to puzzle out what happens in the mind itself that leads to mystical states. Mystics and gurus give us clues about what to do to achieve such states and can tell us what we may perceive is happening, but neither scientific nor philosophic experts are much interested in analyzing how mental processes interact to arrive at the mystical perspective. Perhaps the disinterest comes from an unconscious superstition that looking at the operations of mind in mystical experience might somehow contaminate our appreciations of supernatural experiences. But mystical states need not be studied in terms of mechanical processes of brain; we can instead, examine some operational features of mind characteristic of mystical experience that neither philosophers nor psychophysiologists have described. As a matter of fact, learning more about the nature of mystical experience, how it occurs and how it achieves its insights, might be one of the most productive exercises we can undertake.

Let me make it clear that my analysis has nothing to do with either the content or the objectives of mystical experience. It is concerned only with the nonmystical features: the operations of mind and thought and perceptions that can be inferred to underlie, or be associated with, the generation of insights; how the experiences are appreciated in consciousness; and how they can be recalled to be communicated.

There are, surprisingly, several previously unnoted but quite important and unusual mental activities leading to or accompanying mystical states. They follow from an analysis of commonly observed qualities of mystical states: their dissociation from ordinary states of consciousness, their insights that synthesize knowledge in a nonordinary way, their ineffability, and the curiously different nature of the way the experience is perceived, put into memory, and recalled.

Mystical states are so called because they are most often associated with religious pursuits, yet their occurrence is much more frequent in the more philosophic, nonreligious searches for an understanding of the nature of life, and perhaps should be called "quintessential consciousness" states. I feel, in fact, that mystical experience may be much more common than is generally believed, and that many people have such experiences but do not fully recognize them or appreciate or communicate them because their reservoirs of concepts or words are too limited to bring them into full flower.

The knowledge that the mystics and saints report from mystical experience is knowledge that the elements and events of the universe are all manifestations of a universal order and pattern. The idea that information about the relationships of material elements can be reordered (information being knowledge understood through the activity of the brain) becomes difficult only when no orderly process causing the reorganization can be detected. Virtually every human being since the beginning of time has learned about the world through teaching or by verifying observations of direct experience. Yet some of our most profound insights into the nature of the universe have come through altered states of consciousness, either of a mystical nature or closely related states.

What we can deduce is that during mystical experience the mind makes (or accepts) an extraordinary synthesis about the essence of life and about relationships among things and happenings within the natural universe—a synthesis that transcends expression except as it can be expressed by analogy and by behavior in the larger dimensions of time and space, yet a synthesis that contains recognized harmony and order.

Despite its mystical, supernatural nature, we must also admit that the phenomenon of reordering relationships among the essences of things or events in the universe that lies at the heart of mystical experience depends upon physical, orderly processes in the brain. When an individual comes into an awareness of the flow and pattern and oneness of all in the universe, that awareness would seem most logically to be related to a process of reorganizing information already within the memory banks of brain. *That* part of the process can validly be considered to be a natural physical operation. What may be supernatural is either the impetus to begin the process, or the unique ordering of information contained in the physical substance of the brain that causes it to flow into unifying coherence and the special way the information is then put into memory so that only the essence of the experience is available for recall.

One persistent enigma of mystical states is the ineffability of the experience. This, of course, represents a tantalizing contradiction. If, as it is universally agreed, the mystical experience defies accurate description, how is it that the memory of the experience is so completely appreciated that the memory impression seems to be permanently embedded in the consciousness-unconscious structure so that those experiencing the states do, nonetheless, try to and do communicate something about them? It would seem that the experience is not only put into memory (impressed on neural tissue), but can also be recaptured from memory in a way that, through analogy and relationships to sophisticated, evolved philosophic concepts, allows the conscious mind to approximate the experience abstractly.

Since we human beings are so constructed that the transmission of ideas and feelings occurs only with intact neural substance, we are almost compelled to deduce that the cohesive, organized information representing the experience becomes impressed on neural tissue, the only source and mechanism we possess that allows us to recapture experiences and communicate them.

The absoluteness of this law makes it difficult, if not impossible, to explain or accept mystical states as anything other than a reorganization of knowledge, learned and experiential, accomplished by the natural faculties of human minds. That it is a special state is clear, but it is not clear whether mystical states are accidental or are contrived by desire, teaching, or by other unknown activities of mind. Regardless, it is impossible to separate out the elements of mind and consciousness that initiate the process, knowing as little as we do about the realm of the unconscious and its push-pull relationship with conscious awareness. All desire to know the unknowable can reside in unconscious awareness equally as well as in conscious awareness.

Another observation about the altered state of mind we call mystical experience is that there is an apparently paradoxical impression of sensations. While it is agreed that during mystical states there are no ordinary sensations, the fact that the state is appreciated and can be recalled as an experience means that some sensory apparatus of the brain can sense (detect, appreciate) thought, and that some organizing mechanism is also available to detect the "ineffable" and understand it (organize it) even though the meaning and type of sensation does not translate into ordinary forms of communication. Nor are these the kinds of sensations scientists can measure and classify.

This brings us to the basic difficulty in our efforts to understand unusual mind states. We have no suitable words to describe our appreciations of "pure" thought, yet appreciate them we do. I believe this results not so much from the limitations of language, as from the restrictions of scientific notions of mind study, which are not appropriate in examinations of the higher-order processes of the mind. The term sensation is usually reserved by scientists for perceptions associated with stimulation of a sense organ or with a specific body condition, while "perception" is most often used to express awareness of the meaning of things or events.

But mystical states are not simply the source of a special awareness. The impression for the human being is also one of feeling—much as are sensations that are recognitions of other events impressed upon the body. The difficulty in the language is that "sensation" is used rigorously for responses to physical stimuli. But the fact that mystical experience impresses itself on the physical substance of the body (the brain) should be enough to qualify the response as a sensation, albeit one originating from an apparently intangible stimulus. For it does appear that we do have sensations about abstract thoughts and experiences.[1]

It is not enough to discuss thoughts in terms of their *meanings* only; from reports of mystical experience and of other states of dissociation of consciousness come clear indications of a true *sensation* of thoughts and concepts, as if we possessed an ability for "mental auto-appreciation." Certainly this could qualify as a legitimate sensory process of man, for the brain's neural tissue is, in fact, the seat

---

1. It can be argued, of course, that the sensations about mystical experience arise as a result of emotional appreciations of the difference between depersonalized and physically identified states, but I doubt those who experience mystical states would agree.

of all perceptual activity, where sensations are appreciated and felt. The existence of thought-sensations would explain the deep imprint in memory that such experiences have.

The same could apply to the mechanisms of self-awareness. In other sections of this book, I have discussed some of the "evolved" senses, such as a sense of biological awareness and a sense of order. Philosophers have long recognized the aesthetic sense, but there would seem to be others, such as the sense of self, of identity, the senses that recognize harmony and continuity. Hindu philosophy recognizes many levels of consciousness, some of which seem to be way stations to samadhi, and it also recognizes nine *nava rasas*, the basic aesthetic "emotions." Indian philosophy recognizes sensations of the mind's activity; Western science does not. Yet the mind-brain processes that evolve such sensations as compassion, a sense of justice, etc., from experiential information would seem to be not so different from those that could produce our appreciations of beauty or harmony or order. It seems to me that if we were to study these more sophisticated appreciations with the same fervor as we study the more primitive emotions of hate, anger, and fear, we could come much closer to fulfilling the human potential.

There are many experiences in daily life that approximate mystical experiences. We can, for example, intellectually, consciously come to an understanding of the Taoist concept that the flow of life *is* and that no human intervention can ever capture that is-ness, and later have moments of sensations of that is-ness. The same unconscious recognition is evident in the creative process—art, literature, music, landscaping, molding, inventing—when the artist-creator becomes lost, absorbed in the creative process and the flow and harmony and order of the creation. These states of mind bear a remarkable resemblance to mystical states.

Assuming that the insights of mystical experience do not appear fully developed (as in revelation), the remarkable synthesis and *experience* of complex, abstract, quintessential ideas reveals the capacity of mind to reorganize information to evolve higher-order concepts, concepts that are ordinarily beyond conceptualization. If the capacity for superior, creative, enlightening conceptualization exists, as obviously is indicated, then one of the more exciting questions for human potential is, Can we learn to use this capacity at will, rather than waiting a lifetime for one or another so-disposed individual to experience insightful altered states? We do know that more and more people are experiencing spiritual enlightenment, partly because we now know this is possible for ordinary human beings through mental discipline, and partly because there has been a growing systematization of appropriate mental exercises.

The third—or perhaps first in order of importance—observation is that mystical states are also dissociated, or altered, states of consciousness. The nature of the dissociation is quite different from that in other altered states, save perhaps the nonpathological state of depersonalization and special states induced by mescaline. The mystical state appears to be characterized by: (1) a dissociation of thought from both the emotions and sensations; (2) a total focus of attention and all mental operations on quite special kinds of thoughts; (3) insights and enlightenments that do not usually occur in most states of mind and consciousness activity; and (4) the subsequent usefulness of the insights, certainly to the individual, and often to much of society.

The phenomenon of nonpathological depersonalization (never studied to my knowledge) seems to share the most prominent characteristic of mystical states—that of divorce of thought from body sensations and from an awareness of sensory information from the environment. The feelings of mind being detached from the body and from the body's senses, and the simultaneous absence of all sensory input (or blockage of it from recognition) leave for recall the indelible impression of the *lack* of ordinary sensation. (These nonemotional depersonalization states are not to be confused with neuotic depersonalization, in which emotional anxiety about the mind-body separation is usually terrifying.)

For some individuals certain mescaline experiences can scarcely be distinguished from mystical states, a fact strongly suggesting that information about mystical states is information about some state approaching the desired Void, not the Void itself. Although there are some who deny the similarity between spiritual and mescaline mind states, there is always the question as to whether the critics have experienced both kinds of states, or even either. Or perhaps the denials reflect a spiritual prejudice that excludes the possibility of a drug-induced mystical vision. Aldous Huxley and John Blofeld are two who have described the similarities, and it was as a consequence of discussions with Huxley that my one and only mescaline experience came about. It was as close to the mystical state described by Blofeld in his books *Wheel of Life*[2] and *The Tantric Mysticism of Tibet*[3] as if it had been prepared according to his script, even though I read his books years afterwards. In a discussion I later had with Blofeld in Bangkok, he indicated few, possibly no, differences between his mescaline experience and the satori he achieved after years of training in the tantric Buddhist (Vajrayana) tradition.

Although the events leading into and out of my mescaline experience were typically drug-related (nausea, changes in perceptions), the bulk of the experience was, by clock time, a prolonged state of complete detatchment from all sensations, and a state of total depersonalization. There were no sensations of any ordinary kind, only the "knowing" and the "sensation" of being a part of the essential nature of the universe. As the drug waxed and waned in its effect, there also came an awareness of the chaos and disorder of the familiar, "real" world, conceptually, in understanding and appreciation only, with no words or emotions or logical thinking, and between the detached state and this awareness of the real world there developed a conflict. It was short-lived at first, but, as I remember, as the awareness of the man-made and disharmonious elements of the world grew and the drug effect diminished, I was seized by the realization that I was not sure of wanting to return to the real world at all. When it became inevitable that I would, I became increasingly immersed in the swells of the mystical state. The enlightenment of the experience was so profound, so pervasive of being and all life, that, like Blofeld, I never felt even a twinge of desire to repeat the drug experience. There were more insights in those hours than I could ever hope to fully appreciate in the whole of my life.

I suspect that the unity and harmony that is perceived during such experiences touches and is absorbed into being in a way that is quite different from the way ordinary sensory stimuli are appreciated, although I'm sure most neurophysiologists would disagree with me. Certainly the curious access hypnotic suggestion or religious conversion or peak experiences have to impact on neural tissue for appreciation of the material communicated and to be put into and recovered from memory suggests a Gestalt, patterned impress

---

2. Berkeley, Calif.: Shambala Publications, 1972.
3. New York: E. P. Dutton, 1970.

of information, perhaps a set of triggering, conceptual stimuli that touch the "organizing button" of the mind-brain's highest-order abstracting and consciousness processes.

There has never been a satisfactory explanation for the sudden profound insights from mystical or related states, or from poetry, inspiration and revelation, which appear full blown and developed in consciousness with no connection to conscious thought or even to attention. While we can postulate about concept formation and the mind's ability to use learned abstractions and logic, we cannot yet understand revelatory concepts, especially those that defy known processes, such as Einstein's relativity theory.

The magic of posthypnotic suggestion, or the sudden intrusion of an irrelevant thought into daydreaming (Oh my God, I left the roast in the oven!), illustrates both the potency and complexity of the unconscious intellect, but more, it illustrates the existence of quite different "sets" of intellectual activity concealed from conscious awareness. If the unconscious operations can and do arrange the priorities of thoughts and respond intelligently to an irrelevant command, then surely these unconscious mechanisms, under the right conditions, can reorganize their stored information in many ways, some of which lead to appreciation of fundamental truths about the universe—the kinds of insights and understanding we believe derive from the "mystical" state.

I believe that these processes are aided and abetted by the innate intelligence of man, which has been evolving for a long time, just as his physical structure has evolved. But the intelligence of the individual human being has been repressed by the process of species adaptation for the survival of man as a group, the need for human beings to struggle at a social level for survival. Perhaps the new awarenesses about the capacities of mind augur a new stage of evolution, a stage in which individual innate abilities are emerging to evolve a harmonious state of understanding among all human beings.

Insights into the nature of the universe—those insights and our appreciations we call ineffable, beyond description—can, interestingly enough, leave quite different imprints on an individual's psyche and this too may be a part of the evolutionary process of the psyche. For the most part, we hear only of the heavenly or divine or universal appreciations that dispose man toward saintly paths. But there can be consequences dangerous to the individual as well. Gopi Krishna,

for example, in his book on the kundalini[4] describes his sudden realization of samadhi and the fullness of the kundalini energy within the
highest chakra. Even after seventeen years of preparation through
disciplined meditation, the revelations he experienced at that moment were so pervasive of being and mind and spirit that he suffered
several years of schizophrenia-like behavior and sensations before his
mind-body-spirit became aligned with his enlightenment.

I have questioned many yoga masters about the incidence and
degree of emotional problems among student practitioners of various kinds of yogic meditation, and have been regularly informed that
such untoward reactions are frequent. The same is known to occur
in Christian and Buddhist religious communities.

It is tempting for religionists to interpret such emotional disasters
along the way to understanding the true nature of the spirit as resulting from a lack of proper preparation or lack of truly spiritual motivations. Psychologists also speculate on motivations, but they tend to
emphasize more the conflict between material desires and ways of
life and the spiritual ideal. And it is true that the intense anxiety that
can often occur after moments of mystical experience for some people does suggest a deep conflict between desire for a nonmaterial and
unknown spiritual reality and fear of the loss of the known material
reality.

I favor the latter hypothesis because of a dramatic incident that
occurred in my research laboratory. A prominent visiting internist,
also involved in psychiatry, asked me if he could experience alpha
brain wave biofeedback. (This was in the early days of biofeedback,
when I had the most sophisticated laboratory conducting alpha brain
wave research.)

As the session was proceeding, I suddenly noticed the appearance
of giant alpha brain waves in the EEG recording I was, by habit,
monitoring. I quickly checked the equipment for any faulty operation, and after some ten to fifteen seconds I realized with considerable fear that the giant waves were indeed from the physician's own
brain. He had not given me any signal through either of two inter-
communicating systems, and I dashed madly down the hall into the
isolation room where he was. He was in a frozen attitude, and as I

---

4. *Kundalini: The Evolutionary Energy in Man* (Berkeley, Calif.: Shambala Publications, 1970).

shook him he gasped violently, then gave an enormous sigh as his posture began to relax.

Later he explained that while concentrating his attention on the biofeedback signals of his own alpha activity, he had suddenly lost all sensation of his physical being. His mind or consciousness seemed filled with a "nothing." He had no body sensation with which he could identify his physical self. The state terrified him. He became powerless to move, and could not even press his fingers on the switch beneath them or speak into the microphone by his head to signal us in the recording rooms. He thanked me profusely for saving him.

Still later I learned that he had been a serious student of Buddhist meditation but had given it up after six years of practice because he could never achieve any sign of a mystical state.

I can only surmise that his meditation practice habits returned during the alpha biofeedback experience, and that his single-focus attention to a signal of mind state let his consciousness slip past the barrier that had for so long resisted his spiritual search. Perhaps, also, the greater weight of his unconscious mind during his meditation practice was occupied by the meanings of his material universe and material security, the attachments to material things he needed to maintain a sense of well-being. Whatever unconscious struggle occurred, the victor was fear, fear perhaps of loss of identity, fear of the unknown, fear of losing what his being believed to be life itself. This experience, incidentally, was not unique. Two of my colleagues in biofeedback have reported similar ones, and they are, in a way, similar also to certain LSD experiences where the fear of losing touch with the customary reality sometimes touches off irreversibly distorted perceptions.

There seems to be a common theme in mystical states and depersonalization in that both have the potential to be either unsurpassedly enlightening or to cause mental turmoil. The difference in consequences would seem to be caused by the ability of the unconscious-conscious interactions to accept loss of identity and socially accepted values; this in turn suggests considerable differences in the ways in which conscious perceptions structure unconscious mechanisms and affect their operation. The same effect may be the reason for the differences between hypnotizable and nonhypnotizable people. What this does seem to tell us is that the unconscious mechanisms for reordering information about the universe do exist within the human psyche, and that spiritual or meditative exercises are a way of relieving the weight of a social, consensual consciousness dependent upon agreeing about what is safe or not safe for survival of the human species. The increasing incidence of mystical states may, after all, be evidence of the evolution of a new "creative flash," a new system of life in which understanding replaces competition and possessiveness as the reward and purpose of life.

Imagery, Imagination, and Mental Images

Imagination is by far the most neglected and underdeveloped of the normal abilities of the human mind. The ability of mind to create and re-create mental pictures of things and events not present (which we call imagination and the professionals call imagery), is little understood as a mind resource. Psychotherapists use imagery to dig for psychologic problems and to conjure up better ways of coping with and understanding life, but most people rarely, and scientists virtually never, consider the creative potential of imagination for improving the condition of man. Certainly they rarely try to understand the process of imagining and how to cultivate it to make it more productive or more efficient. More often than not, imagination is seen as the tool of fancy or illusion and only regretfully admitted to be of occasional use. Yet imagination is the forgotten and rusting key to many treasures of the mind. Imagination is the marvelous uniquely human ability of mind to create and re-create life's experiences and life's thoughts and hopes and dreams in infinite variations both pragmatic and chimeric. Imagination can re-create the past with the highest fidelity or transmute it to fit the whims of emotion. It can project its fabrications into any future it chooses. Images are used to solve problems or to gain relief from mind pressures by fantasy, or just to amuse one's self.

Imagery may not generally be considered to be an altered state of consciousness, but perhaps it should be. There are times when imagery clearly represents an altered state, as in dreams, drug states, psychoses, or hypnosis. But there is also the imagery of daydreaming and worry and active imagination, when images intrude upon conscious awareness. The line between imagery directed by conscious intention and imagery arising uncalled for from unconscious activity is uncertain at best. When we engage in imagery and try to construct images intentionally, more often than not the images from the unconscious crowd out the ones we intended. For the most part imagery is the handiwork of the unconscious.

Far more important than its talents for work or play is the power of imagination to determine human behavior. It is called upon to interpret sensations, to analyze experience, and the images of desire hover over thoughts and behavior irresistibly, beckoning toward fulfillment. Images, moreover, don't merely guide behavior, they exert a very real action on the physiology of the body. Any kind of mental image—visual, auditory, tactile, muscular, emotional or intellectual—all determine the physiologic activity of both body and brain.

Imagination is recalling from memory bits of information obtained from all kinds of experience, then shaping them into some kind of meaningful train of thought or reverie. There are as many ways to imagine things as there are ways to perceive things. So little is known about imagination and how it is accomplished in the brain and where it comes from that the general public is, by and large, totally unaware that there are great varieties of imaginative processes.

Imagination—the making of mental images—is nearly always assumed to be a process of conjuring up *visual* images. "Picture that in your mind's eye," or "Can't you just visualize him doing that?" are phrases we learn in childhood. Our early learning is saturated with the teacher's urging us to "Close your eyes. Now, do you have a good picture of that?" A large part of intelligence testing is based on the assumption that everyone can visualize, that they can imagine by using visual images. Yet the real fact is that perhaps only 25 percent of human beings are capable of making reasonably good visual images.

For many people mental images are not visual, but are dominated by memories of sounds, or of touch, body feelings, muscle activity, emotion, or even abstract concepts. Relatively few people have "pure" images, confined to one sense or one emotion. People who have intense, real-as-life, vivid visual images are relatively rare, perhaps less than 10 percent of the population, and just as few possess the ability to make intense, vivid auditory images. Most of us create and re-create images that reflect the way we see, hear, feel and think about experience, with sensations of "seeing" or "hearing" mixed in with sensations or feeling and emotion.

Two remarkable effects of imagery, scientifically validated but woefully underexploited for their powerful effects on human minds and bodies are (1) that the more specific the image, the more specific the effect, i.e., the image excites exactly those physical mechanisms of the body to produce reaction to the image; and (2) the effect of the mental image is to cause *an expenditure of physical energy.*

The imagination makes the body work. Imagine lifting a heavy weight; you can feel the muscles tense. The body is working, it is expending real physical energy. Mental images direct and activate the nerves to make the body work, and work in exactly the way the imagination dictates.

The athlete who concentrates, projecting performance in mental images, uses imagination for something even more remarkable and subtle. He is not just projecting and imagining, he is *preparing* the nerves, the muscles, the heart, and the mind to unify their physical action toward a single-minded, determined objective.

The mind focuses and the nerves respond. Some mechanism somewhere in the profound complexity of dynamic, moving thought pushes aside all interfering and distracting mind and body activities, and this too reflects the power of mind to select its own physical implements for action. The nerves are fed by the electrical impulses from the brain, yet the brain is also the handmaiden of the mind.

The best-known trick of imagination is the unpleasantness of neurosis. The mind and emotions are tricked by imagination into believing the self has insoluble problems. Disturbing images can become so global as to occupy or freeze the logic of the mind. The critical role imagination plays in neurosis and other stress-related disorders is described in chapter 6. Here we need only the reminder of the lemon to understand how mental images can make the body miserable, if the images are miserable. A fleeting mini-neurosis might be the numbing fear of failure in one's first public talk, or the breathless agony of waiting to be asked to the prom. Uncertainty begets anxiety and anxiety begets a rapid pulse, spastic breathing, dry mouth, sluggish gut, and muscles so tense they become tender. Full-blown neuroses are runaway imagination, an imagination so detached from reality that consciousness can no longer make the connection between the worry and the images that the worry has excited.

Images can be exuberant and stimulating, healthful and therapeutic. Just today I read a report on using sexual fantasy exercises by senior citizen groups who had been misled into believing they had seen the end of their sexual lives. If your sexual partner of thirty years is no longer the ravishing beauty or macho strong man of yore, then use the imagination. Re-create the excitement, the physical delights in the mind. A well-oiled imagination is what made the excitement happen in the first place. If you don't think so, try it without images and the feelings those images excite.

Sexual fantasies are the old reliable of psychotherapists and psychiatrists. Nearly everyone has them. But the role of the imagination in sex is far broader than psychology has realized. First experiences are often built up from images built up from hearsay or suspicion; subsequent experiences are generated from memories, fantasies, need for testing, and other emotional-mental triggers. Whatever qualities the experiences give, they are incorporated into new fantasies. And while we know little about all of the mind activities that are not communicated, and lie unexpressed in the subconscious, we do know that the emotions, thoughts, feelings, and actual physical sexual activity become tied together in great complexes. What is not recognized in plain language is that a great share of the *sex drive is in the imagination.* It is a clear example of a feedback system. The drive for sex comes from the images of excitement and pleasure projected by the mind, and the images are fed and strengthened by the sensations produced by the sexual activity. It is the mind that gets it all going.

Images, unformed or repressed or magnified by conscious awareness, are the driving energy of all normal appetites and behavior, but they are, as well, the culprits when human appetites and behavior become disturbed. (The central importance of images in all varieties of reactions to the stresses of life is covered in chapter 6.) It is images that churn the emotions, images that make the body feel and express turmoil, images that set attitudes and behavior. Images are the germ substance of supermind.

The bottom line is that mind controls its creator brain and the product of the brain's activities we call mind, directing them to make decisions, to create images, to conceive desires. These intangibles of mind initiate the flow of nerve impulses and direct their passage throughout the nervous system, including the complex neural networks of the brain itself, with extraordinary precision.

This is supermind at work, a superior mind unrecognized and unrealized.

CHAPTER 12

The Intellect
of the Unconscious

New Insights

In the past the greatest obstacle to discovering the fundamental nature of mind has been the technical inability to measure either the operations or products of private mental activity that are self-generating and self-determining. This obstacle no longer exists; the discovery that human beings can learn to use mental activities to control their own internal physical processes gives us, at last, an accurate and reliable scientific way to explore the unconscious mind.

The discovery of the biofeedback phenomenon has revealed the universal, innate ability of the unconscious mind to control and regulate all physical processes of the body.[1] Not all scientists may yet agree with this conclusion, but it is a conclusion based on fact and scientific logic, and a conclusion that won't go away. A few research-er-theorists believe the biofeedback phenomenon can be explained by older theories of conditioning or physiologic habituation, but most biofeedback researchers are convinced that biofeedback learning depends upon complex mental activity. Some scientists not well acquainted with biofeedback research have not yet taken the time (and courage) to face the unalterable fact that human beings can be given a bit of biological information about themselves and quickly learn

---

1. Described in another context in chapter 5.

how to use it to control a physical body function. No other learning is like the learning in biofeedback; there is no "teaching," but there is learning; there is no example to follow, yet there is learning; there are no specific rewards or punishments, yet there is learning. Biofeedback learning is accomplished by taking nothing other than a symbol and using it to control, with the finest possible discrimination, the activity of physiologic systems or individual cells.

That the elegant intellect of the unconscious mind is the prime agent of biofeedback learning is easily illustrated. I will describe two quite different kinds of learning to control obscure body functions, then will review the learning steps in each example to focus on the remarkable abilities of the unconscious and the nature of the unconscious process. Both examples are amply documented in the scientific literature.

The first example is the now rather common use of biofeedback in the treatment of Raynaud's syndrome, an ailment in which there is vasoconstriction of the blood vessels of the hand, apparently due to overactivity of the sympathetic nervous system and markedly aggravated during stress situations. The patient's hands become cold, blue and very painful. The biofeedback treatment uses a device that feeds back to the patient information either about his hand temperature or about blood flow or about the size of the diameter of the blood vessels of the hand. It doesn't seem to matter as long as there is some indicator of the amount of circulation in the hand.

The patient is given this information almost continuously during the training sessions and is also given some background information about his condition, what caused it, what the instrument does, and how to use it. He is also given clues about how to use his mind and state of consciousness to bring about a change in hand temperature, strategies such as imagery, self-suggestion, or relaxation techniques. After a few sessions of this kind of self-training, the patient learns to regulate the temperature of his hands (and with continued practice learns to control his vascular problem). When the patient is asked how he actually controls his hand temperature, he can't describe how he does it except sometimes to say that he simply puts himself into another state of mind.

This is a clear demonstration of active, intentional unconscious learning. The first provocative fact is that the information used in learning is symbolic, abstract information requiring intelligent interpretation. That is, the information about the temperature of the hand is not any sensation of warmth or coolness detected by the senses, but is instead a man-made measurement symbol of temperature (or blood flow, or blood vessel size).

The information displayed by the instrument must be detected by the visual and auditory senses, interpreted and appreciated by the interpretive cortex, and then related to sensations of warmth or coolness. The involvement of the mind's interpretive faculties is clear because the visual or auditory senses do not directly communicate with the brain areas normally giving rise to sensations of warmth.

The other information the patient has (instructions, background information, and clues about how to use the mind) are all conceptual kinds of information, also requiring interpretation and understanding. Both kinds of information, the biological and the conceptual, must be translated into exactly those kinds of neural activity that can be associated with the mind-brain mechanisms able to appreciate the meaning of the information and make a choice about what to do about it. The entire process is carried out by the unconscious, with the unconscious mind directing the body to perform exactly the task the patient intends to perform, raising hand temperature.

Much the same process occurs in nearly all biofeedback learning to control internal functions.

Learning to Control a Single Cell

The most spectacular display of the mind's ability to perform complicated tasks without conscious awareness is illustrated when human beings learn how to activate and suppress the activity of individual motoneurons (nerve cells sending their fibers to muscle fibers) in the spinal cord that control the activity of muscle cells. In some muscle-rehabilitation clinics this learning to control muscle-cell activity is now an everyday phenomenon, and it is a feat of mind that can be demonstrated in any suitably equipped laboratory.

With simple electrical sensors placed on the skin over a muscle, the electrical activity muscle cells develop when active can easily be detected, amplified, and displayed on an oscilloscope screen (much like a TV screen). It is possible to display on the screen the activity of many different muscle fibers (cells). Muscle fibers act in groups, called motor units, because all cells of the group receive their nerve supply from the same terminal fibril of a strand of motor nerve. Each group may contain as few as three or as many as three hundred muscle fibers, and so when a motor unit becomes active ("fires"), the electrical change produced is specific for that unit. The number of fibers in a motor unit determines the amount and duration of electrical activity when they become active, and so the electrical representation on the oscilloscope screen is of different shape and size for each motor unit. That is, each motor unit writes its own electrical signature, and even though the motor potentials (electrical activity of each unit) fly across the screen rapidly, the activity of each motor unit can be easily identified by its shape and size. The special feature of motor units that makes them so perfectly suited to the study of unconscious mechanisms is the unique circumstance that the nerve supply of each unit can be traced to a single nerve cell (mononeuron) in the spinal cord.

The oscilloscope provides visual feedback information about motor unit activity; the same electrical muscle activity can also be used to activate an audio signal, such as a click sound. Because the motor potentials are of different shapes and sizes and occur at irregular intervals, the "sound" of the muscle activity in different motor units is heard as different volumes and rhythms.

When the average individual is given such visual or auditory information about the activity of a few muscle cells, and is requested to select one or another motor unit and control it, the individual not only learns to control the muscle firings, but learns very rapidly.[2] The feat is all the more astounding when one realizes that each muscle electrical potential represents the action of a single motoneuron in the spinal cord, i.e., the activity of each motor unit is controlled by the activity of a single motoneuron in the spinal cord.

Learning to control the motor units of the muscle can come about in two ways. For therapeutic purposes or in research, the individual is usually requested to select one or another motor unit, identified by shape and size on the oscilloscope screen and by the accompanying audio signal, and learn to control its appearance on the screen "by

2. Children as young as five and mental retardates are equally capable of this learning to control internal biological activities (which is one reason why I believe it to be an innate property of the mind-brain complex).

some mental means." Usually this is all the information or instruction the person receives, yet within a matter of minutes, he (or she) learns to control the selected motor unit. Quite ordinary people can, moreover, learn to control a dozen or more motor units, either individually or in groups. It is also quite easy to learn how to control many different motor units in specific series or rhythms.

Astounding as it is that an individual can accomplish this so quickly upon request, even more astounding is the situation in which an individual learns to control the cells without having any information at all about what is on the oscilloscope screen. This was, in fact, the situation in which this kind of biofeedback learning was discovered, and an experiment I and others have repeated in the laboratory. When sensors are applied to their muscle and the oscilloscope showing the muscle's activity is facing them, and with no instructions or clues whatsoever, many people become curious enough to begin playing mind games to see whether they can influence the activity on the screen; they, too, learn quickly how to pick out a special motor unit and control its activity.

The sophistication of the learned control of motoneurons in the spinal cord cannot be fully appreciated until the anatomy and physiology of these nerve-muscle cells are understood. In the spinal cord there are large groups of such cells clustered together according to the muscles and specific areas of muscles they innervate. In order to produce the smooth, coordinated muscle contractions of normal movements, each cell must fire a tiny bit asynchronously from all other cells it is related to, firing, say, two microseconds "out-of-step." Otherwise, if all cells fired at the same time, the muscle would be a trembling mass. In order that a single cell may be selected out to become active, as in the learning situation, all of the other cells that are functionally related, i.e., that work together to produce coordinated movements, must be suppressed in their activity. So when a single cell is being voluntarily controlled, that one cell is being activated selectively, while at the same time the activity of all related cells is being suppressed.

To me this is a striking example of an otherwise inexpressible intelligence, an awareness, a biological intelligence that is expressed only by changing one's own cellular physiological activity.

A Summary of General Observations

The prowess of the mind to move electrochemical underpinnings of the body with such precision is almost beyond our ability to comprehend. Here is a situation in which there are no elaborate learning aids, no prior experience by anyone; instead, ordinary human beings seize upon the signs of bits of muscle activity displayed upon the oscilloscope screen and the clicks sounding out the cellular activity, and use these visual and auditory symbols to identify and manipulate a cell or two so small that they have never been appreciated by the mind that is now controlling them.

In this remarkable display of learning ability, there are only two observable features of the entire learning process, and only one is necessary to trigger the learning activity: the information about the cell activity. The other observable feature is the result of the learning: the intentional control of the muscle cells. Certainly between the simple perception of the audio-visual clues about the cell activity and the resulting control of the muscle cells there are mental processes of bewilderingly intricate complexity that are not only skillfully directed by the mind itself, but directed without any conscious awareness of how this is accomplished.

Despite the seeming simplicity of this learning phenomenon, where only a sensor to detect muscle cell activity and an oscilloscope are used, it provides more material for identifying covert mental activity than has ever been available before. The analysis is not difficult, but before I describe some of the universal qualities of the unconscious mind we can deduce from biofeedback learning, a brief summary of some of the more obvious implications will help set the focus for the later discussion.

Because the elements needed for learning and the learned performance can be identified so exactly in motor unit learning, we can deduce a great deal about a number of different operations of mind. In the learning situations I described, for example, we can assume that the control developed over the cell was intentional. In some way the unconscious mind established goals to accomplish a specific task (controlling a very specific physiologic activity), and there was as well some projection of what the results of trying to learn the task might be. That is, something in the mind perceived elements in the situa-

tion (the electrical activity on the screen along with either instructions or certain associations made from exploring the situation out of
curiosity), grasped an idea, unconsciously, of what *could* happen,
discovered what it needed to do to accomplish its objective, made a
decision about what to do, and then performed the necessary operations of brain to carry out the intention to control the specific neurophysiologic manipulations needed to achieve the goal. And because
the learner has no conscious awareness of the learning, the process
is one of unconsciously directing all mental operations and all physiological operations to carry out the intentions of the conscious mind.

To summarize the high points of the self-learning process:

There are first, a number of *concepts* presented to the mind. One
concept is contained in the electrical signals representing the activity of a single cell on the oscilloscope screen. The information on the
screen is actually a symbol, a representation of the biological activity
of one cell and the muscle cells it innervates as it becomes active over
time. It is an abstraction of what is happening both in time and the
spaces in the central nervous system, an abstract, spatiotemporal
symbol of biological activity. There are also the concepts presented
to the mind in the form of instructions (or what curiosity found), some
explicit, some implicit, and there are also concepts in the form of
surrounding attitudes, and in the set and setting of the experiment.
All of these concepts are absorbed and dissected into myriad bits of
information and implications for the mind to consider and act upon.

Then, since there is nothing except the internal self between this
array of concepts and the final result of manipulating single cells, we
have to assume that the mind-brain uses all the information—the
idea, the symbols, the decision, the ambience—to accomplish a
predetermined goal, the goal of learning and performing a specific
physical activity. The mind-brain has to project what the result
should be, so the goal itself must be predefined.

This is a very complex operation of mind, turning intention into
action. The mind uses information to produce, effectively and efficiently, an *ordered* alteration of biological activity. The cells, the
chemistry, the electrical traffic of the central nervous system are all
directed to proceed orderly and efficiently to accomplish a predetermined objective that is still in the mind's eye. The result of this action
is control, a voluntary control that changes physiologic activity in
such a way that the changes are compatible not only with what the

instructions call for, but also with the maximal precision the biological system is capable of—the finest possible discrimination of biological activity—changing the activity of a single cell. Voluntariness is suprabiological.

The Unconscious Intellect: The Information It Uses

To appreciate the extraordinary powers of mind used during learning to control body processes, one has only to consider the scanty and vague information the mind has to work with. The information is of two types, and both are unfamiliar.

The visual and/or auditory information *about* the electrical activity of the motor units, which in turn is information about the activity of the spinal motoneurons, is an abstraction of cell activity, an electrical representation that must be decoded and interpreted. The representation of the electrical potential seen on the oscilloscope or heard as an auditory signal, to repeat, really represents events occurring in time and the spaces of the brain. And it is important to remember that the mind has never had a prior sense impression of its own muscle cell activity. It is information relayed to the learner only by wires and authority.

The second kind of information the individual has to work with to learn to control the motor-nerve cells is the instructions he perceives cognitively. The instructions may be a command to control the cells, or a suggestion. Either way the explicit information is minimal and gives no information about *how* to learn the control despite the fact that this is a completely new experience for the individual. In other words, the learning aids given to the individual are minimal. There is, however, a good bit of implicit information contained in the command or in the instructions to learn to control the cells. Implicit in the instructions, for example, is that the task is possible to perform, that it can be learned in a reasonable period of time, and that the learner has the capability to learn the task.

Learning occurs, as we noted, whether or not instructions to learn are given. In the presence of information about any phenomenon, human beings spontaneously extract and abstract relevant and related information (exploratory behavior), form concepts, explore various manipulations, and usually select some effective procedure to control the phenomenon. When the available information is about the self, although there may have been no prior experience, identification of the new information with existing self-image information appears to catalyze innate drives to achieve or impose order.

The need for intelligent action on either explicit or implicit instructions can be illustrated by the kind of instructions usually given in psychological experiments. In motor unit learning, for example, instructions are often a modest, "Those are visual and auditory symbols of your muscle-cell activity; select one or two and try to control them." Such instructions contain a statement about the situation and the goal, and require translation by intelligent mental capacities. What learning instructions do is give information that can be intelligently used to accomplish a desired goal. The instructions given to learn can never zero in on the essential processes of learning; they can only give background or provide clues or set a direction or confirm the learning.

One characteristic of biofeedback information that most people fail to appreciate is that it is substitute information. Remember that the feedback information about the muscle activity was visual and auditory—tracings of electrical activity flying across the oscilloscope screen and the accompanying auditory signals. But, normally, muscles are controlled largely by means of information fed to the brain from sensor cells located in the muscles, sensors that detect the tension in muscles. That is, under normal circumstances the body's automatic control-regulating physiologic systems use internally sensed (proprioceptive) information about physiologic functions directly to effect the control regulation. But in biofeedback learning, information about the physiologic function to be controlled is perceived through quite a different sensory route, i.e., visual or auditory; hence it is substitute information. This means that the brain mechanisms that implement any intended action can use any *form* of information so long as it provides reasonably accurate information about the function.

The facility for using "substitute" information in biofeedback experiments demonstrates that the mind can substitute different packets of sensory information for the innate, primary information packet, and suggests that the mind-brain may have many different kinds of packets of sensory information about our physiologic functions available and ready for use when appropriate or needed. The blind and deaf appear to substitute different packets of sensory information for the one they are lacking, and this allows them to compensate for their sensory losses and learn to heighten their remaining senses. We might consider such packets of sensory information as kinds of back-up systems that operate somewhat independently of the systems normally used to carry out physiologic functions. Under special circumstances any substitute packet of sensory information can be used to sense situations and provide information for making decisions in systems that don't normally use or need this "extra" information.[3]

Another enlightening observation is that the learner can learn many different variations of motor unit control. He can, for example, learn to activate different sequences of motor units, or he can learn to activate different units at different specific times, such as one per second. These performances mean that the learner not only controls the activation and suppression of motor units selectively, but also exactly when they are activated and suppressed, demonstrating the unconscious mental ability for a rapid *intentional* ordering of both the place and time of nerve-cell activity.

Clues to Unconscious Abilities from Observing the Performance

Each of the observations routinely made during learned motor unit performance has startling implications.

The first observation is, of course, that people learn easily and quickly, often within two to five minutes. This must mean that the incredibly complex mental operations needed to carry out the learning occur with extraordinary speed. Since the process that occurs between the intention to perform and the learned, voluntary performance itself is perfectly ordered, the implication is that the intention to learn and to perform in some way *anticipates* the order in which the neural events must occur so that the performance can match intention.

---

3. If we look at sensory information this way, it may help explain certain mind-brain problems, such as that of brain-damaged children, certain learning problems, or such inappropriate muscle responses as laughing when one really wants to cry. It is perhaps a perceptual dissonance, in which packets of sensory information get mixed up and affect systems they shouldn't.

Next, the fact that learning to control motor units and the single cells that innervate them, then performing the control voluntarily, at will, are carried out wholly by the unconscious mind has extensive implications for understanding the nature of mind. The fact that the ability to control body activities can be carried out by unconscious mental activities through conscious intention is easily confirmed using motor unit learning. I have previously described (in *New Mind, New Body*) Basmajian's experience with a TV interviewer who insisted upon trying to learn motor unit control while at the same time conducting an interview and being filmed for TV. Despite Basmajian's admonitions, the man insisted; happily, during the thirty minutes of interview that fully occupied his conscious awareness, he also learned to control his motor units!

Another intriguing observation is that when a faultless performance is maintained constantly, say for five minutes or more, extreme mental fatigue occurs, indicating an expenditure of energy. Since the work involved in activating a few muscle cells is infinitesimal compared to the energy used to move a whole muscle, the energy expenditure may represent the energy used in intense concentration. The fatigue is puzzling in view of the fact that the learner has no conscious awareness of working at the task; the learning is accomplished and performed without any conscious awareness, although as we noted earlier, the performance is precisely compatible with the instructions and with the maximal capabilities of the biological systems involved.

These observations demonstrate why the biofeedback phenomenon lends itself so readily to the study of unconscious mental mechanisms. The only information the learner has available to use is abstract, requires complex cerebral processing, is substitute information remote from any prior experience; yet the learner learns, and puts into unconscious memory the ability to change the electrochemical activity of cells so he can reproduce the performance at will.

All of this means that there is a remarkable amount of complex mental activity that is never appreciated in conscious awareness. Obviously, in order for one to learn, the information relevant to the task must be perceived, then sorted out in order to make the appropriate associations; there must also be mind-brain processes that evaluate both the representational information of the biofeedback signal and how the cognitively perceived information relates to it, and there must be processes that select the appropriate neural networks to implement the learning, and finally, processes that activate these networks with remarkable specificity. All of this is carried out "unconsciously." The miracle of the mind's activity is that *it learns how to intentionally control the flow of electrical impulses in any nerve it chooses.*

A Sense of Order as a Fundamental Property of Mind-Brain

One of the most striking features of the biofeedback phenomenon, particularly as exemplified in the learned control of nerve-muscle cells, is the consummate orderliness with which the learning is accomplished. With no more than the mechanical representation of the muscle cells' activity and an explicit or implicit command to control those cells, somehow mental mechanisms excute the instructions with remarkable precision and with remarkable rapidity. The result is an *ordered* alteration of physiologic activity. Through the brain's neural networks of trillions of nerve connections, exactly those nerve filaments and their chemistry and electrical behavior are selected and directed to proceed with incredible efficiency to accomplish an objective still in the "mind's eye."

The rapidity, the specificity, and the efficiency with which this learning occurs (sometimes within two minutes or less) imply the existence of a mechanism for ordering the most molecular of the body's physiologic activities toward a new objective conceived and defined by the mind-brain's intellectual functions. This ordering action, moreover, *takes precedence over the effects of all spontaneous or automatic activity,* and is a strong indication that the mind-brain possesses a separate function capable of evoking and putting into effect orders for physiologic activity to follow, orders specifically tailored by either the mind-brain's own resources or by another of the mind's self-governing faculties. Since the result of the ordering process is completely compatible with the intention to change the physiologic activity and even though consciously there is no knowledge of how to proceed, the result is the most precise and parsimonious use of the available physiologic mechanisms. One can now begin to think in terms of some highly developed innate qualities of the mind-brain complex, one of which could be called a sense of order.

A sense of order can be distinguished from other evolved senses that are subconsciously appreciated only. A sense of order is an awareness of the sequence of proceeding, and implies an ability to sense how things *will* fit as contrasted to a sense of continuity, or that things *do* fit, once fitted. It is also different from a sense of harmony, which is the sensation and awareness of the appropriateness of elements to a particular pattern. A sense of order implies *an innate ability to anticipate orderly sequences.*

A sense of order can also be inferred from the *disorder* that can be observed in conscious awareness under different circumstances. The curiously disordered logic of dreams and the disorder of perception and of subjective sensations under the influence of hallucinogens are well known. Both cases of disorder imply that when sensations and perceptions are undisturbed, they function in an orderly way.

In the dominant theories explaining faculties of mind, it is postulated that the sensations or awarenesses of being arise from or parallel the actual neural events of the brain. Exactly the same assumption could be applied to a sense of order, i.e., that since the neural processes are orderly, some awareness of orderliness can develop. But this does not explain how the ordering developed in the first place.

One can only guess that if animals and man evolve new senses, such as the sense of beingness or the sense of awareness of self, then perhaps the sense of order that seems to operate in motor unit learning is also an evolved sense. That is, the evolved, innate awareness of the natural order of all biological events within the self can evolve further through accumulation of experience. It seems likely that the original orderliness of the physiologic entity is established through the substances of genes and chromosomes, and that the physical, functional orderliness is appreciated by the organism in some way (see discussion of biological awareness, pp. 45–48). If this is so, then the innate sense of order could be modified through experience and learning. This would seem to be a logical development that would benefit the organism by shaping the ordering process for its optimal effectiveness and use in ensuring its survival and well-being.

One of the insights into the cosmic consciousness is the inexpressible knowledge of the unifying order of the universe. A sense of order would be the ability to sense, biologically and unconsciously, if not consciously, the order of the body's chemical the electrical events necessary to achieve an objective that is only vaguely known to consciousness. What implements the sense of order must be twofold: intention and direction, discussed in the following section.

The Will and the Will Executor

Another deduction that can be made about events in the unconscious mind during biofeedback learning is that intention, the will, appears to operate as an independent function of mind. Intention is the decision to take a certain action, which, of course, can be a decision to take no action at all. Another term is voluntary action. The usual definition or description of intention is that it is a decision to take action based not only upon consideration of the value of the goal (a specific objective), but also upon estimates of the relative effectiveness of possible alternative actions and a consideration of what the consequences of different actions will be. Too often psychologic theory dismisses the will as nothing more than motivation; however, motives are simply the urges or drives to take action, and they neither decide nor make a determination to take action.

To be sure, the decision to take action depends upon an appraisal of information that is relevant to some goal, but the decision itself does not necessarily supply the energy either to initiate action or to carry through with the decision, or, as a matter of fact, the decision *not* to take action. For intention can be either implemented or denied by mental action itself. Intention, moreover, can be either passive or active, i.e., the internal mental mechanisms can be "relaxed" to allow one or another sensation or awareness to emerge, or other mental processes can be excited for immediate action.

Intention anticipates goals, often when there has been no previous experience or direct knowledge about the goal. There are probably several distinct mental operations that comprise what we call the Will: the ability to project actions mentally before they are taken, the ability to compare alternative actions for relative effectiveness, and the ability to evaluate the merits of goals. That the will is an emergent function of mind capable of independent operation is demonstrated by the fact that it can be exerted on any body system, each differing remarkably from the others in chemical and cellular composition.

One of the most extraordinary capacities of the will is its ability to regulate its own underlying substance, the brain. When intention directs behavior, it is directing the activity of brain.

The will, however, does not implement (execute) commands, it simply gives them. To carry out commands of the will requires a separate mechanism to direct the events involved, i.e., in order for the will to act, another independently operating function of mind, a coordinating director or will executor, is required to turn volition into action. It is the mechanism of direction that selects the correct channels of neural networks to effect an appropriate action and produce a change in body function. For example, if I want to take a bite of sandwich while I'm working but am distracted at the moment of implementing my intention, I might end up with a pencil in my mouth. The intention was present but there was no direction for the voluntary action.

It is a very complex process, turning volition into action.

The Brownenberg Principle

In biofeedback, when people learn how to control a physiologic function, all they can tell you is that they know how. They can't tell you *how* they perform the control. As a matter of fact, the same situation occurs for everything we have ever learned. We cannot describe the internal learning process.

We cannot know or experience or have any conscious awareness of the nature of our own mental processes. That is, we cannot be aware of *how* we are thinking *when* we are thinking. Conscious awareness is the awareness of doing, not the awareness of how something is done.

In learning, all you know is that when you have certain bits of information and make some mental effort, you learn something. You have no idea of how you accomplished the learning, i.e., you have no awareness about *how* you are learning *when* you were learning.

In thinking about this puzzle, I developed a principle to explain it that is modeled after the Heisenberg principle in quantum mechanics.

The Heisenberg principle of indeterminacy states that if we know the momentum of a particle, we can't know its exact location in space, and if we know the energy of a particle, we can't know its exact location in time. For my own amusement, I've called the situation of the inability to objectify an awareness of how one performs voluntary control, i.e., performs a learned task, the Brownenberg principle.

The Brownenberg principle says: If you are busy processing information in your brain, you can't know you are processing the information because the information being processed is occupying the same neuronal space that is needed to become aware of what is being processed.

And of course, conversely, if you are aware of information that *has been* processed, you can't be processing new information at that moment of awareness because the mechanisms for awareness occupy the same neuronal space needed to process the new information.

But enough of amusing theories.

The Unconscious Mind—Master of Mind Functions

Learning to control a single cell is no doubt the supreme example of the ability of the unconscious mind to absorb information, interpret perceptions, make associations, evaluate meanings, decide the most parsimonious execution of its intentions, and finally to set a selected activity in motion.

Mind-brain science has scarcely touched this extraordinary universe of the unconscious mind. It has argued that it has no reliable, physically documentable index to reflect the more obscure events of the mind.

It can argue no more. We now have new techniques that open up innovative ways to study the unconscious. Motor unit learning can be used to demonstrate unconscious processes with unqualified precision. We can now, for example, measure the effects of subliminal perception much more directly than ever before, measure the influence of suppressed and unconscious motivations, measure how experiential memories color perceptions, measure how the "intelligent" mind is distorted by false information, and explore processes of mind that we were never really sure existed.[4]

We are just now entering a new era of understanding the mind

---

4. I have previously described (in *New Mind, New Body*) the ingenious experiments of Dr. David Kahn, who combined learned motor unit control to operate subliminally presented ambiguous or conflict material. Although remarkably promising as a technique, the work was terminated before final completion. The enormous complexity of the procedure apparently has deterred others from similar research.

because we have new techniques to isolate and characterize the component activities and potency of mind in a way that can satisfy the criteria of science. We can now document in quantitative physical terms the effects of mental activity on the physical functions of the body. We can now study more systematically than ever before the mysterious events that lie below the level of conscious awareness, such phenomena as subliminal perception, hypnosis, the mechanisms of awareness and insights, and a hundred other phenomena of mind that have puzzled man since his beginning. The mind-brain barrier can now be broken.

Appendix A

The prevailing theories about stress aren't much help in trying to understand what we mean when we say something is stressful. Biomedical, psychological and even biochemical theories talk around stress, some theories being concerned with the origins of emotional reactions to stress, not the nature of the stress, while other theories concern themselves with what physiologic changes occur in the body under stress, rather than with what stress itself is.

Psychodynamic theory, for example, proposes that stress reactions arise from certain kinds of psychosocial circumstances that cause unconscious conflicts and these in turn produce unconscious defenses against the agony of the conflicts. The theory fails to extract the essential qualities of psychosocial circumstances that make them stressful, and worse, the theory ignores the critical point of how unconscious machinations can shift the molecules and chemicals of the body's physiology to cause such problems as asthma or ulcers.

Cognitive theory postulates cognitive "intermediaries" between stressful events and the body's reactions to stress, which is about as informative as saying there is a combustion device between the gas pump and the car's accelerator. Cognitive theory is ironically ambiguous because cognition actually means *all* ways of knowing, from imagining to judging moral values. But somehow cognitive theorists haven't gotten around to spelling out *what* cognitive activities are involved in stress reactions or how thinking can transform mental events into physical changes.

From psychophysiologic research comes the "arousal" theory, which assumes that "stress" stimulates (arouses) the physiologic systems causing the physical signs and symptoms of stress disorders. The theory conveniently fails to suggest how "stress" performs this feat.

And finally, there is Selye's stress theory, contained in the description of his General Adaption Syndrome (GAS), which describes the physiological, biochemical, and immune system reactions to *physical* stress, such as chemical or bacteria, but not to psychological or social "stress."

Appendix B

If it is the mind that manufactures "stress," the next question is, How does the single entity of stress become transformed into the many *different* kinds of stress reactions listed in table 1?

As I mused over this question it became clear that the different ways stress is expressed in different people must depend upon their private mental reservoirs of experience, learning, culture, memories and personality and behavioral traits all stored in their intellectual memory systems. The principle behind turning one cause, "stress," into many different kinds of emotional and physical disorders reminded me of Selye's original observations about physical stress.

Quite possibly, one of the most significant intuitions about modern man came when Dr. Selye, as a young medical student, puzzled over the parade of patients used to illustrate the diversity of illness. While every patient suffered a different disorder, there was some look, some quality that they all seemed to share in common. As Selye mused, his observations crystallized into a conclusion so fundamental as to strain the limits of scientific sophistication. All the patients, regardless of the nature of their illness, shared signs of a syndrome he called "just being sick."

It may not sound like much of an observation, recognizing that sick people look sick, but what Selye saw was that people were not sick in *different* ways; they were all sick in the same way. One look at them and you could see they were sick. There must be, he reasoned, some process in the body that responded to *any* assault or invasion of the body always in the same way; the signs of "being sick" were the same no matter how the sickness was caused. From this unpretentious, unadorned observation came Selye's concept of stress.

For what Selye found was that varieties of physical stress are converted into varieties of specific physical reactions by physiological mechanisms that produce also a stereotypical response we recognize as "being sick." This is not an easy concept to grasp, simple though it is. What Selye showed was that no matter what the physical stress is (heat, cold, injury, infection), in addition to the specific reaction (vascular change, tissue swelling, migration of white blood cells), there are also changes in the body that are nonspecific, i.e., that are the same for any physical stress. It is the nonspecific biochemical changes of the body that express the total involvement of the body as "being sick."

I do not mean to put myself in Selye's class, but he did break the ground for looking beyond the complex to the simple, and it is with his example before me that I have been persuaded that what I call the "worry syndrome" involves common processes of mind that convert varieties of social stress into varieties of stress illnesses.

The "worry syndrome" may involve much the same kind of general principle as does the "just being sick" syndrome. There are hundreds of specific social problems, each of which can cause an emotional or physical illness, but no specific social problem causes a *specific* emotional or physical illness. It seems reasonable to assume that certain personal actions are required to transform a specific social problem into a particular reaction of the many that could be produced. One person converts the stress of a work situation into ulcers, while another converts it into a neurosis, while still another converts it into high blood pressure. The processes that transform psychosocial influences into neural or visceral or muscle distress are the intellectual processes of problem-solving (worry) deprived of the information they need to function normally.

The mechanisms that operate in the "worry syndrome" differ from those that operate in the "just being sick" syndrome. The latter are physiological mechanisms, while the "worry syndrome" involves mental mechanisms. But the principle would seem to be the same.

Appendix C

The role of information for the person under stress is paramount to his relief. Most people are denied the information most critical to their relief by the established policies of medicine and psychology that usurp the capacity for human understanding of one's own thoughts and feelings and body by adopting the role of sole protector and healer of the society of man. For far too long the prevailing attitude of the health sciences has been that the patient or the person counseled should receive only that information about his condition that the specialist diagnosing his problem believes he should have. This peculiar attitude comes from the misguided notion that only the specialist can appreciate the meanings of man's difficulties and only he then can prescribe the remedies. Usually this attitude is ascribed by the specialists to their concern that the unknowledgeable patient, without the "right" information, may bring harm to himself by inappropriate health practices. In truth, it is only in recent times that the patient has been given half a chance to help himself find relief from his emotional and physical difficulties.

The scheme I have outlined to explain how stress and stress reactions develop is essentially one of intellectual activity gone astray, and gone astray only because the intellect lacks information to solve the problems it perceives. The intellect keeps trying. The first step in the process is the worry that comes from recognizing a disparity between expectations an perceptions of one's social activities. If the problems cannot be solved reasonably or if psychological defenses against disappointments and conflicts cannot be adequately developed, worry proceeds to rumination. With inadequate information rumination becomes circular and results in perceptual distortion and perceptual obstruction, ending in stress disorders.

As with any theory, if the scheme I have proposed is a valid account of how emotional and physical disorders can develop through a series of normal intellectual activities to intellectual malfunction, then the concept should point directly to the means to repair and prevent the disorders.

In the scheme, unproductive intellectual function first arises when the interpretive mind defines a problem in social relationships or in the social dynamics. Assuming fairly normal expectations and perceptions, the perceived problem represents mental distress because the conflict between expectations and perceptions is not understood, rationalized, defended against or explained away with reasonably convincing logic.

The entire burden is on the interpretive mind. It must analyze, evaluate, and judge what it perceives for special meanings to the individual, and then, when it perceives, the interpretive mind must attempt to understand why there is a difference, or how to live with the difference or how to minimize its impact on the psyche. To perform these complicated functions the mind requires appropriate, relevant, meaningful information, and when the information necessary to resolve the conflict or to understand it is lacking, the mind, impelled to conjecture and imagery, searches for answers with the information it has. The only reason for unproductive problem solving—and stress—is lack of information.

The stress process starts and worsens because people really perceive only the tips of the icebergs of their social situations, i.e., they build mental pictures with inadequate information, they misinterpret, they ruminate, and they are, literally, tied up in knots inside without being consciously aware of it. But mainly people become sick because they do not have accurate information about their social situations and how their bodies are reacting. Without these kinds of information they cannot devise coping mechanisms. So the answer should lie in giving them information.

Appendix D

Stress Reduction with Awareness Techniques

Any technique that gives an individual information about body states can effectively reverse (or prevent) stress reactions, emotional or physical. The internal mechanisms that make this possible are some of the most interesting of the mind-body's abilities.

There are many new techniques that teach how to become aware of the many different aspects of the psychobiologic self. The psychological techniques are well known, from the Esalen techniques, touching, holding, group encounters, to EST or assertiveness training. These concentrate on feelings about the self and other people, about the social reality, and having that information makes it much easier to develop coping mechanisms.

Still newer interests focus on awarenesses of internal states, including awareness of what the mind does and awareness of states of consciousness. I happen to separate the new techniques into three main categories: body or muscle awareness, visceral awareness, and cerebral or consciousness awareness. The reason for using these categories is because many people, including many thereapists, believe they are interchangeable and they are all able to produce the same results: stress reduction, relief from stress.

They don't all do the same things.

Progressive Relaxation, known popularly as tense-relax exercises, deals exclusively with the muscles of the body, and while the relaxation it can produce after years of practice can have an effect on the viscera, the effect is a secondary one, and it takes quite a long time to generalize the relaxation training from muscles to viscera.

It is, however, true that many, possibly most, stress problems are accompanied by muscle tension, but muscle tension is pronounced and is the

271

principal physiologic change mainly in anxiety states and in stress problems accompanied by marked anxiety. The troublesome problem of muscle tension in stress reactions is that it is generally *unfelt* muscle tension. The tensions are not generally felt as sensations for many reasons: because the muscle masses of the body are so great, because the tension is not the kind of tension generated to begin moving muscles, because the tensions can be spread throughout many muscles, and because physiologic structures like muscles tend to adapt to altered states after a time. The tensions of stress are usually felt *after* the stress, when the attention can begin to turn again to the body state.

The objective of the many body awareness techniques, especially progressive relaxation, muscle biofeedback, yoga exercises, and structural integration is to increase the awareness of the level of tension in the muscles that is not usually felt. When body awareness techniques are used in the treatment of stress-related disorders, the attention becomes focused on the body rather than on the stress. As attention is maintained and various strategies such as imagery or relaxation exercises are used to increase awareness of tension, both unconscious and conscious awareness begin to recognize the tension, and with continued practice lower and lower levels of tension can be detected. The strategies are aimed at the patient's becoming aware, consciously or subconsciously, of different levels of body tension. With practice, the individual first develops a subconscious awareness of tension which displaces enough of the cortical preoccupation with the "stress" to allow some activity of the muscle-tension governor to return and the automatic regulation of function begins to be restored. The effect of this is relaxation. With continued practice, awareness of lower and lower levels of tension can be detected and thus more and more relaxation results.

Just why physical relaxation of tensions invariably causes a relaxation of mental tensions is not known, but one can speculate that as physical tension diminishes and the attention is directed more toward internal activities, there is concomitantly less attention on the social sources of stress and the cortical circuitry becomes more accessible to other types of intellectual information and activity. Many years ago Edmund Jacobson postulated that anxiety (the reaction to stress) and relaxation are mutually incompatible. Exactly why this is so can only be speculated, but it appears that one factor is that body tensions create a subjective sensation of tension, and if body tensions are absent, as during relaxation, then there is no sensation of tension. It would also follow that if one does not feel tense, there would then be a consequent improvement in all intellectual functions.

The advantage of muscle biofeedback over other body awareness techniques is the accuracy and directness with which muscle-tension levels are detected. When the muscle (EMG) biofeedback instrument is used, it detects actual muscle activity and measures tension levels down to zero. This means that the person learning to become aware of muscle tension has a precise detector and measuring instrument to help him. He can watch numbers on a counter or hear tones or watch lights that signal tension levels and learn to associate these signals with the internal sensations, and over time can learn to detect and then sustain, voluntarily, the low tension levels of the relaxation state.

On the other hand, biofeedback of muscle tensions is limited to working with one, at most two, muscles at a time. The other body awareness techniques may sacrifice specificity and sensitivity for detecting tension but they in turn have the advantage of directing the attention to nearly all the muscles of the body and, an important plus, some techniques use large groups of muscles or whole-body muscle activity to give an awareness of sensations of whole-body, integrated tension and relaxation.

Awareness of internal states of the viscera is much more difficult to achieve. The internal organs and systems are not only encased deep within the body and muscles, but their nerves to the brain connect mainly with rather primitive, lower brain control centers; the neural information, after these connections, about viscera activities is both sparse and communicated diffusely to higher brain areas that detect internal activities. Reducing the tensions of the viscera, for example, lowering blood pressure, decreasing heart rate, regularizing breathing, or calming gut motility, thus needs techniques directed especially toward these body functions. Obviously tense-relax exercises do not affect the viscera directly, although well-learned muscle relaxation does seem to generalize to the viscera. A more direct approach is the use of techniques such as Autogenic Training or guided imagery. These techniques tend to focus on states of internal activity supported by the viscera, such as learning to become aware of finer degrees of body warmth (change in circulation) or visualizing the state of activity of specific internal organs and systems.

Awareness of the operations of mind and consciousness is a type of awareness that has not yet been formally recognized as a special kind of awareness but I think we can no longer avoid the evidence that awareness of one's own mind and consciousness is indeed a special awareness. In various forms of meditation and even in the more advanced autogenic exercises, the objective is to eliminate physical awareness and other distractions as a way of learning how to appreciate the operations and content of the unconscious mind. There are many reasons for recognizing awareness of central, subjective conscious or unconscious tensions as a separate kind of awareness that need not be associated with either muscle or visceral tensions in stress reactions, or if it is, body tensions may be proportionately less than the cerebral, subjective reactions to stress.

Evidence for one reason for treating subjective tensions separately by focusing awareness on mind and consciousness comes from certain anxiety reactions in which the body is not primarily affected, or the individual has learned ways to inhibit or suppress body tensions, and the mental anguish exists apart from body involvement. Another bit of evidence comes from clinical studies reporting successful treatment of various kinds of neuroses and anxiety by brain wave biofeedback that affects subjective states only. And a final bit of evidence comes from the therapeutic effect of various kinds of meditation. Certainly in meditation there is no active attention to muscles or viscera; meditation techniques are directed mainly toward an understanding by consciousness of the totality of being and the place of the being in nature. Whatever physical changes of the body that follow this practice must be indirect and secondary.

The Awareness of Patterns

There is still another area of "unconscious" awareness that is neither recognized nor utilized. We have no convenient descriptions of this kind of awareness, but it seems, as in Gestalt concepts, to be an awareness of patterns of events, things, or situations as wholes rather than awarenesses of specific elements within the wholes. In some way, the perception of patterns leads to an unconscious direction of activity and behavior that is appropriate to a total situation or event. The phenomenon suggests that the mind appreciates, extracts, judges, makes decisions, then acts with considerable relevance and specificity to elements in the pattern but with no conscious awareness of the elements within the pattern.

I suspect this phenomenon can be explained on the basis of the concepts I have presented, that the unconscious mind is marvelously adept at perceiving and understanding and acting upon information that is not admitted to conscious awareness. The phenomenon is tacitly acknowledged by most psychologists as important in adverse reactions of human beings, but little attention has been paid to useful outcomes. Journal keeping is an interesting example of how perceptions of patterns can lead to useful insights.

In a previous book on biofeedback I discussed the incident of the researcher attempting a biofeedback study to determine the effectiveness of biofeedback in headache. Subjects were asked to begin keeping records of the frequency and severity of their headaches and to report to the laboratory twice before beginning treatment, once when they had no headache and once during a headache. All subjects reported, to be recorded for physiological data, when they had no headache—recordings to be used as control data. But after a considerable time period, no one reported for study when he did have a headache. The single change in the subjects' daily regimen was keeping records of headaches, and we are left with the rather obvious deduction that the record keeping had some influence on the frequency and severity of the headaches.

Journal keeping has also become a popular technique for dealing with various personal psychological problems and for dealing with stress, as well as being a technique used in conjunction with biofeedback. While we can only guess at why record keeping is an effective therapeutic tool, one good guess is that by bringing together events and situations happening at different times in different places and under different circumstances in a record or journal and paying attention to it, we begin to appreciate a pattern that is especially related to a headache or some other problem. We may, of course, gain a conscious insight, but often the insights occur unconsciously.

In the headache study, the record keeping may have given the subjects clues about what was causing their tension headaches, and it is likely the headaches stopped because the unconscious mind either decided to avoid stress situations or developed other ways to cope with the stress.

One of the most dramatic examples of this phenomenon is a study done using video feedback for patients with psychomotor epilepsy. During the video taping, the neurologist-psychiatrists conducted in-depth discussions about various emotional situations with the patients. Once or twice during these interviews the patients apparently reacted to the emotional material and suffered brief seizures. All patients had long histories of frequent seizures. Subsequently the patients returned and were shown the video tapes while the researchers discussed with them what they were doing. The result of this procedure was astounding. Even though there was no concrete discussion of the emotional triggers that caused the seizures, the patients promptly became almost seizure free.

Here again is the remarkable operation of the unconscious mind that can absorb great patterns of circumstances and meanings, extract the elements most significant for well-being, then take appropriate action to utilize what it has learned. Why didn't the patients do this for themselves? Probably for the hundreds of reasons why we rarely take time to analyze things of mind: we have been discouraged by the sciences from such self-examination; we have lacked the background knowledge to use common information; and most important, we have not had our attention drawn to the situation as a special one that could produce a solution.

Bibliography

When one explores for unknowns, as I have done in this book, there are few neatly packaged concepts that can be cited from existing scientific literature. While my conceptual sympathies lie with such scientists as Sperry, Hall, Montagu, Lorenz, and Leakey, perhaps more stimulation to attempt new formulations about the human mind came from the volumes of arrogantly oversimplified statements about mind-brain function that have so long dominated (and inhibited) understanding human beings. Few representatives of the latter persuasion are included in the following, and partial, list of references that inspired me to search for a new perspective on the human potential.

Alland, Jr., Alexander. *The Human Imperative.* New York: Columbia University Press, 1972.

———. *Evolution and Human Behavior.* New York: Anchor/Doubleday, 1973.

Ardrey, Robert. *The Social Contract.* New York: Atheneum, 1970.

Barnett, S. A. *Instinct and Intelligence.* Englewood Cliffs, N.J.: Prentice-Hall, 1967.

Baron, Robert A., and Byrne, Donn. *Social Psychology.* Boston: Allyn & Bacon, 1977.

Brady, John Paul, and Brodie, H. Keith H., eds. *Controversy in Psychiatry.* Philadelphia: W. B. Saunders, 1978.

Campbell, K. *Body and Mind.* New York: Anchor/Doubleday, 1970.

Corcoran, D. W. J. *Pattern Recognition.* New York: Penguin Books, 1971.

Dawkins, Richard. *The Selfish Gene.* New York: Oxford University Press, 1976.

Day, R. H. *Human Perception.* New York: John Wiley & Sons, 1969.

Dimond, S. J. *The Social Behavior of Animals*. New York: Harper Colophon Books, 1970.

Dobzhansky, T. *Mankind Evolving*. New Haven: Yale University Press, 1962.

Dodwell, P.C. *New Horizons in Psychology, 2*. New York: Penguin Books, 1972.

Dröscher, Vitus B. *Mysterious Senses*. London: Hodder & Stoughton, 1964.

Elliott, H. Chandler. *The Shape of Intelligence*. New York: Charles Scribner's Sons, 1969.

Fincher, Jack. *Human Intelligence*, Capricorn Books, G. P. Putnam's Sons, 1976.

Foss, Brian M., ed. *New Horizons in Psychology*. New York: Penguin Books, 1966.

Gergen, K. *Social Psychology*, CRM Books, 1974.

Globus, G., Ed. *Consciousness and the Brain*, Plenum Press, 1976.

Goodfield, June. *Playing God*. New York: Random House, 1977.

Gould, Stephen Jay. *Ever Since Darwin*. New York: W. W. Norton & Co., 1977.

Hall, Edward T. *The Silent Language*. New York: Doubleday & Co., 1959.

———. *The Hidden Dimension*. New York: Doubleday & Co., 1966.

———. *Beyond Culture*. New York: Anchor/Doubleday, 1976.

Hanson, Earl D. *Animal Diversity*. Englewood Cliffs, N.J.: Prentice-Hall, 1966.

Hass, Hans. *The Human Animal*. New York: G. P. Putnam's Sons, 1970.

Hinde, Robert A., ed. *Non-verbal Communication*. Cambridge: Cambridge University Press, 1972.

Kohler, Wolfgang. *Gestalt Psychology*. New York: Mentor/New American Library, 1947.

Leakey, Richard E. *Origins*. New York: E. P. Dutton, 1977.

Lindsay, Peter H., and Norman, Donald A. *Human Information Processing*. New York: Academic Press, 1977.

Lipowski, Z. J.; Lipsett, Don R.; and Whybrow, Peter C., eds. *Psychosomatic Medicine*. New York: Oxford University Press, 1977.

Lorenz, Konrad. *On Aggression*. New York: Harcourt, Brace & World, 1966.

———. *Behind the Mirror*. London: Methuen & Co., Ltd, 1977.

Mandler, George. *Mind and Emotion*. New York: John Wiley & Sons, 1975.

Marmor, Judd. *Psychiatry in Transition*. New York: Brunner/Mazel, 1974.

Mazur, Allan, and Robertson, Leon S. *Biology and Social Behavior*. New York: Free Press/Macmillan, 1974.

McKellar, Peter. *Experience and Behavior*. New York: Penguin Books, 1968.

Montagu, Ashley. *The Human Revolution*. Cleveland: World Publishing Co., 1965.

———. *The Nature of Human Aggression*. New York: Oxford University Press, 1976.

Morick, Harold, ed. *Wittgenstein and the Problem of Other Minds*. New York: McGraw-Hill, 1967.

Murphy, Gardner. *Outgrowing Self-Deception.* New York: Basic Books, 1975.

Parsegian, V. L. *This Cybernetic World of Men, Machines, and Earth Systems.* New York: Anchor/Doubleday, 1973.

Pohemus, Ted., ed. *The Body Reader.* New York: Pantheon Books, 1978.

Rosenfeld, Albert, ed. *Mind and Supermind.* New York: Holt, Rinehart & Winston, 1973/1977.

Sagan, Carl. *The Dragons of Eden.* New York: Random House, 1977.

Salk, Jonas. *The Survival of the Wisest.* New York: Harper & Row, 1973.

Selye, Hans. *The Stress of Life.* New York: McGraw-Hill, 1956.

———. *Stress Without Distress.* Philadelphia: J. B. Lippincott Co., 1974.

Silverman, Robert E. *Psychology.* Des Moines: Meredith Corp., 1974.

Simpson, George Gaylord. *Biology and Man.* New York: Harcourt, Brace & World, 1964.

Smith, Anthony. *The Human Pedigree.* J. B. Lippincott Co., 1975.

Smith, John Maynard. *The Theory of Evolution.* New York: Penguin Books, 1966.

Vernon, M. D. *Human Motivation.* Cambridge: Cambridge University Press, 1969.

———. *The Psychology of Perception.* New York: Penguin Books, 1962.

Wescott, Roger W. *The Divine Animal.* New York: Funk & Wagnalls, 1969.

Wolman, Benjamin B. *The Unconscious Mind.* Englewood Cliffs, N.J.: Prentice-Hall, 1968.

Index

Adaptation of species
  to environments, 141–43
  and evolution, 140
Aggression instinct, and Lorenz,
  182–83
Altered states of consciousness
  classification of, 227–31
  and consensual consciousness, 196–
    97
  as dissociations of consciousness,
    196–97
  and mystical states, 232, 233–43
  nature of, 200–201
Animal behavior
  and behavioral scientists, 188–89
  human compared to, 181–82
  as patterns of mind-brain activity,
    190–91
  and scientific study, 185–86
Animals, domestic, evolution of
    intellect in, 187–88
Ardrey, Robert, 186
Arnold, Magda, 54
Attitudes toward mind, 8–10, 75
Autonomic nervous system (ANS),
    34–35
Awareness
  biological, 45–48
  evolution of, 191–95
  of internal states, 58–60, 76–77
  and perceptions, 42–45
  of unconscious mind, and control of
    body, 55–57

Basmajian, John Varoujan, 258
Behavior
  as adaptive mechanism affecting
    evolution, 162–63
  complex, evolution of, and Lorenz,
    192
  human, Gestalt view of, 180–81
  intelligent, unconscious control of,
    63–65
  and learning, 158–61
  maladaptive social, 128–29
  primitive, and primitive mind,
    183–89
  See also Animal behavior; Human
    behavior
Behavioral scientists
  and animal behavior, 188–89
  and feedback system concepts, 37
Beliefs about mind, 8–10
Biofeedback
  and biological awareness, 46–47
  as intentional unconscious learning
    process, 249–50
  learning
    and control of motor units, 251–52
    implications of, 253–54
    and information used by
      unconscious intellect, 255–57
    situation, 78–79
    what is known vs. how learned,
      262–63
  and observations on motor unit
    performance, 257–59

Biofeedback *(cont'd)*
  self-learning process in, 254–55
  phenomenon, 248–49, 259
Biological awareness, 45–48
Biological communication systems, and
    genetic change, 148–51
Blofeld, John, 239
Body
  awareness of, and well-being, 77–80
  and characteristic dominance of one
      side, 49
  control of, by mind, 30–32
  functions
    and feedback control systems,
        36–37
    and science, 56–57
  image, as sense of physical body,
      48–49
  intelligent unconscious control of,
      66–67
  as mirror of the mind, 51–53
  operations and systems, 33–36
  physical change in, and unconscious
      mental activity, 172–73
Brain, 43, 119, 120
  -to-consciousness theories, 120–27
  evolution of, 164, 184–85, 192
  hemispheres of, and mental
      operations, 123, 124–25
  mind as function of, 163. *See also*
      Mind

Central nervous system (CNS), 35–36,
    41
Charcot, J. M., and unconscious mind,
    177
Communication
  and animals, 189–90
  evolution of, and environmental
      change, 154–55
  and genetic change in evolution,
      147–48
  systems
    biological and genetic change,
        148–51
    and evolution, 137, 153–55
  by time-space patterns, 189–91
Concepts and conscious mind, 15–16
Conscious awareness, 67, 123
  vs. inner unconscious, 73–74
  and mental processes, 262–63
  and perceptual distortion, 104–105
Conscious intention and imagery,
    243
Consciousness
  compartments of, 12–18
  consensual, 58–59

Consciousness *(cont'd)*
  consensual *(cont'd)*
    vs. altered states of consciousness,
        198–200
    effect on expectations, 94–95
    interference in operation of
        unconscious mind, 67–69
  cosmic, 2
  dissociations and resources of mind,
      196–97
  and mind-brain scientists, 123–24
  roots of, 181–83
  skills of, 10–12
  subjectively appreciated, 59
  theories of, 121, 122
Consensual consciousness. *See*
    Consciousness, consensual
Control, unconscious. *See* Unconscious
    control
Cortex, function in tension states,
    109–11
Cosmic consciousness, 2
Cousins, Norman, 57
Cybernetics, 37–38, 50

Darwinian theory of natural selection,
    136, 139. *See also* Natural
    selection, theory of
Déjà vu, 10, 216
Depersonalization, nonpathological,
    238, 239
Discovery of the Unconscious
    (Ellenberger), 177
Dissociation
  of consciousness
    vs. altered states of, 196–97
    and hypnosis, 227
  of emotion and intellect, 209
  of mind and body, 208
  of perception from self-perception,
      215
Distress, mental steps to
  expectations, 93–95
  images of worry, 99–100
  perceptions, 95–97
  rumination, 102–104
  self-deception, 104–107
  uncertainty, 98–99
  worry, 97–98
DNA
  and feedback, 150, 151
  as genetic memory material, 146–47,
      150
Dreams, 10, 172
  vs. out-of-the-body experiences,
      214–215

Eccles, Sir John, 52
  and hemispheric activity of brain,
    124
Ecological balance, and adaptation to
    environment, 142–43
Ellenberger, Henry, 177, 178
Elliott, H. Chandler, 33
Emotion, 209, 214
Emotional problems due to meditation
    and mystical experiences, 241–
    42
Emotions, 91–93
Energy responsible for mind, 126
Environment
  change in, and evolution of
    communication systems, 154–55
  and evolution, 141–43, 167–68
  and learning, 144
  and mind, 41
  social vs. physical, in evolutionary
    change, 163–64
ESP, 4
Evolution
  biological, foundations of, 136–39
  of behavior and evolutionary theory,
    159
  of brain and biological systems,
    132–33
  of cognitive apparatus of man, 195
  of complexity in species, 144–45
  consensus theory of, and science,
    143–45
  and cooperation of systems, 165–66
  of environmental change and
    communication, 154–55
  of human senses, 48–50, 51
  influences on, 159
  of intellectual processes in animals,
    187–88
  of internal communications systems,
    155–56
  and learning, 143–44
  and natural selection theory, 139–46,
    153, 165
  of nerve tissue, 156–58
  phylogenic scale in, 144
  and social activities, 160, 161–62
  of social mentality, 161–64
  of supermentality in man's evolution,
    167–68
Evolutionary development in
    organization of systems as
    wholes, 151–52
Evolutionary process and mind, 135–
    36
Evolutionary theory, evolution of
    behavior and, 159

Expectancy, and intellect, 97
Expectations
  influenced by consensual
    consciousness, 94–95
  and perception of reality, 54
  role of, in stress reactions, 93
Experience, 12, 13, 14
  of internal states and technology,
    51–53

Feedback
  as communication, 148–49
  control systems and operations of the
    body, 36–37, 38–39, 149–50
Flying saucers, 219–20
Freud, Sigmund, 228
  and unconscious mind, 177, 179

Genes, 146–48
Genetic change, 140, 147–48
Genetic code, as basis of evolution,
    137
Genetic theory, problems in, 150–52
Gestalt view of human behavior,
    180–81

Human behavior
  compared to animal, 181–82
  functions of, and psychology, 179–81
  and imagination, 244
  origin and nature of, 166
Human mind
  obstacles to understanding, 19–20
  power over brain, 24–25
  See also Mind
Hypnosis, 224–27
  and unconscious mind, 177–78
Hysterias, and unconscious mind, 22–23

Idiot savant, 220–24
Illness, Second Illness as reaction to,
    111–14
Imagery
  conscious and unconscious, 243–44
  hypnotic, 10
Images
  mental, 244–45, 246
  in reactions to stress, 99–100
Imagination, and mind, 232, 243–47
Insights
  and mystical states, 240–41
  and unconscious mind, 203–204
Intellect
  hidden, and ability to solve problems,
    203–206
  and stress, 92. See also Distress,
    mental steps to

Intellect *(cont'd)*
  unconscious, 240, 255–57
Intellectual processes, evolution of, in
  animals, 187–89
Intelligence, effect of, on systems in
  evolution, 151–52
Intention, as function of mind, 261
Internal states
  awareness of, 74–77
  control of, through biofeedback,
  78–79, 80

Jacobson, Edmund, 99
Janet, Pierre, and the unconscious
  mind, 178–79
Jones, Jim, 198
Journeys Out of the Body (Monroe),
  211
Judgment, and subliminal perception,
  65
Judgments, conscious and unconscious,
  53–54
Jung, Carl Gustav, 228
  and unconscious mind, 53, 178

Keller, Helen, 44
Knowledge, from mystical experience,
  234

Learning
  and control of a single cell, 250–53
  and environment, 144
  and evolution, 143–44
    of behavior, 158–61
  and evolving neural tissue, 184
  as spontaneous, 255
  See also Biofeedback learning
Lorenz, Konrad, 167, 228
  and aggression instinct, 182–83
  and evolution of complex brains and
    behaviors, 192
  and mind of man, 193–94, 195
LSD, 197, 229, 230, 242

Meditation, emotional problems due to,
  241–42
Memory
  characteristics of, 215
  -consciousness units, 215–17
  operations of, 14–16
Mental activities
  and mystical states, 233
  unconscious, and motor unit
    performance, 258
Mental images, 227, 244–45, 246
Mental processes
  and conscious awareness, 262–63

Mental processes *(cont'd)*
  of self-deception, 10, 104–107
  and stress, 89–90
Mescaline experiences, and mystical
  states, 238–39
Mind
  altered states of, 200–201, 230–31
  beliefs and attitudes toward, 8–10
  -body
    operations, nature of, 36–38
    problem, 118–20
  brain, 14, 39, 41, 237
    effect of, on body, 119–20
    and process of association, 62–63
    and sense of order, 259–61
  characteristics of, and Lorenz,
    193–94
  concept of, and science, 3, 5–6, 19,
    33–34
  and consciousness
    compartments of 12–18, 20
    experts' view of, 119–20
    and science, 17–18
    skills of, untapped, 10–12
  and control of body functions, 21–25,
    56, 254–55
  and control of brain, 127, 246–47
  control of physiologic systems, 38–39,
    41
  definitions of, 117–18
  divided, and idiot savant, 220–24
  and drug abuse and use, 129–30
  effect of, on body, 75–76
  energy responsible for, 126
  enigmas and paradoxes of, 1–4
  environment and, 41
  evolution from brain, 132–36
  healing, discovering, 20–25
  imagination and, 232, 243–47
  intention as function of, 261
  -is more-than-brain, 133, 134
  and mystical experiences, 234, 237
  -over-body phenomenon, 42–43
    experiences, 29, 30–31
  in hypnosis, 226
  and stress reactions, 106–107
  power of, to control the body, 6, 29,
    30–32, 79–80, 193
  powers and potential of, 2, 6, 7, 19,
    127, 164, 167–68
  primitive, and primitive behavior,
    183–89
  as product of brain, 119, 127, 163
  resources of, 18–20
  scientific materialist vs. mystical view
    of, 126–27
  states, nonordinary, 197–200, 203

Mind *(cont'd)*
  See also Human mind; Unconscious
    mind
Monroe, Robert, 211
Moon, Reverend, 198
Motor units
  learning to control, 251–52
  performance of, and biofeedback,
    257–59
Mystical experiences, emotional
  problems due to, 241–42
Mystery of the Mind, The (Penfield),
  126
Mystical states, 232, 233–43

Natural selection theory of evolution,
  139–46, 153, 165
Nerve tissue, evolution of, and
  expansion of communication,
  157–58
Nervous system, 34–36, 41
Neural tissue
  and evolution, 136–37, 140–41, 163
  and evolving internal
    communications systems, 155–56
New Mind, New Body (Brown), 258

Order, sense of, in motor unit learning,
  257, 260–61
Out-of-the-body experiences, 211–17

Parasympathetic nervous system, 36
Pavlov, Ivan Petrovich, and
  experiments in learning, 61–63
PCP, 229
Penfield, Wilder, 52
  and mind, 126
Perception, 12–13, 43
  and rumination, 104–107
  subliminal, 63–65
Perceptions
  and sensations, 43–44, 54
  of social situations, 95–97
Phylogenetic scale in evolution, 144
Physical self, primitive nature of, 33–36
Placebos, effect of, on consciousness
  and unconscious mind, 70–72
Pribram, Karl, 5
Primitive behavior, and primitive
  mind, 183–89
Problem solving, 10, 103, 172
Progressive Relaxation, 99
Psychology, and functions of human
  behavior, 179–81

Reflexes, and self-regulating systems,
  157

RNA, 146
Rumination, 102
  effect of, on body, 103–104
  and self-deception, 104–105

Scientific method vs. descriptive
  science, 228
Scott, John Paul, 186
Second Illness, as reaction to illness,
  111–14
Self-deception, and distress, 104–107
Self-learning, in biofeedback, 254–55
Selye, Hans, 5, 57
  theory of stress, 85–86
Sensations, 12
  in mystical states, 235–36
  and perceptions, 43–44, 54
Senses, new evolved, 48–51
Sensory information, interpretation of
  by science, 13–14
Shape of Intelligence, The (Elliott), 33
Sheen, Fulton, 189
Sleep talking, 211
Sleep walking, and mental activity,
  210–11
Social behavior, maladaptive, scientific
  approach to, 128–29
Social distress, 87–88, 90
Social mentality, evolution of, 161–64
Social organization, and
  communication, 160–61
Species
  adaptation of
    to environments, 141–43
    and evolution, 140
  evolution of complexity in, 144–45
Sperry, Roger, 5
  and mind, 122–24
Stress, 81, 83–86, 88–89
  arousal-alarm theory of, 87–88
  disorders, and internal perceptions,
    109–10
  illnesses, 81–84
  as logical, 108–11
  manufactured by mind, 90–93
  reactions, 93, 110
  See also Distress, mental steps to
Subconscious, and Pierre Janet, 178
Subliminal perception, 64–65
Supermentality, evolution of, in man,
  167–68
Survival
  and evolution of senses, 48–49, 145
  of fittest, 139–46, 153, 165
Sympathetic nervous system, 35
Systems
  analysis, and evolutionary process,
    138. *See also* Cybernetics

Systems *(cont'd)*
  and evolution, 151–52, 165–66,
    194–95

Tantric Mysticism, The (Blofeld), 239
Tension states, and cortex, 109–11
Tinbergen, Nikolaas, 186, 228

Uncertainty, and arousal of physical
    mechanisms, 98–99
Unconscious abilities, 257–59
Unconscious anxiety, as mental
    struggle, 174–75
Unconscious awareness, 51
  techniques of tuning into, 55–56
Unconscious intellect, 240, 255–57
Unconscious mental activity, 23–24, 44,
    175
  in biofeedback learning, 258–59
  and changes in the body, 63, 172–73
  and imagery, 243
  and motor unit performance, 258
  and Pierre Janet, 178–79
Unconscious mental operations, and
    physiologic response, 54–55
Unconscious mind
  ability of, to direct behavior, 55,
    59–60
  and animal behavior, 189
  and behavioral scientists, 171–72
  and biofeedback learning, 249,
    253–54, 255
  capabilities of, 175
  caring, 206–10
  and consensual consciousness, 25,
    67–69

Unconscious mind *(cont'd)*
  and control of body, 60–63, 66–67
  and control of intelligent behavior,
    63–65
  deception of, 72–73
  and dreams, 10, 172
  and emotion, 208
  historical insights into, 177–79
  and hysterias, 22–23
  intellectual abilities of, 55, 203–204,
    208
  logic and intellect of, 23–24
  as master of mind functions, 263–64
  as resource, 202–203
  and science, 17, 21
  and sense of order, 259–61
  and social demands, 60, 98
  and subliminal perception, 64–65
  victimizing, 72–74
Unconscious operations, 204–205, 240
Unconscious reality, 173–76
Unconscious thought, power of, 173–74

Wheel of Life (Blofeld), 239
Will, mental operations of, 261–62. *See
    also* Intention
Worry
  definitions of, 82–83
  and distress, 97–98
  images of, and distress, 99–100
  reasonable and destructive, 100, 102
  and rumination, 102–104
  and stress disorders, 107, 109
  and stress reactions, 91–93
Wundt, Wilhelm, and psychology as
      study of conscious experience,
      180